T0369027

The Plane Truth

from an

American Airlines Flight Attendant

by

Alicia Lutz Rolow

iUniverse, Inc.
New York Bloomington

iUniverse books may be ordered through booksellers or by contacting:

iUniverse
1663 Liberty Drive
Bloomington, IN 47403
www.iuniverse.com
1-800-Authors (1-800-288-4677)

ISBN: 978-1-4401-0655-2(pbk)
ISBN: 978-1-4401-0656-9 (ebk)

Printed in the United States of America

iUniverse rev. date: 12/16/08

Contents

Dedication

For Shanon Lee Rolow, my husband, best friend, and the one person who gives me the strength to face my sometimes insurmountable odds with courage, conviction and the tenacity to write this book in the hopes of one day giving my profession the respect that it so much deserves. For my beautiful granddaughter McKaylah Rae Lutz. I strive daily to be an example for you of how strong a woman must be, in order to be able to co-exist in what is still to this day, very much a man's world. For my sons Isaiah Shanon Rolow and Brandon Samuel Lutz, who are and will continue to be the loves of my life. Most importantly, for the memory of Amy Sweeney and every crew member who lost their lives on September 11th 2001, so that their deaths on that fateful day will not be in vain and their incredible courage will not be forgotten. Thank you Amy, Thank you everyone. We will never forget!

NYC World Trade Center
American Airlines Flight 11 Crewmembers
Captain John Ogonowski
First Officer Thomas McGuiness Jr.
Flight Attendants Amy Sweeney, Betty Ong
Diane Snyder, Karen Martin, Bobbi Arestegui
Kathy Nicosia, Jean Roger, Sara Low,
Jeffrey Coleman

US Pentagon

American Airlines Flight 77 Crewmembers

Captain Charles Burlingame

First Officer David Charlebois

Flight Attendants Michelle Malkin

Ken and Jennifer Lewis

Renee May

Somerset County Village of Shanksville, PA.

United Airlines Flight 93 Crewmembers

Captain Jason Dahl

First Officer LeRoy Homer, Jr.

Flight Attendants Sandra Bradshaw

Lorraine Bay

Wanda Green

Cee Cee Lyles

Deborah Anne Jacobs Welsh

"Father forgive them for they know not what they do"

(Words of Jesus Christ at his crucifixion John 19:17-24)

Foreword

As I write these words I can only pray that they reach every *American Airlines Flight Attendant* as well as all other commercial airline flight attendants and passengers. May the tremendous responsibilities that *"flight attendants"* have as *"guardians in flight"* cause for all of us to quickly wake up and realize the importance of our presence on board every aircraft we take up in flight. Allow no one to intimidate or harass us into making compromising decisions that could allow for another catastrophic scenario at *39,000 feet* needlessly costing not only our lives, but the lives of the passengers we transport on a daily basis from one destination to another. *Please God, please let us not continue the complacency I begin to once again see on our aircrafts. Help us to keep strong and vigilant and constantly reminded that while we take to the heavenly skies we are "The Last Line of Defense" up there.*

Introduction

I am not a novelist or professional book writer so I beg indulgence from all those who read this book and ask that you please accept my humblest of apologies in advance, should this book not follow the formatting and criteria of that of a professional writer's traditionally published manuscript. Although I have attempted to write it in a manner that allows for all who read it to understand its contents and message, this book is written expressly for all American Airlines flight attendants. With that said, allow me to tell you a little bit about who I am. I am an *American Airlines* flight attendant and have been one for over thirty two years. I began my flying career on *May 27, 1976* when I graduated from the place that we flight attendants at *American* call the *"Charm Farm"* better known as the *American Airlines Flight Service Academy*. During the time that I sought out this profession, it was an extremely difficult and competitive career to acquire. For me, as I am sure it was for many other young women and men who were being accepted for this career, becoming a *commercial airline flight attendant* was a dream come true. The *elite* status attached to the profession gave me a tremendous sense of accomplishment and great pride in myself, which was extremely important for me since coming from the tumultuous background I called my life, it helped validate who I was. The era in which I was born and grew up in was notorious for giving the false impressions of widespread *familial bliss* throughout this country. Appearances of *"all is well on the home front"* were very important to people during these times, even if it existed only on the surface. There were deeper, darker and more ominous agendas going on within most family households, but you never aired out any of that laundry to anyone, ever! As children, the very adults we depended on for guidance and leadership during our upbringing such as our parents for instance seemed to master the art of hiding unsavory and taboo family secrets that were occurring within our very homes. A great example of this was the very common problem of *parental alcoholism.* Other forms of more serious *parental dysfunctional behavior* ran rampant during these times as well, but the widespread *alcoholism* problem among head of households, left many of us in a broken or in a somewhat delicate and vulnerable state. It was a prerequisite for most of us growing up in that time frame to always be the perfect little soldiers suffering silently through it all, and we were expected to make sure that all family secrets stayed just that; *secret!* Needless to say, the profession of the commercial airline flight attendant, was the perfect job for so many of us because it opened the doors for us to be able to gain our independence from all that was not kosher at home, while at the same time, it provided us the many opportunities that were out there, to experience the vast world outside of our own. Well, what more could any of us possibly ask for right? Little did we know that we were about to embark on a very mentally abusive relationship between *flight attendant employee* and *commercial airline company employer* similar to the one many of us already had at home and were trying to escape. Don't get me wrong. *There were many wonderful times I've experienced in my career and still do, but those wonderful times have everything to do with my fellow crew members and passengers and have absolutely nothing to do with American Airlines management, at least not in the last ten years anyway.* Every flight attendant out there, whether they work for *American Airlines* or any other airline company knows that what I will share in this book is the absolute truth, and whether they want to admit it or not doesn't really matter because the truth is just that, **TRUTH!** It is not opinion that could be interpreted in different ways by different people. My hope is that this truth brings us all together so that it allows us to gather the strength that we will need in order to **STAND!**

CHAPTER 1

DEAR AMY.....

November 14, 2007

Dear Amy,

I know that my writing this letter to you is going to seem a bit crazy to a whole lot of people because it is one letter that you will never receive since you are no longer with us. Nevertheless, I have to write it to you anyway hoping that what I want to convey in it somehow reaches you wherever you are up there. I don't know if I ever had the honor of meeting you personally when you were still among us, but considering the fact that we fly with so many flight attendants during the course of our careers, I sincerely hope with all my heart that I did. From everything that I have read about you regarding the person that you were, I'd like to think that we would have been the best of friends and we would have immediately formed that incredible flight attendant bond that so many of us have with one another. I am aware of the fact that I am not responsible for the blatant lack of security that our company's upper management so called leaders at American Airlines provided you with on that God forsaken day, but I still feel a strong need to tell you how very sorry I am that those extremely disturbed animals who claimed to be crusaders for their absurd cause were able to board and then hijack your flight that day. That just NEVER should have happened! No one will ever convince me that American Airlines management took every security precaution that was available to them on that day because if they had, the entire monstrous situation would not have occurred. Our company is in the business of commercial air travel for Pete's sake! They had been aware as well as your government had been aware for a very long time that the horrifically devastating scenario that all of you had to deal with up there was coming! They knew it was only a short matter of time before such a hijacking would come about. Many of our passengers as well as our crew members had reported to our company officials on numerous occasions that they had noticed suspicious behavior coming from passengers of Middle Eastern ethnicity on many of our flights just days prior to the morning leading up to your flight. When American Airline's management received that information, they should have responded immediately by going through passenger manifests looking for any and all information that would bring up red flags and obviously there were plenty! What makes me so furious with them is that to this day they don't feel any responsibility for what happened to you and all of those people who lost their lives on that day. There is never any accountability with them but Lord knows we are expected to be accountable for everything. That is absolutely outrages! Someone needs to keep explaining the very important fact to them that they keep refusing to understand and that is that when we are at work, their main responsibility has to be about protecting us and our passengers in any way that is necessary to keep us as safe as possible at all times. American Airlines management official's negligent indifference caused you and everyone else on board that flight to pay the ultimate price. Your government offered you the same exact negligence and indifference. I suppose that is what causes this incredible anger and disgust I feel towards our company as well as our country's leaders. The fact that they all felt your life, as well as the lives of all the others who died on that horrible day and in that horrible manner was expendable. Outside of your loved ones, the two most important entities in your life, your company and your country failed you miserably! Here we are six years later and American Airlines corporate management has returned to their greedy mentality of back to business as usual barely skipping a beat and using that day as an excuse to pull off all the shameful corruption for anything they can get away with. The incredible heroism that you displayed on that day leaves me speechless. Your contacting American Airlines on the phone, even before you called your husband and your babies, giving this company's worthless management employees a blow by blow account of the horrific

*events that were literally unraveling before your eyes as you were
speaking all the while staying calm, collected and so unbelievably
focused in the midst of what certainly had to be the most
unimaginable desperation any human being should ever have to
endure, speaks volumes about your selfless character and your
amazing courage under fire. Your final thoughts in those solemn
final moments of your life were about trying to protect your
passengers and crew.   It was you Ms. Amy Sweeney, who gave
them that incredibly accurate account of the hell that was going
on up there. Everything! From the description of the attackers to
the seat numbers they occupied to the number of attackers on
board and the weapons they were using, etc. etc. etc. all of it. I
am so damn proud of you girl! So much so that I cannot even
find adequate enough words to describe how I feel about you. Let
the next illiterate moron out there come up to me and tell me how
we are nothing more than glorified waitresses in the sky and see
what happens! I know I certainly can't wait until our very own
avaricious company CEO or any of his gluttonous, desirous
buddies try and tell us at our next contract negotiations how
overpaid we are! Yeah! I am sure you were thinking about how
much you were overpaid on September 11th weren't you Amy?
Bastards! Am I making you laugh up there? I hope so Amy
because you are giving me strength down here and I really need it
right now because I have been fighting the fight for what seems to
be a lifetime and I feel myself tiring and I know that I don't have
that option right now because I still have so much work that
needs to be done down here. You would think September 11th*

would have been enough to shock this company's leaders into re-thinking the disgusting manner in which they continuously choose to engage in, when communicating with all of us right? Not a chance Amy, not even close! It all continues to be about the almighty revenue and about how much of it they can line their own pockets with at the end of the day! What you and all of those people went through is still not enough to shame corporate management into acknowledging that we the crewmembers are absolutely vital for the safety and the well being of those hundreds and thousands of passengers we transport every day on those aircrafts. There should be nothing but respect and gratitude shown to us instead of the continuous disrespect and total disregard for who we are and what we do! To this day, virtually no viable training is in place or has been made available to us at our yearly Emergency Procedure Training (EPTS) that teaches flight attendants how to deal with this "new wave" type of hijacking, then to top off all of the above, our country's leaders are fighting over who is going to inherit our current egotistical rootin tootin cowboy wannabe buffoon president's job next year when instead, their number one priority should be concentrating on correcting the problem of our unsecured borders which no doubt will be the next totally avoidable huge catastrophe to hit our country since September 11th. Jesus Christ Amy, these crazy radical Islamic extremist "self locked and loaded killing machines" are coming in through our unsecured borders like a swarm of locust! Did that just make you laugh? Are you somewhere up there laughing with me right now? God Amy, it is all so very ridiculous and out of control down here. There is so much arrogance and greed all around us. It is not only destroying our beloved country but it is destroying our very lives. Every time I look into my beautiful granddaughters face and see her little innocent eyes, I think about your little babies eyes. I am so afraid for all of them. They look to us for answers and guidance. They are so little and so wondrous and innocent. What legacy and foundation are we leaving for them to stand on? There are times when I feel so guilty for bringing them into this world. On the morning of September 11, 2001, you got up to go to work and you did all your usual morning routines with your family. When it came time to get ready for work you repacked your suitcase, showered, blow dried and styled your hair, put your make-up on and finally slipped into your American Airlines uniform. You kissed your babies and husband good-bye and told them you loved them and would see them tomorrow. You took one last look around making sure you had everything you would need for your trip and you drove away for your flight never thinking it would be the very last time you would see your loved ones. I go over it my mind again and again because I picture myself with my own kids, doing the very same thing. Why you? Why not me? As I am writing these very words to you I can't stop the uncontrollable tears that are falling on my computer keyboard. I keep picturing the incredible hardship of your husband having to process the horrific information he is now witnessing first hand on the television screen as American Airlines flight 11, your flight, scheduled from Boston's Logan Airport to Los Angeles

International Airport is instead hijacked and diverted to New York City where it slams into one of the World Trade Towers and burst into a raging inferno, while at the same time having to come up with the words to tell your babies that their mommy is never coming home again. You were an incredible human gift that was bestowed upon this earth only to be taken away so violently and needlessly before you could even finish living your life. You had so much of it left. All the plans and dreams of watching your kids grow up, violently taken from you. The grandchildren that you would have earned every right to spoil rotten but instead will never get the chance to even meet. I am so angry Amy for the loss of you and for the tremendous loss as well as pain that your husband and children have to deal with on a daily basis. I am grief stricken for your mother and father who never once fathomed the day you were born, that you would be taken from them in such an unnecessary and tragic manner. My heart is heavy with sadness for all of the people that loved you so much and are now finding themselves without you trying to make sense of why? I hope your children's father never lets a day go by without telling them what a brave and selfless human being you were and how you carried them in your heart until your last breath. I know there isn't a day in my life that goes by that I don't think of you and the rest of those people that showed such heroism on that day. It is because of all of you that I can go up there now so much more mentally prepared for what was once to all of us the unthinkable. I will be forever grateful to all of you for that. I realize that unless people were directly affected by

September 11th, they have moved on. I suppose that's just what people do, I don't know. What I do know is every flight attendant and crew member out there lives with September 11th front and center as I do and I do not expect that to go away for as long as I live. Most flight attendants remain very much in a post-traumatic state. I cannot tell you the amount of times in a day that something or someone triggers a thought that puts me on that airplane with all of you on that day. If I'm not awake then you come in my dreams. After it first happened I carried a tremendous sense of guilt in my heart. I had truly convinced myself that had I been with you, it would not have gone down that way. I rationalized in my mind that I would see the hijackers coming at us and we would all fight like hell, ruin their hijacking attempt and bring all those people and ourselves down from the skies safely. I now realize that I would have been as unprepared and caught off guard as all of you were, because we never had the "heads up" from our company leaders that we should have had. I still think about the strangest things that come to me at the most unexpected times. For the last twenty to twenty five years of my flying career I have been flying transcontinental flights and have been working on the 767 aircrafts since we acquired them. My trips in the last few years have consisted mostly of the LAX-JFK runs, but I can't tell you the number of times I have worked American Airlines flight 11 BOS-LAX. I know as certain as I know my own name that the aircraft that you flew that morning was the very same aircraft I had flown back and forth many times as well. I almost always work the business class galley flight attendant position on the 767 and I would be willing to bet my life that my own fingerprints were probably in numerous places in the galley of that 767 you flew that day where the cabin service employees who cleaned that aircraft before you boarded it, perhaps possibly missed when wiping it down. I guess what I am trying to say to you Amy is that a part of me went with you that day. A part of all of your American Airlines flight attendant family went with you that day. I really wanted you to know that. I need you to know that you were not alone in your final moments of despair because we were all with you. I pray for you everyday as I do for your family as well. I know that the God that I believe in, took you in His arms along with everyone else on board that day and held all of you together through the impact. I know that you closed your eyes and when you opened them again you saw only the light of His eyes and the proud smile on His face and all you could feel after that was the warmth of His embrace and the complete, undeniable feeling of peace and that's when you knew that you were home. Maybe when the time comes for me, I will be given the privilege and the tremendous honor to be able to embrace you myself. Until then, from the bottom of my heart I thank you so very much Ms. Madeline Amy Sweeney.

Love,

Alicia

CHAPTER 2

THE CHARM FARM
EXPERIENCE

It starts at the ***American Airlines Flight Service College*** better known to most of us as ***The Charm Farm.*** As perspective ***American Airlines*** flight attendants, we already had the prerequisite basic *"self-esteem"* problems required for that particular position in tact, which we had previously acquired from our early years of living in our dysfunctional homes. ***The Charm Farm*** had such a powerful impact on all of us and we struggled through it the best we could because we felt so lucky to have gotten that far. At the time that we were going through the flight attendant training, this career had to be one of the most difficult and elite occupations you could land. Thousands and thousands of people applied for the position but few got selected. Many of us were coming from homes that were not happy and stable by any means. There were some of us that were broken from divorce, always absorbing the blame for our parent's miserable failed marriages. Then there were those of us that had to deal with physical or mental abuse which was a daily staple in our households. Then there were the majority of us who had alcoholic parents; usually one but sometimes two and that one needs no further commentary or explanation on the life long devastating affects it had on us. To sum it up, the kind of parents most of us had while growing up were the kind that never missed an opportunity to remind us of how we were never good enough and would never amount to much of anything. Unfortunately for us, our backgrounds left us prime targets for *The Charm Farm.* Once there, we were able to continue to receive the same kind of desecrating treatment we were so accustomed to receiving at home except with a little different twist here and there. The majority of us who were at *The Charm Farm* training to be *American Airlines* flight attendants were made up of mostly women and we were very young and clueless. We had absolutely no idea of how to put the dynamics of the whole situation we were about to get into together, until much later on in our lives and careers. My personal stay was in *1976.* During my stay there I was able to witness so many of my future co-working flight attendant piers humiliated by the *Farm's* over zealous and mean spirited female instructors who couldn't handle the incredible beauty of some of the young female students who were there for the training. Most of the student body was made up of very attractive young women but it was the ones who were beyond attractive and were in the category of incredibly stunning who would be the ones that would have it the hardest. It is all still so vivid in my mind even after all these years. The excitement of *"having arrived"* so to speak, along with the incredible feeling of anxiety mixed with fear, trepidation and a tremendous desire to please is what made every single one of us completely vulnerable for the demeaning treatment we would receive while we were there. To this day, most of us still get that sickening feeling in the pit of our stomachs when we have to return there for our yearly *EPT's (Emergency Procedure Training). The Flight Service Academy* aka *The Charm Farm*, is no longer set up or managed in the manner in which it was back in *1976.* Things have definitely changed since then but regardless of that fact, it still doesn't erase the unpleasant memories from that place we all took with us which makes for a stressful yearly **EPT**'s visit every time. When we first arrived at the **Farm** and checked in at the *"welcome desk"*, we were given our dorm room keys along with the names of the other students who we be rooming with us in our dorm. It was at that time that we were informed by the certain individuals who had the positions of overseeing and running the **Farm** of what would be expected of us during our eight week stay. We were also made very aware at that time of the curfew hour that existed which was set up for us to adhere closely to in order for us to not be locked out of the college at night. They went on to sternly mention that if in fact any of us should find ourselves in that locked out predicament at any given time, there would surely be consequences that would immediately follow. These individuals continued for what seemed like hours with a myriad of rules and regulations that all perspective flight attendants were expected to follow but the absolute golden rule that could not be broken under any circumstances was the one that stated there would be no drinking of any alcohol at any time by any one of us while on the school premises. That information was quickly followed by the consequences for the failure to comply with any or all of those rules as well. I suppose that I should mention the fact that the consequences we would face for non compliance of any and all rules should we get caught or any type of behavior they deemed as "**insubordination**", would be exactly the same. Our training would immediately terminate and we would be sent home on the next available flight. Hey! Now that I think about it, I've just realized that **American Airlines** management has been holding our careers over our heads as collateral even before we actually got the job. Imagine that! Anyway, after what seemed like an endless amount of hours of being preached to on what we could and couldn't do, every one of us were then assigned what was called a *"personal instructor" (supervisor)* and we were informed that they were there to not only assist us with whatever guidance we might need while undergoing and receiving our training, but to also help expedite our transition of becoming *American Airlines* flight attendants so that we could accomplish that as smoothly as possible. Luckily the *personal instructor* that was assigned to me was one of a handful of male instructors that were teaching at the *Farm* and believe me when I tell you that in this particular instance, it made all the difference in the world whether you were assigned a male or a female for a *personal instructor* because it seemed like a lot of the female instructors were on a self righteous mission to discombobulate the young and beautiful women that were passing through, ultimately annihilating what little confidence and self pride they may have managed to bring to training with them. If you paid close attention and most of us did, it was always very apparent that whatever negative and condescending communication or tactics these caustic female instructors chose to use on these young women on any particular day, was always driven by the complete and undisputable jealousy that they possessed. That was my personal opinion then and it shall remain my personal opinion forever. Of course, not all the female instructors who worked at the *Charm Farm* at the time had this jealousy monkey on their backs. There were some who were actually really quite helpful and showed genuine concern and excitement for us. Nevertheless, there were those few bad apples in with the bunch, and we all know what happens to a bowl full of perfectly good apples if you put a bad one in the same bowl and mix them up! There were so many days I remember walking through the hallways following my regimented class schedule and I would catch a glimpse of someone sobbing in a corner over something terrible that had either been done or said to them by one of these *capricious* and *mean spirited* instructors. They were constantly threatening to send us home for one thing or another they'd claimed we had said or done. Come to think about it, the *Farm* was the first place where I began hearing *American Airlines* management employee's favorite word; **insubordination.** It was a word that was reiterated for us numerous times a day and it was almost always followed by how it would not be tolerated! It was so terribly heartbreaking as well as disturbing for me when I would see these young women being berated into such a beat down and submissive condition. We wanted this career so badly that for some, it didn't even register at the time that we had already begun the all too familiar process of selling our *self respect and dignity* to this company for it. I suppose it was because I had spent some time with a few of these young women when we had first arrived and that had allowed me the ability to see first hand how sweet they all were and how they were so full of excitement. I just couldn't understand why this was happening to them or what they could be experiencing, which would cause that happy, enthusiastic disposition they had all brought with them to the training that I had witnessed just days before, to all of a sudden change so abruptly. It didn't take long though, before I quickly realized that the reason that they were being targeted by a handful of these shameful and envious female instructors, was for absolutely no other reason than the sheer fact that these women were young and beautiful. As a matter of fact, it would be soon thereafter when the all consuming jealousy belonging to these *nefarious* female instructors would show itself, making it very apparent to the rest of us. Most of these young beautiful women who had been singled out by their instructors precisely for this horrendous treatment were, in their early to mid twenties and when they were initially interviewed for the flight attendant position with American Airlines and then later accepted for the training, these young flight attendant trainees felt so lucky to be realizing the dream that was shared by many of the other young women that remained in their small towns who had not been selected and who would not be as fortunate to get the same opportunity to realize theirs. Not this one anyway. These young women were incredibly honored to have been chosen from hundreds of applicants to be there for this training. The rest of us knew exactly how they felt too, because we felt the exact same way. The difficulty of having even gotten that far was still very fresh in all of our minds. We had to overcome some very stiff competition along the way. I know many of my co-working flight attendants today who are close in years to my seniority or senior to me will remember the **"grooming"** portion of our training that we managed to survive, but not without our battle scars to show for it. *The American Airline's "one look fits all"* was the look they were going for. It was the **"generic"** and **"controlled"** appearance the company's management people wanted us all to have. When I think back and reflect on it now, I realize that it was just one of the many ways they came up with to keep us from bringing our own unique and different personalities to the career because different personalities would mean different view points which in turn would enable us to think outside of the box they wanted our thoughts and opinions to be kept in. *American Airlines* management didn't want flight attendants out on the line that had their own mindset, they wanted flight attendants out on the line that could follow orders and do exactly as they were told! To this very day I can remember the hell this one particularly beautiful young woman in my class was made to endure the entire time she was training at the *Farm,* for reasons that not only had no validity to them but also had absolutely nothing to do with her at all. To my surprise, there have been times in my life when I have found myself thinking about her and I feel the same sadness come over me now that came over me then. I find that to be amazing considering the fact that over 30 years have passed since the last time that I saw her but the memory I have of her never leaves me and I think it's partly because I've carried with me the guilt of knowing that I should have spoken up for her during those times when she could not speak up for herself and no one else would speak up for her either because of their fear of retaliation. Today I would have handled it all so differently but then again, today I am not the frightened and intimidated young woman that I was then. The woman I have become today would have found her audacious voice and used it all the while standing by that beautiful young woman regardless of whether or not anyone else did too! Today, I would speak up for her not only because it would be the right thing to do but also because of the fact that the many years I have had of constantly dealing with these **"*less than decent*"** types of people that ***American Airlines*** management insists on employing, my personality has developed into one which would never allow me to sit quietly on the sidelines while injustices are being committed either to myself or anyone else. The incredibly ominously disturbing and covert circumstances which surrounded this young woman over thirty years ago is still prevalent in the work place today but it is especially so in ours, which only solidifies the conclusion I have come to which is that I believe at times human nature isn't so human after all. There were a number of these dark deplorable stories provoking sadness similar to hers that were going on at the exact same time with other perspective young flight attendant trainees but in this chapter, I will only share her story and try to tell it in such a manner that will allow for your complete and unequivocal understanding of the injustices we were dealing with, along with everything else we were up against during our time spent in that place. This one particular young woman I will speak of was only one of a handful of **"beyond beautiful"** and absolutely **"stunning"** young women who had been accepted for training at the ***Charm Farm***. She was about 5ft. 10 in. and had this gorgeous long flowing blonde hair as well as this *"killer body"* that went along with her gorgeous face! She always looked liked she had just literally stepped out of the nearest *Vogue Magazine.* When we began our training, she always showed up for classes looking impeccably put together and polished. What amazed me the most about her was that she was as unbelievably sweet and humble as she was beautiful. I really believe that she wasn't even aware of her breathtaking beauty. Every time this young woman entered a room, all conversation in that room would immediately come to a complete stop *(no pun intended)* and all eyes were on her. To this day, I consider her to be the most beautiful woman I have ever seen in my entire life and I have seen many, yet in spite of that fact, she never once flaunted herself to anyone or acted conceited or self absorbed; at least not any time that I ever saw. I distinctly recall an immense fear that would come over me whenever I was around this young woman. I knew that the fear I was feeling was not for me but for her, but I didn't understand why I was feeling it. As time went by I began observing the interactions between this young woman and her *personal instructor.* In the next few paragraphs of this chapter that immediately follow, I will be referring to the **Charm Farm's** *personal instructor* that was assigned to the respective young and beautiful flight attendant trainee I am speaking to you of as *Cruela DeVil* because of the fact that she bore a striking resemblance to her. Now for those of you out there who may not know who *Cruela DeVil* is, she was the villain in the *Walt Disney* animated movie classic entitled *101 Dalmatians* who was obsessed with owning and wearing real animal fur. In this movie, *Cruela* has a niece who lives across town and owns two Dalmatian dogs, a male and female. Well, the female Dalmatian delivers a litter of puppies and when *Cruela* finds out about it, she hires two thugs to break into her niece's house, steal the puppies and remove their polka dotted skin in order so that she can have a Dalmatian polka dotted fur coat made for herself from their fur.

(Luckily the Dalmatian pups get rescued and find their way back home). Taking the Dalmatian equation *(no rhyme intended, just got lucky)* out of it, the reason for the correlation is that a more perfect name than *Cruela DeVil* as well as a more perfect description of the character belonging to the *personal instructor* of this young flight attendant trainee does not exist. I began noticing that no matter what topic of conversation or situation transpired between this young woman and her *personal instructor Cruela,* the conversation always ended in the exact same way every single time with **Ms. DeVil** expressing only negative and condescending remarks to this young woman regarding anything she was involved with whether it was that she didn't shout out her evacuation commands loud enough during the *"evacuation drills"* portion of our training, or she didn't have correct hand placement at the window exit of the *Boeing 707* aircraft simulated trainer we performed our emergency landing drills on, or yada, yada, yada, not to mention that she had the tremendous nerve and audacity to constantly complain about this beautiful trainee's personal appearance as well, telling her that she looked completely unprofessional, which of course was not only ludicrous of her to say in the first place, but it was an outright lie! As I stated earlier in this chapter, this particular beautiful and young flight attendant trainee's grooming was impeccable every single day since the minute she had arrived at the *Charm Farm.* It didn't matter what this poor young woman did to try and please *Ms. DeVil* because even though she did all the things and made all the changes that *Cruela* asked of her, such as wearing her clothing in a matronly manner for example or tying her hair up in a tight matronly bun, none of it would ever be good enough for *Cruela* because the issue that was always in question was not really about the flight attendant trainee's inability to do anything right. The *real* issue was about the self loathing, homely, fat ankles and power tripping *"straight from* *hell"* instructor *Cruela DeVil,* who was so consumed and beside herself with the insane jealousy she felt over the stunning, tall, thin and young trainee that was assigned to her that she couldn't see straight, so needless to say and much to the demise of the flight attendant trainee, *Cruela* took much pleasure in her negative and vile treatment of her trainee and she wallowed in her deprecation as she watched her flight attendant trainee crumble a little at a time from the non stop criticism and harassment that she provided for the young beauty. By the time our training started winding down towards the end of its final weeks leaving its mark, it was very apparent to the rest of us that the constant abuse inflicted on this young girl was definitely taking its toll. *Ms. DeVil* was busy with her plans of making sure that there would be no graduating with the rest of us for her trainee. As if watching and realizing this terrible situation wasn't bad enough, what was worse was the fact that I didn't know how to help her or if I even could. At first, all I could feel was a sense of desperation for her and that eventually turned into an increasing anger that I began to feel towards the *Farm's* instructors who although were not behaving in that same sadistic manner themselves, they could clearly see what *Cruela* was doing to this young woman and they chose to look the other way while it was happening. That only fueled her ability to continue undisturbed with her despicable abhorrent behavior. There was nowhere for me to go with my new found observation and no one I could report it to because I had absolutely no way of proving it since no one would back me up and I knew that! Furthermore, I knew without a doubt that I couldn't approach any of these above mentioned *cowards* masked as *personal instructors* because it was clear to me that if I even so much as attempted to speak up in this young woman's defense, I would have been informed that it was *"none of my business"* and I would have then found myself immediately holding an *American Airlines* **ONE WAY TICKET** in my hand with my name printed on it reading destination **HOME** and the worst part about that would have been not the ticket itself but rather the fact that it wouldn't have even been a *first class* ticket for my troubles, it would have been *coach*! At this point in the game we were in either our fifth or sixth week of the training course and *Cruela* had been patiently but anxiously waiting for this next "*personal grooming*" portion of our training to begin. *Ms. DeVil* had spent the previous weeks scoping out the prettiest women assigned to her group and had already made up her mind about who she would select, what she would do to her and when she would strike! She was ready! *The Charm Farm* hired hairdressers and make-up artists who were just students themselves that were attending some beauty school or other in town, learning how to cut hair and apply make-up on people. The first day we started the "*personal grooming*" training, *Cruela DeVil* didn't waste a moment of time in executing her plan on her unknowing first victim. Well, I am sure you can guess by now who that was going to be. She called out the girl's name, smiling at her the entire time as the young woman came towards her with that typical insincere and hypocritical ear to ear grin that disgusting and spineless people like her who happen to posses a small amount of power over others always seem to have plastered on their faces. She sported bigger hair on this particular day compared to the prior times I had seen her, and she reminded me of a wild animal with its hair standing on end right before it strikes its prey! She began speaking in that *annoying Texas drawl language of her very own* and proceeded to inform the young woman of how lucky she was to be the first one selected from her group to receive her *American Airlines* flight attendant makeover. *"Idin it xidin",* she drawled at the young woman with much glee. Sure. It was just peachy, I thought to myself. Along with the others, I took one last good look at this beautiful young woman with the beautiful long blonde hair before she descended into that *"personal grooming" classroom from hell*, because we all knew that no matter what hideous things *Cruela* was about to have done to her, that beautiful hair would be the first to go. Boy, did we call that one right! *Cruela DeVil* had the hairdresser severely chop off that girl's hair. When the haircut was all said and done, it measured about three inches from her scalp all the way around. As if that wasn't enough entertainment for *Ms. DeVil*, she also had the hairdresser dye it to a jet black color. Needless to say, it left the young woman in a massive state of hysteria and the rest of us in severe depression. We had all been, in a word, *"controlled"*. I have to say that I truly believe that was definitely the most defining moment in that young woman's life during her stay at the *American Airlines Flight Service College in 1976!* They had succeeded in not only breaking her spirit but that of many of the others. She, as well as a few of the other perspective flight attendant trainees would never make it to graduation with the rest of us. To give you an idea of just how prevalent this unscrupulous behavior was at the *Charm Farm* during the year I attended, when I first arrived there and they issued me the key to my dorm room along with the names of the other three trainees who would be my roommates, we were a total of four. By the time our graduation day rolled around there were only two of us left in that same room; *Miss Sabrina Hansen* and me. The other two just magically disappeared. Somehow I managed to personally escape the bulk of the entire *Charm Farm* nightmare pretty unscathed. I suppose it had a lot to do with the fact that I was lucky to have been assigned a male *personal instructor* while I was there as opposed to one of his *Broom Hilda* colleagues. I do have to say in all honesty though that I also had the good fortune of having had somewhat of a *"heads up"* conversation about the *Charm Farm* with the flight attendants who were working the flight which flew me to Dallas Fort Worth for my initial training and that most definitely worked to my advantage as well. I don't remember any of those flight attendant's names, but the advice, the warnings and the information they provided me with in the brief conversation we shared on that flight, would prove to be invaluable to me once I arrived at **The Charm Farm**. The most important instructional words they conveyed to me as I was getting off that flight and heading for the Flight Academy were basically *"to lay as low as possible as if to almost make myself invisible and to remember that only when I graduated and went out on the line as a full fledged flight attendant, would I know what a great career I had chosen because all of the nonsense that went on at the Charm Farm was not indicative of how things really worked once you got out on the line and if I could get through that, it would all be worth it in the end"*. Well, I have to say that if it wasn't for those ladies who were on that flight that day, I probably would not have been one of the **Charm Farm** survivors who were able to make it to graduation! Today, I am not so sure that would have been such a bad thing! Today, I think that maybe those young beautiful women who didn't make the cut 30 years ago went on to bigger and better things and *they,* not *us*, were truly the "*lucky ones*". Hopefully they are not presently finding themselves in the terrible position the rest of us are all in, which is that of having our flight attendant careers threatened by the greed and corruption of corporate management employees who happen to be in control of our livelihood and should otherwise be guiding us and our airline company to prosperity and success but are instead making despicable decisions that adversely affect all of us as well as our company. Today, I and others like me must fight to take back what has been stolen from us and from our careers by this company's shameless corporate leadership. Instead of being able to look forward to the retirement so many of us were once promised in return for our diligence, company loyalty and hard work that we gave for so many years of our lives, we are faced with the debilitating consequential issues that our company's corporate leadership has brought to our table, which has been completely manifested by their ***insatiable greed***! Needless to say, the rest of us made it to the graduating ceremonies and amazingly enough still feeling so proud of ourselves and each other. Even after all that we went through, we were ecstatic with joy at the fact that we had finally made it and were now full fledged "***American Airlines Flight Attendants***." That proud feeling that we felt on that day is one that most of us have not experienced in a very long time. At the graduating ceremonies we were given an ***award/diploma*** stating successful completion of the training course for flight attendants. We were lucky enough to have our diplomas signed by ***Mr. Albert Casey*** himself, who at that time was still chairman and president of American Airlines, Inc. **(there was no AMR)**. Had they been signed by ***Mr. Casey's*** successor, **Mr. Robert Crandall**, I would have burned mine by now! We were also given a graduation picture that was taken with all of us in it as a memento of our memorable stay at the ***Charm Farm***. Posing for that graduation picture was an event all by itself. I remember all of us being crammed in together on this wide, huge winding staircase. We were all dressed in our American Airline's uniform looking just like the "***Stepford American Airlines Flight Attendants***" they had created but even that fact couldn't cramp our style that day. Nothing could! After the picture taking time was over, someone started playing the baby grand piano that was located at the bottom of that staircase and before we knew it, they had us all breaking into a chorus of that infamous American Airlines jingle that was used to advertise the airline on television commercials during that time frame. "***We're American Airlines .....Doing What We Do Best***". Then, just like that, we were crying and hugging each other while saying our goodbyes. We would make promises of keeping in touch with each other forever not knowing that most of us would never be able to keep those promises. We told each other how much we loved one another and then after a few more tears and a lot more hugs we were off and running to our new lives and the new cities and destinations where our own personal journeys awaited us. We were unstoppable and felt invincible. We were on our way to change and conquer the world starting with **New York City, Boston, San Francisco, Los Angeles and Dallas Fort Worth** to name a few of our conquering destinations. Let's face it, compared to where most of us had been during our young lives those big cities were the world! As great as the adrenaline was in those early days that made us feel so alive and vibrant, American Airlines management harassment and intimidation started way back then. We wanted the job so badly and the company knew it. They used that very fact to their utmost advantage. The harassment and intimidation tactics that American Airlines management used on us then continue to be used on us to this day. It is the way they controlled us then, and they continue to control us now. Consider the very important fact that this company that we work for always chooses to interact with us in such a demeaning and disrespectful manner because it is what ultimately keeps them in charge while we are constantly under their thumb doing their bidding. Their tactics are really nothing new. It's what I've dubbed "***The American Airlines Management Syndrome***". It is extremely similar to the "***Stockholm Syndrome***" that we flight attendants are well familiar with except of course in this case, we are the ones being hijacked and this company's corporate leaders make us feel so grateful for not taking our jobs that we actually begin to sympathize with their absurd cause of slowly but surely wiping out all our benefits and cutting back our pay while at the same time paying themselves bonuses off our tired backs and then, we take it a step further and actually ask them via **(APFA),** if there is anything else we can give them or we simply offer to just let them take away from us whatever they haven't already taken, in return for allowing us to keep our jobs. What our actions are actually really translating to them is: "***take everything you want from us just please, please let us keep our jobs***"! So now that they've allowed us to keep our jobs we are so grateful for their kindness and we demonstrate that gratitude to them by allowing them to do whatever the hell they want with us and take whatever the hell they want from us! ***American Airlines flight attendants out there; doesn't what you just read sound not only immensely co-dependant which is exactly what it is, but completely spineless and cowardly as well? Are all you out there taking this in?*** I know damn well how hard it is for you to come to terms with the fact that we have all been beaten down so badly through harassment and intimidation by the very people who are running this company and their greed ridden counterparts, but we have to take ***responsibility*** for the fact that we have allowed ourselves to become this weak group of people who can't even muster the strength and conviction to fight for ourselves, much less stand up for each other. ***We have to own this situation before we can begin to get on the path to fix it, otherwise, by continuing to display our constant cowering behavior we will continue to keep sending the same message we've been sending this company's management over and over again for what is now too many long years and that message is, that we don't matter, we are expendable, we will take whatever you want to give us instead of whatever we have worked hard for and earned as well as deserve!*** As difficult as it is to think of ourselves in this manner, our co-dependency is something that we had better start re-evaluating about ourselves and quickly because we are running out of time. It was somewhat excusable back in the days of the ***Charm Farm*** years when we were such young dumb asses afraid of our own shadows. We were inexperienced, unaffected, and extremely vulnerable then but now it's over thirty years later and we are not so young, not so unaffected and not so extremely vulnerable and it's not excusable anymore it's downright sickening! We all need to take our heads out of *"la la land"* and start paying closer attention to what we have and continue to let these corporate greed mongers do to our careers and lives! If this company's management we currently have in place that dares to call themselves the American Airline's Corporate Leadership is allowed to continue to oversee and run *"OUR"* airline in the manner in which they have been, ***they are going to run it right into the ground like a dart along with our jobs, benefits and pension, and no matter how you slice that, it's sure not pizza!*** Lately I've had to ask myself some serious questions concerning the way we flight attendants have allowed ourselves to be treated so disrespectfully by this company's management people for so many years and when I use the word WE here, I'm using it loosely because I for one decided along time ago that I would be treated with the respect and integrity that I deserve and it has been a long hard struggle, at times fighting huge battles that almost always left me out in the cold standing alone, present time not excluded! So the million dollar question I am always asked by others is *"why do you stay"*? ***Why do any of us stay?*** Well, it's like someone in our flight attendant family whom many of us happen to know and whom I happen to love very much would always reply when asked that very same question from some of our passengers. When it comes to working for American Airlines, ***"our job is a lot like an abusive marriage; you know that you should leave but you stay for the children."*** Besides the fact that for most of us, working as flight attendants is in our blood, many of us have a tremendous amount of years invested in this airline company; certainly more than that of our current CEO. Flight Attendants, don't you think the time has seriously come for all of us to stand together united and strong and start taking back from corporate management what is and has been rightfully ours all along instead of running the first chance we get for our retirements that we are not even ready for yet or we to try to find other careers or jobs that we have no doubt become obsolete for? If corporate management takes what is not only theirs but ours too, and then bankrupts this airline, which seems to me to be quite possibly what they could end up doing especially when you look at the way in which they have been *"choosing"* to handle things in the last few years, I hate to tell you this but running to your respective retirements is not going to guarantee you will be safe from the incredible financial mess that our *genius greed ridden corporate leadership* has tail spinned this airline company of ours into. When any company completely bankrupts, eventually there is no more money because there is no more company; therefore, if there is no more money or company, than there is no more retirement! It's pretty basic really! Those of you who are opting for a retirement of the *"early out"* kind as a quick fix, well, all you are accomplishing by doing that is basically allowing yourselves to get swindled from much of your retirement *"early out."* Isn't the current mentality we are beginning to develop, which is that of looking out for *"me"* instead of for "*one another*" one of the reasons why this airline situation of ours has escalated to the current problematic dimension it is currently in? Isn't that what American Airline's corporate leadership has done to us? Why then, would we want to turn around and develop the exact same attitude towards each other that corporate has towards us? Aren't we sick of running yet? *When does the time come when we no longer come to work constantly running scared for our jobs?* This is our careers as well as our lives these people are **annihilating** daily. Hey, fellow flight attendants out there! Do we have to be reminded of what exactly it is that we do for a living and how much of it is done at *39,000* feet? Probably *80%* or more of our lives are spent at that high altitude! *Have American Airlines Flights*

11 and 77 and the passengers and our fellow crew member family who were on those flights and died, slipped your minds? I think the constant *minimizing* of who we are and what we do for a living by this company's management is deplorable unacceptable and **insubordinate** and furthermore, *it will not be tolerated!* You guys, come on! *For the people that lost their lives on September 11, 2001, for our families and loved ones, for our passengers everywhere and for our very selves and each other my fellow flight attendants the time has come when we need to STAND!*

"From the sunrise in the East, to the sunset in the West,

we're American Airlines, doing what we do best."

(American Airlines advertising jingle)

American Airlines
Flight Service College

Awards this Certificate of Graduation to

Linda Alicia Garcia

for successful completion of the training course
for
Flight Attendants

<u>May 27, 1976</u>
DATE

CHAIRMAN & PRESIDENT-AMERICAN AIRLINES, INC.

DIRECTOR-FLIGHT SERVICE COLLEGE

"My Ticket out of

the Charm Farm Nightmare!"

"Graduation Day"

CHAPTER 3

THE FLIGHT ATTENDANT BOND

Those of us who have been around for 15 years or more have truly witnessed the demise of what use to at one time be one of the most incredible industry this country has ever known. To have been a part of it then, is what I believe in my heart keeps me fighting furiously for its **restitution.** I have worked in this industry when it was at its best and it was during those early years that we the flight attendants at **American Airlines** formed this incredible bond that holds us together. *This bond is also universal in the sense that it reaches outside of our own flight attendants to the other commercial airline flight attendants as well.* The reason I can make that last statement is because after September 11th 2001, I attended many memorial services that were held to honor the fallen flight crews that had died on that horrible day and a couple of those services were to honor the **United Airlines Flight 93 crewmembers. *Although they were not my own, I mourned for them with just as much intensity as I did for my own fellow crew members. There was absolutely no difference whatsoever in my level of sadness.*** I realize that to the normal (non-crew member) person that might sound a bit incredulous, but you can ask any flight attendant if what I speak of is so and they will tell you every time that it is. We are all one in the same. It is *the flight attendant bond.* It was formed years ago and was already there even before I started with **American Airlines.** At the time American Airlines hired me in May of 1976, (I' am sure if they had to do it over again I'd be working for Delta), **Mr. Albert Casey** was the man in charge. Although we had to fight **Mr. Casey** on many company policies that were implemented at the time due to their nature in regards to being **sexist** or just plain **unconstitutional**, such as the one where you **had to resign as a flight attendant if you got married or had a child while you were employed as a flight attendant,** in other aspects **Mr. Casey** was a very kind and respectful man towards his employees. I think that most employees who were around in those early years would wholeheartedly agree with that. **Mr. Casey was old school and he was the last of a dying breed, such as Howard Hughes, who truly had a tremendous respect and love of aviation.** It never became routine for him. He was in awe of it much the same way that the rest of us were. **The bond we have among flight crews was able to come into existence because of the manner in which Mr. Casey ran the operational part of Flight Service at American Airlines which is the department that flight attendants and Cockpit Crew Members operate under.** He kept the entire flight crews together while we worked our trips not only for however many days of those trips we happened to be working, but for the entire month. When you flew with the same people for days or weeks or months at a time, you not only got to know and love some of those people, but they also got to know and love you as well. You felt privileged and honored to be able to work side by side with so many of them. One of the statements I make quite often when I am describing my co-working **flight attendants** is that they **are really good people who genuinely care about others.** We are loyal and fiercely protective of one another. **American Airlines is lucky to have such wonderful people working for them and they do not deserve us.** We formed these incredible ties with each other that at times were much stronger than the ones we had with some of our own family members. In fact, *we actually became each others second family* and because we were all so young at the time we started flying, we grew up together. We attended each other's weddings. We were there through the births of each other's children, always keeping one another informed of their growth, achievements and accomplishments. We confided in each other from coast to coast and supported each other through thick or thin, in sickness and in health as well as through the losses of our parents or loved ones. Those of us from that era that still remain on board with this company are still very close and work hard to keep that bond alive and thriving as much as possible even though *we are finding ourselves at a serious disadvantage these days since the flight crews are not kept together in the same manner in which they were at one time. That was all in the big corporate scheme of things that started emerging after Mr. Casey relinquished his power to the new CEO that would take over American Airlines, Mr. Robert Crandall and as we all well know, Mr. Crandall had different plans for all of us and he started those plans with division.* He saw the tremendous closeness and camaraderie we had with one another and realizing that, he immediately went to work to change that situation as quickly as possible. There were too many of us and he knew that besides the known fact that there is a great power in numbers, *dividing us would give him the ability to control us more completely and with much less protest.* During those years that *Mr. Casey* had the say so, we looked forward with much anticipation when our bids came out and we looked up the names of the crews we would be flying with the following month. So many times we would hold a bid that would reunite us with crews we had previously worked with the month before and we would literally scream from excitement! If that weren't enough

35

icing on the cake, as they say, to add to our adventure we would hold these incredibly paired trips that would take us to fantastic cities such as New York, Boston or San Francisco for example, which we would get to explore on our 24 hour layovers. The minute the limo would pull up to whatever hotel we were laying over at, we quickly signed in, got our room keys from the front desk and scurried off to our rooms to freshen ourselves up because someone in the crew had called *"downstairs 15 minutes!"* and we were off and running. Sometimes for dinner, other times to a Broadway play or both and there was always shopping and sightseeing all depending on the city you were laying over in. *There were so many times we would look at each other and acknowledge how wonderful it all was and how glad we were that we were so persistent and determined to attain this incredible flight attendant career we now had.* No matter what trials and tribulations we had to overcome to get there, every single one of us knew it had all been worth it in the end. We marveled at the sheer thought of how we were technically at work getting paid while we were on these outings loving life because the layovers were part of the job description. Now looking back as a 54 year old flight attendant, I realize that the way it was then is as it still should be now. These days, having so much more life experience under my belt as opposed to the amount I possessed in those early years, I understand all too well why those perks were established for the fight attendant career in the first place. It's not like we perform our jobs from a work cubicle in a nice safe office somewhere on solid ground. *We perform our jobs thousands of feet into the skies, strictly confined in a large silver tube which is emitting continuous radiation contaminants. We breathe filthy recycled air from the aircrafts "dirty" air conditioning system and dehydrate ourselves from the combination of the dry air found at that altitude along with the pressurized cabin climate. Then of course, there's the sleep deprivation, as well as the high stress that goes with the job! Most important of all, lets not forget that we work under the potential risk of emergency landings complete with emergency evacuations (those are always fun), fatal airplane crashes and aircraft hijackings, and hijackings these days those don't end up working out where we find ourselves being hijacked to some sunny tropical place, before the hijackers decide to let us all go and surrender to the local authorities. The era of those type hijackings are OVER! We run a much "higher risk" of meeting up with AlQueda up there than those who work on solid ground and for the flight crewmembers today, that certainly doesn't play out to be like the old "Las Vegas charter party flights" we use to work in times gone by!* All that said, it is shameful how this company's upper management has disappeared all those little benefits that made this career so worthwhile. I truly believe it has been our amazing *flight attendant bond* that has really kept us here for so long. I will forever remember this one particular trip I was flying one month. I literally had nine co-working flight attendants assigned to work the trip with me and as luck would have it, they all happened to be some of my closest friends! That just doesn't happen that often on its own. The trip was *American Airlines Flight 10 from LAX to JFK (the all nighter).* We had close to a 30 hour layover right smack in the middle of downtown *Manhattan* in December no less! I cannot even begin to describe the excitement we were all feeling at the fact that we had all ended up on the same trip for such an incredible layover. I remember laughing so hard on that *McDonnell Douglas DC10* aircraft we were working that night as we flew to *New York City.* It's just a given that when you put nine flight attendants together on the same airplane working the same flight, who not only happen to be great friends but also have these diversified and highly animated personalities and can totally entertain themselves, at times even corralling in a couple of passengers into the mix, that scenario just guarantees that we are all in for a wonderfully fun and memorable trip and that goes for everyone who is on that airplane! The almost five hours in duration of flight time went so fast that it seemed more like five minutes to us. We were having so much fun on that flight that it had seemed as if we had just taken off before the next thing we were unbelievably hearing was *"flight attendants prepare for landing."* When we arrived at the airport in **New York** and made our way through the **JFK** terminal and outside to where the crewmember hotel limo pick up area was where we could board the limo that would drive us to our layover hotel, we were still splitting our sides from laughing so hard as we were recalling the events that took place on our flight that night, and we continued that wonderfully uncontrollable laughter through the entire ride into the city. Once we arrive in the city, we already knew that it was going to be very difficult to make ourselves settle down and go to sleep so we could rest for at least three maybe four hours after being up all night, and then make ourselves get up, get showered and get going again because we were still really tired, but that was exactly what we had to do if we wanted to make the most of our layover time and see and do all the things in the city that we wanted to see and do, and boy did we have plans! It was *seven a.m.* in **New York** and the city was already awake and bustling with enthusiasm. It was **Christmastime** after all and as we drove towards our layover hotel, the streets looked like something out of a **Hallmark greeting card** with all the lights and trimmings of the holiday season everywhere you looked. The store windows were dressed with beautifully ornate Christmas decorations; the kind that you only see on the **East Coast,** that made you immediately think of such movies as *"Miracle on 34th Street"* or *"It's a Wonderful Life"*! Residing in **Southern California** most of my life has really helped me to appreciate an **East Coast Christmas** especially one in

New York City. The splendor of it all just made us all the more anxious and excited about being there. The anticipation of getting out there and not only enjoying it, but actually becoming a part of it was tremendous. That's what you do in the City at Christmastime; you become a part of the Christmas season's experience. Nevertheless, we knew that because we had been up all night flying, in order to be able to **double sleep** that same night *(sleep twice in the same day),* we had to force ourselves to get at least a few hours of rest before engaging in our *New York City* escapade, especially knowing that we did have to eventually work the flight back home to *Los Angeles* at some point, and we certainly didn't want to scare our passengers when they boarded our airplane by looking like a bunch of haggard flight attendants, which we knew was exactly the way we would look if we didn't get any rest on our layover. So after finally arriving at out hotel (**still laughing**) and obtaining our room keys from our *"great"* and *"dearly loved"* little British hotel clerk named *Doty,* who worked at the front desk and never once missed checking us into the hotel without showering us with her *incredible warmth* and the *genuinely sweet smile and candor* that she always had waiting for us when we arrived, the decision that we would all meet in the lobby at *high noon* was made, and we all set off to our respective rooms so we could get some shut eye. As tired as we were, when the alarm clocks went off in our rooms a few hours later, we didn't require much prodding to make ourselves get up because we couldn't wait to meet downstairs so that we could be together and start laughing all over again! That laughter would quickly become very "*slap happy*" all day long. When we were all accounted for in the hotel lobby, we donned on our *American Airline's* navy blue trench coats *(with the liner in it),* put on our scarves, hats, ear muffs, gloves and anything else we brought to keep us warm for that very cold weather outside that we were about to enter with some trepidation but certainly most willingly. The laughter started almost immediately when one of us made a comment about how *"we all looked like a bunch of penguins in our navy blue trench coats"*. We were momentarily deceived by the way in which the weather outside appeared because the sky was completely cloudless and it was a striking cobalt blue color while the sun was brighter than bright. That deceitful moment was over in a flash when we stepped out of the hotel and into the street though, because we quickly realized that things aren't always what they seem, and in this case, the weather proved that statement to be literal. We could see our cold breaths blow in front of us and immediately decided that finding walking partners among ourselves to huddle up close and get personal with, would be a necessity for this little escapade of ours, so each one of us locked arms with another as we quickly walked to our first destination because it was so very cold. Our first stop turned out to be just around the corner to the first neighborhood deli where we *"unanimously"* decided that the short walk past a couple of buildings and one or two establishments near our hotel was just far enough. We were on a quest to acquire our first cup of **strong hot steaming java,** before we set off on our big adventures for the day! We were already freezing at this point, and we had once again started deliriously laughing at the fact that we hadn't even been outside for very long! *"We are all nothing but a bunch of California wimps"* one of us yells out loud, and of course that only creates more laughter. When we found ourselves standing in front of the deli, we began pushing and shoving each other **(in jest of course)** in order to get through the front doors as fast as we could because we knew that it would be nice and warm inside that deli. Up until the point where we were all finally inside, we were completely oblivious to the fact that we were making a huge scene and providing a *morning show* for the deli's patrons that were already inside, enjoying their first cups of coffee while reading the daily morning newspaper, or simply enjoying each others conversations. Everyone in that deli just stopped in their tracks and all of a sudden, there was this dead silence that engulfed the room. We all froze and quietly stood there looking out into the room at the faces that were staring back at us, realizing then and only then, that all of those faces had eyes that were now fixated on us and it seemed as if they were momentarily being held captive by the total amazement of what they had just witnessed. What they were looking at, were a bunch of **dressed alike freaks wearing navy blue trench coats** that were deliriously **slap happy** and completely **out of control!** Well, as tired and **slap happy** as we all were, that reaction from those people certainly didn't help us in our situation one bit, and it only served to make us start laughing even harder than we were before! The owner of the establishment recognized some of us from previous visits and he was genuinely happy to see all of us come in to his deli, and his reaction when seeing us, made us feel happy too. He was most hospitable towards us and even joined us for a few minutes while we would drink our coffees and teas or whatever the hell it was that we were drinking to warm ourselves up. *This moment in time, this feeling of friendship and camaraderie of which I know to be of the truest kind; the hugs, the laughter and love we shared among each other, all of it, is "undeniably" the best part of our jobs as flight attendants and will be what I will choose to take with me and keep close to my heart for as long as I live, when it is time for me to go.* It is not taken for granted by any of us. When I sometimes stop and try to think about what other employment out there could possibly provide me with even a fraction of such an incredible **benefit** or **perk** or whatever you want to call it, I can tell you with all that is certain to me that no other such employment exists. **Not like ours!** So after we warmed up and finished our hot drinks, we bundled back up, said our **"thank yous"** and did our **"see you next week"** routines, and once again went venturing back outside into that frosty day, so that we could begin our big day in the City, starting with our Christmas shopping. We headed towards the nearest subway station where the plan was to take a train all the way down to *Canal Street.* Of course me being the obsessed *fitness freak* and *avid runner* that I am, wanted to see if I could get my daily workout in while I was on this layover. I would try to convince all my lazy friends of how it would really be good for us to just walk all the way downtown instead of taking the train, but that idea was quickly squashed, and I was then informed by all of them that I must have become oxygen deprived from flying on so many airplanes for too many years because it had seemed to them that I had finally lost my marbles *(more laughter).* So I reluctantly went with the majority vote and I proceeded to the nearest train station with those losers, where we boarded the *"E" train* headed downtown and we were finally on our way to our much anticipated *Canal Street* shopping escapade. We spent a few hours there, checking out designer *knock off* watches, bags/ purses, sunglasses and *"real"* sterling silver jewelry. Some of us had shopping lists that were given to us by our family members and friends back home in *Los Angeles*, of what they wanted us to bring back home for them. They knew that we had a long layover in the city, and that we were planning this *Canal Street* shopping extravaganza. Others just had their Christmas shopping lists with them and were seizing the *Canal Street* bargains, and crossing off the names of the people on their Christmas lists who they were buying for. Before we knew it, three hours had passed and it was time for us to leave *Canal Street* and head back to the train station once again, where we would then board another *"E" train* only this time we would be heading uptown until the train reached the *34TH Street* and *Broadway* exit, because we still had much more shopping to do! This particular area of *Manhattan* has miles of shopping boutiques and department stores on both sides of the street and of course, that was where we would be making our exit off the train! We hit every store we came across on **Broadway,** including the infamous **Macys Department Store** and I have to say that compared to all of the other stores in **New York's Manhattan** adorned with the beauty and the magnificence of the blessed holiday season, **Macy's** always made all the rest of them seem pale in comparison, with the exceptions of maybe **Sacks Fifth Avenue** and **FAO Shwartz!** The minute we stepped off that train, climbed the stairs and hit that bright sunlight, our hearts started pumping with excitement at the sights and sounds of the hustle and bustle that was already in motion long before we got there. The streets were filled with Christmas holiday shoppers, carrying arm loads of gift boxes and shopping bags filled with presents. They were walking, talking, laughing and running to catch taxi cabs. Makeshift Santa Clauses stood on street corners playing Christmas music and ringing bells to attract your attention and remind you to kindly put your spare change in the donation box they had that was collecting money to help those that are less fortunate. The delightful aroma coming off of the street cart food vendors from their **New York** hot dogs and sausages **(my favorite)** managed to get me every time. I would lather my dog up with that spicy mustard they have on their cart, some onions, and top it off with that incredible **sauerkraut concoction** they invented. **Amazing!** That always had to be followed up by those delicious **hot roasted caramelized nuts.** I could **never** pass those up. Then you had the street vendors on every block selling anything and everything, signaling and then seducing you over to them with their crafty **"I'll give you a good deal"** sales pitch and their big warm smiles in order to solicit their goods to you, and goods they had! Watches, purses, hats gloves, ear muffs, scarves, sunglasses, music and movie CD'S, books, art, jewelry, sweatshirts with a variety of **New York City** logos on them. You name it and they were selling it! We Christmas shopped but *flight attendants never drop*! After shopping a few more hours *(actually, quite a few),* it was dinner time and everybody was famished, so we momentarily argued about where our dinning experience would take place that evening, and we quickly found ourselves at **Carmines on 44TH** and **Broadway.** After sharing a wonderful meal with my wonderful friends, most of us, including me, were done for the night so we headed back to our hotel, the Mildew Plaza *(The Milford Plaza)* as we affectionately called it, with the exception of a brave and tireless few who unbelievably carried on further into the evening, and took in a Broadway show. As for the rest of us, the time had definitely arrived when we would call ourselves a *"done deal"* and call it a night! My God, at what point in our careers did we lose that wonderful *perk* that came with this profession? How did we let these corporate people take that away from us? This job of ours is not one that entails having both feet on solid ground. Flight attendants are not consumed with monetary greed the way our corporate executives are. **American Airlines** flight attendants are not difficult employees. We seriously don't ask for much. If we make a descent *"living wage"* and are provided with *"medical"* and *"dental"* insurance for ourselves and our families along with our little measly retirement, and pass benefits, what else have we ever demanded or asked for? Considering the risks we take with our very lives every time we come to work, I don't understand why it is that corporate has to take away our few, and at this point very limited *"perks* and *"benefits".* That's just shameful on their part. **How many millions do they need to make?** We all miss those days terribly and what is really not only sad but terribly unjust as well, is that those trips paired in that manner have all but disappeared because of the insatiable greed of the CEO's that have come up the corporate ranks after **Mr. C. R. Smith**. Up until now, that *flight attendant bond* that some of us senior flight attendants are desperately trying to hold on to, is beginning to fray and is getting harder and harder to keep alive and thriving among us. There is so much adversity being thrown our way these days, along with the company management's constant unreasonable demands that many of the *"old school"* flight attendants are looking to find their way out of this career either through *retirement* or just simply *early out*. The flight attendants that have been hired in the last few years, understandably *do not* have that strong connection that we have with one another because *they have never known this career in the same manner in which we have known it*, therefore, it is not possible for them to have the capability to demonstrate the same allegiance that the rest of us have and lovingly display towards each other, and at times, that very situation creates *dissention in the ranks*, so to speak. That dissention between some flight attendants is exactly what this company's corporate management leadership, past and present, has kept diligently enabling for so many years, in order to maintain control over us and they have been quite successful I might add! *American Airlines* corporate management would like nothing better than to see me and others like me, who *stand up* and *protest* against *unjus*t company disciplinary tactics and the *unethical* corporate stance they maintain, to just go away. *The threat of being caught by the general flying public, committing the reprehensible and immoral offenses they commit on a daily basis, not to mention the blatant disregard they maintain towards passenger and flight crewmember safety, is what keeps them on their toes, every time they publicly address the airline travelers with their excuses and LIES! I am sure that they can't even begin to "fathom" the idea of being forced to become accountable for the despicably shady and borderline criminal form of overseeing this airline company that they have engaged in for quite some time now.* The powerful force that they know would inevitably materialize from all of us standing together against them, is not anything that they want to see happen anytime soon and it frightens them. Although I had heard that very statement from different people at different times in the past when discussing the dire situation we have been in for quite some time now, and are still currently finding ourselves in with this airline, I have always had trouble believing it to be true, I suppose because of the intimidating size of **American Airlines** and the powerful corporate management executives that oversee it. That view has changed dramatically for me in the last two years however, due to the fact that it has been **reiterated** to me in the last few months, not by just one **California Labor Attorney** that I have contacted, but by several, that there is immense power in numbers, and that has put it all in proper perspective for me! Flight attendants, we cannot allow **American Airlines** management executives to take that incredible *flight attendant bond* away from us the way they have slowly but surely taken everything else. From a passenger's standpoint in this day and age, especially with all the **terrorism threats** and the **safety** and **security** issues that are not being taken seriously or addressed properly by our current aviation industry's leadership; then adding to that mix everything else that can go wrong up there, it has to be a frightening feeling for them every time they have to board an aircraft and fly anywhere. *"Dear passengers believe me when I tell you, that it is this bond between the flight attendants that will make the difference in the outcome you experience, should you find yourself in any horrific and catastrophic situation up there. If you are ever on an unfortunate flight with an entire crew made up of flight attendants that do not know this bond that I speak of, my serious advice to you would be that you start praying very hard, because I guarantee that you will quickly come to know and understand the difference in your flight attendants"!* The time has truly come flight attendants, when we all need to **STAND**!

"My Beloved Airline Family"

Flight Attendant Camaraderie

Persuaded to run the New York City ½ Marathon by Fellow Flight Attendant on a layover.

Survived It!

"A Lifelong Bond"

"32 Years in the Making"

The Alnighter Gang Reunion 2008

I will remember you

Will you remember me?

Don't let your life pass you by

Weep not for the memories

Remember the good times that we had?

*(Singer and songwriter Sarah McLachlan)

CHAPTER 4

THE CHANGING OF THE GUARDS

The "*Changing of the Guards*" is what I like to call the big event that takes place at *American Airlines* every five to six years give or take a year, when the employees have the honor of watching yet another **CEO** retire from this company, jumping happily into the gigantic *golden parachute* the company has provided for him *regardless of his job performance while he was there*, due to a little safeguard clause in his contract), and moves on. The next corporation that hires him has their own board members who will be *salivating* from the anticipation and excitement at the thought of the millions this guy is going to make for them. Yeah, he's that good. Hell, the **CEO** we presently have, *Mr. Gerald Arpey*, has had his face plastered not only on the cover of *Fortune Magazine*, but he was *named CEO of the year in the September 2007 issue of the Dallas CEO Magazine!* As a matter of fact, he made a direct quote in that magazine on that date that stated as follows: quote: *"I think it is a real credit to our unions and employees that they executed that plan that allowed us to rebuild against the strength of the company."* End of quote. *Wow! What an understatement!* I wonder if every one of us grasped what he meant by that? I hope we're all paying close attention these days, because although I am sure that our present *CEO Mr. Arpey and his buddies* *are financially quite sound, the rest of us are heading for dire straights if we don't start making things change around here.* Corporate may not like our attitudes about the way things currently are, but at this point, seeing as how they are the ones responsible for our company's current condition, who really cares what they like, right? *They have managed to literally make it a sink or swim situation for the rest of us so we better start swimming FAST!* Like I was saying earlier, this is a huge event only in the sense that it *gives the employees a bit of hope for a little while anyway, that maybe, just maybe, someone honorable, forthright and decent could take over the job of running this company and all of its employees not only with the respect and dignity that each and every one of us deserves in their own right, but also and most important of all, with a complete sense of fairness which is all any of us really ask for.* We quickly realize though that all that hoping is purely in vain and that very soon after their induction, it is quite indubitable that the abusive and one sided financially rewarding *(not our side)* working conditions we have allowed ourselves to remain in for such a very long time resume once again under new leadership. In case anyone could possibly be wondering exactly what all that means, let me break it down for you so you can understand how that works. *WE make a lot of money for this company, through our hard work and commitment, for the benefit of its success.* This of course is everyone's goal considering it is the company many of us have been working at for a considerable amount of years and had hoped to retire, at some point in our later lives from. *We* accept unnecessary salary cutbacks, *we* start paying more for our medical insurance, (*which by the way was completely provided by the company as one of the benefits of the job when I started in 1976),* and as for our wonderful stand-by pass privileges, well that's the perfect name for them *STAND-BY* because that's exactly what we do. *We* stand-by flight after flight after flight, sometimes not ever reaching any destination we're trying to get to due to the fact that the passenger loads are almost always oversold making it impossible to accommodate non-revenues, that's us. More often than not *we* end up buying full fare tickets so we can get where we are going without all the stress. Some pass privileges, huh? I wonder if *Arpey,* or any one of his buddies or family members get bumped off airplanes the way the rest of us non-important employees do, you think? Please! All *they* do is get *richer and richer off our backs.* *They* buy two maybe three vacation homes aside from the primary mansion residence they already live in, maybe a yacht here and there, a brand new Rolls Royce for the high maintenance of their much younger wives, you know, to make their lives happy and comfortable so they will stick around awhile. Basically, *they* do minimal for us, and *they* compensate us as little as they possibly can, since they know they have bred that pathetic *"I am so lucky to have a job"* syndrome in us which we are constantly displaying for them and *we* get to go home and live paycheck to paycheck always trying to make ends meet, which of course for many of us they don't meet! Doesn't that just sound great? Well, that's exactly what has been happening to us for quite a while now. It is the way it has all been purposely designed to work. Don't you guys see that? *"The Rules of Engagement"* as I love to call the whole monstrous situation, was set into motion back in the day when our very own dear *Mr. Robert Crandall* took over this airline. During his reign, he *managed to destroy everything we held sacred and cared about in this career and turned it into the dreaded job we currently know and show up for.* *Mr. king of "B" Scale* himself with all his lies and empty promises, managed to convince us that in order for the company to grow and be able to compete with the other existing major air carriers all of us would have to submit to *concessions and sacrificing (temporarily of course).*

He made grandeur speeches telling us that by all of us doing so would give the company the ability to generate higher revenue, which would then make it possible to purchase bigger and better fuel efficient aircrafts, which in turn would give the company the capability to acquire more routes, which would then ***blah blah blah***, finally allowing us all to reap the benefits that would come from our unselfish sacrificing. Boy! That was some ***reaping*** we did, huh? It was more like him ***raping*** us, wasn't it? What is so sad is that the lies and deception that ***Mr. Robert Crandall*** bestowed upon us back then, continue to this day with our current ***CEO, Mr. Gerald Arpey*** who is doing the fine job with his own lies and deception. ***Arpey*** and ***Crandall*** are made from the exact same mold and there is no doubt about that! The winners for committing the ***biggest stupidity*** of all time, are us, and we win the prize for seriously thinking that every time they uttered that ***WE*** would have to sacrifice in a sentence, ***THEY*** were **NOT** including themselves in that equation. Whatever possessed us to go along with all of that, when they had proven to us time and time again on so many prior occasions of so called contract negotiations, that they are all a bunch of lying crooks of the most serious kind? ***They attended the Lorenzo (remember him?) class 101; "How to royally screw your employees over and walk away from them a millionaire ten times over with their own money"***! History keeps repeating itself and it is constantly trying to teach us over and over again that ***"WE"*** does not mean ***"THEM!"*** It just means ***US***! Why then, do we not pay attention and learn from it? We all know that anytime any of our money grubbing ***CEO*** says the word ***WE*** in any of his speeches or memos or newsletters or any other form of communication he chooses to use to convey his ***LIES*** to ***US***, he is ***never*** including himself or his greedy corporate upper management buddies in the equation of ***WE***! That analogy I just gave you not only refers to our present tense ***CEO Mr. Arpey,*** but our past tense ones as well. How much more do we lose, before we wake up and smell the freaking coffee? It's not like they aren't putting it right smack in our faces! Haven't they done just exactly that for so many years? Did you not feel absolutely outraged when you learned that on *April 18, 2007, our current CEO, Mr. Gerald J. Arpey and his top four upper corporate management buddies found it completely justified to pay themselves those enormous bonuses to the tune of $19,183,270! That amount was paid out to just the TOP FIVE! Let me put that dollar amount into words for you so that you completely understand those numbers. 19 MILLION, 183 THOUSAND, TWO HUNDRED SEVENTY DOLLARS! A Star-Telegram staff writer by the name of Trebor Banstetter* wrote a news article on *March 14, 2007* about *American Airlines* flight attendants protesting these very same executive bonuses. He wrote: *"Forth Worth- Hundreds of American Airline flight attendants descended on the airline's corporate headquarters Friday, chanting about executive greed and vowing to regain wages and benefits they lost four years ago. The rally was organized by the Association of Professional flight attendants, which represent 20,000 American Airline attendants. It was indeed a showcase worker outrage over a slate of lucrative stock bonuses for top executives and managers scheduled to pay out next week. The protesters who arrived in buses at American's Fort Worth headquarters, carried signs and chanted slogans like "Arpey's got the gold mine, we got the shaft." The bonuses which are based on American's stock price and other performance measures will benefit 874 executives and top managers. Estimates vary, but union leaders say the payoffs could be worth more than $200 million. American officials defended the bonuses as a crucial part of top manager's compensation packages and pointed out that the managers don't collect if the company doesn't perform well."* Did you all read that last absurd statement **AA** officials made about not collecting unless the company is doing well? *ARE THEY KIDDING? American Airlines* is beginning to fall apart at the seams while this very article is being written because of the money these same greed obsessed corporate executives *are taking out of this company* to pay themselves these *ridiculously unearned* bonuses, instead of *putting the money back into the company* where it needs to be in order to begin replacing, or at the very least overhauling our aircrafts that are presently the second oldest fleet flying the skies of the *United States of America and Europe,* and are in dire need of attention, preferably before they start falling out of the skies with all of us in them! How dare those **AA** *idiot* officials make *blatant lying comments* like that? I don't know about the rest of you, but besides finding these people completely reprehensible as well as absolutely vacant in the moral department, it is insulting that *Mr. Arpey* would even imply by collecting that massive amount of so called bonus money, that the only reason this company made such a tremendously huge profit this year is due solely to the financial genius of himself and his buddies? Can he really be that *delusional,* or is he just a *worthless lying crook just* like all his *Wall Street bank loan buddies/criminals* that have sent this country's financial economy into a downward spiral tailspin with their contributions to society of *non stop corruption* and *insatiable greed*, and now we the taxpayers, are going to be the ones who will have to pay the price for their corruption, when we are forced by Congress to bail out those *sons of @#*&=$$!* Don't address that statement. We already know the answer! *Mr. Arpey* and his friends who have been living *"high on the hog"* must be having a *"brain freeze"* because they can't quite seem to remember that *WE,* the insignificant little flight attendants of *American Airlines,* put up *$1.6 billion annually in concessions that we cannot afford by the way, but nevertheless contribute, because we were told it would be* *temporary, and it was a necessity for the continued success of our airline company. Those "labor employee concessions" that were made by all of us, is what has kept American Airlines out of bankruptcy court.* The fact that *American Airlines* is still up and flying today, has **nothing** to do with *Mr. Gerald Arpey* and **his corporate entourage**, yet they are justifying paying themselves that enormous amount of money that they have the audacity to call *"bonuses that they've earned"* for keeping the company from going into bankruptcy, when the reality of it is that they did not contribute one dime to be put back into this company to keep it afloat, and now they think they have the right to take the profits of the company *"off of our backs!"* Is that not just the most incredibly unbelievable thing you've ever heard? It is for me! They have a history of using the media for their malicious propaganda against their own labor employees, and they have these little public conferences to spew their lies and make their excuses for their **corruption and criminal behavior.** According to them, that huge bonus money they are paying themselves is not **coming from the labor employees' concessions, but is based rather, on** *American's* stock price and other *"performance measures"?* What the hell are those exactly? The only people at American Airlines that have taken any kind of *"measures"* so that the company can show some **performance** and not end up in the bankruptcy courts system of the United States of America is the *American Airline's* labor employees, and I certainly don't remember being included in any of that bonus money, do any of you other labor employees out there remember seeing yours? I think **NOT!** I searched everywhere on that list of theirs to see if I could find my name, or any of your names for that matter, anywhere on that **bonus breakdown list,** and I have to tell you that I was completely *shocked* and *flabbergasted* when I realized that our names were **NOT** on that list! **I KNOW!** *It's hard to believe right?* I have the list right here, check for yourselves if you don't believe me. Those so called **"performance measures"** that *American's* officials and company spokes people are talking to the press about, will benefit about 874 executives, but the real beneficiaries are the *"top dogs"*. Here are just the names and the bonus dollar amounts of our *top five greediest* corporate execs; **GERALD ARPEY $7,695,428, THOMAS HORTON $4,649,251, DANIEL GARTON $3,721,986, GARY KENNEDY $2,345,989,** and finally **ROBERT REDDING $770.616.** *Now I personally think that last guy got screwed along with the rest of us when you compare his cut to the others,* wouldn't all of you agree? How do these people sleep at night? They must not believe in a *"higher power"* that will one day no doubt be giving them a serious talking to. There was a news article that appeared in the *L.A. Times on April 14, 2007 written by staff writer Peter Pae,* who wrote about just exactly why it is that there is currently so much anger and outrage coming from the *57,000 "rank and file employees" (as he put it), who are seeing red at American Airlines, from corporate executive greed driven bloated bonuses that are going to be paid out. Mr. Pae* writes in his article that *"when the airline industry went into a deep slump after the 2001 terrorist attacks, American Airlines pilots, flight attendants and mechanics agreed to billions of dollars in cuts in wages and benefits to keep the carrier afloat. Now, AMR (American's parent), is back in the black, so much so that 874 top executives will receive more than $150 million in stock bonuses. American Airlines started making big money again in 2006 and executives are cashing in setting the stage for contentious negotiations with employees whose labor contracts* start expiring later this year." *Michael Boyd,* an industry consultant, said *"it's going to get nasty; the airlines have really messed this up. The labor employees worked hard, gave back, and it looks like management is now basically* *saying to them; thanks for the givebacks, suckers!"* As if all of that weren't bad enough, *American* sent letters to its unions warning them not to disrupt operations or otherwise violate federal laws that govern relations between the airlines and their workers. Like there has ever been a time where we just decided it would be exciting to be disruptive, *Please! Arpey doesn't stop there.* He then has the tremendous audacity and arrogance to so graciously send each and every one of us his very own *"Dear Fellow Employee" letter dated October 17, 2007* informing us of how *"American Airlines (AMR)* earned a net profit of *$215 million"* (which by the way exceeds last year's profit during the same time period by over *$101 million* by his own admission). The letter continues with his usual *rhetoric rant* about *"the problematic situations that are causing this company so many financial troubles, such as the high cost of fuel, the work and installation costs of aerodynamic parts on certain types of aircrafts and the funding of our pension plans,"* never once mentioning that the real problems for our financial troubles comes from their incessant *greed.* He even tries to make the one about funding our pension plans sound like that is something he's taking care of out of the goodness of his heart, as if we didn't earn every penny of that pension fund that their greed continually jeopardizes! Then he hits us with his amazing finale of asking us, his *lower food chain* employees to: *"allow him to solicit our ideas to help him in order to keep the airline's fuel costs down"!* Well, as much as I want to believe that every other *American Airlines* employee out there is as upset and disgusted at *Arpey's detached* and *shameless* attitude towards us as well as our passengers, I am *regrettably* aware of the fact that there will actually be quite a few employees out there that will be more than willing to give him all the help and ideas they can, in order to help *Mr. Arpey* out and send him on his merry way with *plausible* information that he didn't even have to think of or figure out on his own! *"Piece of cake, wouldn't you say so Mr. Arpey? Hell, that's easy money for you and a no brainer at that".* Do these few *idiot* employees really think that the *elitist hierarchy* otherwise known as *American Airlines corporate executives* are really going to reward them with something tangible that they can really use such as a, oh, let me think, I know, *A much needed pay raise?* I think **NOT!** Although I can bet that I have a pretty good idea what they will receive in exchange for all of their butt kissing information. *How about a couple of free passes so that they can fly standby anywhere they would like on our oversold flights.* That's always fun. Oh yes, and it will be accompanied by that *"thank you so much for your hard work and ideas" letter (keep 'em coming fools)* they will no doubt receive, along with a certificate including those participating employee's names printed on it, stating how they have been selected as *"Excellent Employees of the Month".* Just think what the rest of us troublemakers are missing! I, for one, am so jealous! *Here I thought that seeing extra money in my little measly paycheck, and getting a little respect once in a while would get me excited but really, a "thank you" letter. What was I thinking?* The best part yet for those *idiot employees's rewards deal,* is that their letter will be official and from no other than the desk of *American Airlines CEO, Mr. Gerald J. Arpey* himself! Just think what they can do with that! For instance: They can run right over to Wal-Mart and pick out one of those diploma/degree frames, put their awesome *"best butt kissing employee"* letter/certificate in it and hang it in their offices at home for all their family and friends to see! *WAKE UP out there! For those of you flight attendants who just can't grow what it takes to do something about our deplorable one sided and at this point very ridiculous working situation we keep calling our jobs, at least have the decency to stay the hell out of the way of the rest of us employees who do have what it takes and are desperately* *fighting to make change happen, or at least try! Stop throwing stones directly in our path! You don't have to stand tall with the rest of us. Just MOVE!* Don't worry, even though you will have had no participation whatsoever in our fight to try and get these *executive greed hogs* who are currently running this company, and the entire aviation industry Into the ground for that matter, to do the right thing, you'll still be able to *ride our coat tails* like you always do. Who knows, when we get all the concessions we have made through the years back, you can just do what you did a few years ago when *WE* went on *STRIKE* and *YOU* went on *SCAB*. Just pretend you stood united with us all along. In time people will forget that you in fact didn't, and you can once again try to pass yourself off as one of *US* instead of the *SCAB* that you really are. *You are the ones that have to live with yourselves every day for the rest of your lives, but hey, not having decent principles, integrity and a strong conviction about anything doesn't seem to bother you so there you have it in a nutshell, and why should it bother me, right? It Does!* Because of the unfortunate manner in which *ALL* flight attendants are considered one group or entity if you will, of labor employees and your *STUPIDITY* affects *ALL* of the rest of us. When you make a bad decision, we *ALL* pay for that bad decision. Those of us that are intelligent can *not* separate ourselves from those of you who are *STUPID!* Do all of you really think that this company's corporate executives and greedy stockholders would be getting away with the shameful things that they are doing, which is ultimately causing the demise of this company, if every single employee stood strong and held those individuals accountable for their actions? As for the rest of us who do want to change things and make them better, who do want these corporate individuals to stop the destruction of our airline, and who do want to know that we are flying *SAFE* at all times, we better start to rally around each other and come up with the lucrative plans we are going to need to safely arrive at our final destination *(pun intended)*. We know it is not going to happen on its own. **It is a well known fact that almost all corporate CEO's including ours, are all about keeping their greed obsessed stockholders happy with the "money numbers" he/she produce on their strong balance sheets.** Making lots of *self interest* money is a ***top priority*** for them and they will mow down whatever gets in the way of that, and that includes us! If that's not ringing true for some of you these days, take a good look at what is happening on Wall Street and this country's economy, and the toll that its present situation is about to take on the rest of us. It is that *self absorbed greedy corporate mindset that has annihilated this country's economy and that is the exact corporate mindset that will annihilate our aviation industry, it has already begun, and for those few of you idiots that haven't noticed, let me repeat that for you, it has already begun!* These corporate executives who have severe *entitlement issues,* will pay themselves millions and millions of dollars off your backs and mine, and after they have exhausted most of our airline company's financial resources, they will **bail** on the *"golden parachutes"* they have been guaranteed by the stockholders, *whether they performed financially sound for the company or whether they ran it into the ground. It doesn't much matter to them either way as long as they get what is theirs!* The bottom line for *Mr. Arpey* and his buddies is that it isn't about spreading the wealth, which by the way, all of us happened to play a *significant* part in keeping *American Airlines* prosperous and thriving so that the wealth could exist in the first place, it's about the *almighty revenue* and the cut backs after cut backs of labor employee salaries and benefits and anything else they can think of, to get the magic numbers they want, because they certainly aren't going to go into their own millions to make that happen! *I am not* *suggesting that Arpey and the rest of them disperse that wealth evenly.* Lord knows I would never suggest anything that bold. After all, we all know they are at the top of that food chain I mentioned earlier, and we are at the bottom, *but I am suggesting that they disperse it fairly!* Okay. Pipe dream I know. He couldn't possibly even conceive of that premise on his own and trust me it shows. When I look at the benefits today, if that's what you still want to call them, as compared to *1976* when I started flying, it makes me sick to my stomach to think about the fact that in regards to what I feel was once an incredible career, *presently we don't have much of anything left to even begin to infer that it was ever anything like I remember.* I would venture to say that those of us with a significant amount of seniority feel that we are trapped in the inevitable situation of having to remain on board with this company and see it through until we reach retirement age, or early retirement age at best. The fact that we have given so many personal years to this ungrateful corporation that we *work* for, is extremely disheartening. What is even more troublesome than that, is the other even more important fact that *as flight crewmembers we have acquired the small problem of becoming obsolete in the outside job market since flight crew jobs after all, are not likely careers that you are going to find listed in the want ads of your local newspaper.* Ours is an entirely *non mainstream, seniority accumulating based career* and one that at our age is not possible to start over and besides, the way that things are these days in the airline industry, who would want to anyway! *Mr. Crandall who by the way has since taken off in his "golden parachute" to make way for the new "breed of greed", is whom I like to think of as the wonderful person responsible for the beginning of the end of this career and company as we once knew it.* We have allowed ourselves to be talked into giving up so very much with every contract negotiated and settled between *American Airlines and APFA* during his rein. In my heart of hearts, I truly believe we can turn this baby around to be a reasonable facsimile of what it was years ago. I am not naïve enough to think that it will not be the battle of all mother lode battles, or that things could be *"exactly"* the same as they once were many years past, because our times have certainly changed and there are some things such as the *security* part of this profession that must remain our number one priority, but as far as the *camaraderie* and *unity* we all once shared with each other, and the *perks* that attracted us to this career in the first place are concerned, I know we can win those back. *It will take courage, conviction and most importantly UNITY among all of us, in order to begin the huge and ugly battle of getting our careers and company back to the way it should be, for not only ourselves, but for our passengers as well!* When I speak to flight attendants out on the line about how we all have to stand up united, and fight these *unscrupulous* executives that are currently overseeing our airline, and how we have to hold them accountable for the mess they have made of this industry and our company and lives, and start turning things around, the overwhelming standard response I get from many of you is; *What, are you kidding me? Turning this company around would take nothing short of a miracle!* Well, I am here to tell all of you that *"Miracles happen every day, sometimes you just have to work a little harder to get them to happen".* We have to begin the *once familiar* process of believing and trusting in ourselves and each other! Boy, what a concept! What is it going to take in order for us to realize that if we keep allowing the slow and willful destruction of our airline company to continue, we are going to wake up one of these mornings not too far down the road, and our airline is **NOT** going to be there! If you don't think it can happen to us, think again and while you're thinking, go talk to the ex *Pan American Airlines* flight attendants or *Trans World Airlines,* or

Continental Airlines, or **Eastern Airlines.** Need I say more? Come on you guys! Let's put all of our heads together and find the way to take our airline company back! It has always been ours anyway. All that *corporate* has done to it since they arrived on the scene is to financially exploit and drain it. **We** helped build it and have kept it successful through the years. Don't you guys understand? *We are American Airlines! It cannot operate without all of US; you know that, I know that and they know that! We need to hang on to that knowledge when we doubt ourselves or they try to rattle us and you know that they will. Our strength is there, inside every single one of us and always has been. We've just forgotten how to tap into it because they have had us running scared for too long. My God, stay focused on what it is we do for a living. Much of our existence happens at roughly 39,000 feet! So very much is asked of us and we ask for so little in return. You know this is the only job we ever want to do for a living and how much we love it when it's right!* Why would we continue to allow anyone to further destroy or completely take it from us! Once again my fellow comrades, I pray you feel as strongly as I do about our careers and our very livelihoods because if you do, the time has come when we need to **STAND***!*

CHAPTER 5

THE DISAPPEARING PERKS

There are quite a number of reasons why so many people sought out the commercial airline flight attendant career. There is definitely a certain kind of personality this profession attracts. Besides the fact that most of us are extremely independent and very self sufficient, a lot of us have always had this fascination with airplanes. When I was a young kid, I remember going with my parents to the airport either to pick up friends or family that were coming to visit us, or to drop them off when their visit was over and they were returning home. *I still can recall to this day the sound of my heart pounding from the excitement as my Dad got closer and closer to the airport.* The minute we were within earshot of the aircrafts powerful engine sounds and I was able to see them either taking off or landing, I was mesmerized. As far as I was concerned, my Dad never drove fast enough when we were going to the airport. My parents told me it was a complete nightmare for them anytime they had to take me along on these airport *pick ups* and *drop offs* of family members who would come out to visit us because my excitement was so uncontainable, that I would literally talk about the airplanes non stop all the way there and by the time we arrived, both of them were mentally exhausted! After I became an adult and actually became a flight attendant, my parents went on to confess to me that there were many times when they would quietly make arrangements for someone to watch me at home while they had to make those airport runs, because they didn't want to have to subject themselves to their airplane obsessed daughter! I have to say on my Dad's behalf though, that he would feel guilty about the times he would be talked into leaving me behind, and after he got home from work, the two of us would sneak out and he would drive us out to the **LAX** airport, where he would park the car off of **Imperial Highway,** where we had an excellent view of the aircraft traffic and we would sit and watch airplanes take off and land for hours. I remember just staring in amazement as they took off one after another, all the while wondering how something that large and heavy could lift off so effortlessly like a bird taking flight. The landings were equally as mesmerizing for me. At first, from a distance, the lights on the airplanes coming in for a landing reminded me of fireflies blinking on and off the way fireflies do in the summertime. Then one by one the lights got bigger and brighter until this enormous bird like machine gracefully glided down from the heavens and met its mark on the runway. I would watch this process over and over again never tiring from it. I have a pretty good feeling that my Dad enjoyed watching them too because there were some nights where it seemed that we would park and stay there for quite a few hours just talking about the awesomeness of it all. He would tell me about his young days in the Merchant Marines and about all the different countries he had visited. There were many times when my Dad took us out of school for weeks, sometimes months at a time, depending on where we were going, so that we could all travel the world with him. When my Mom would start to protest about her fears of having her children fall behind academically in school from missing so many days of attendance, he was always able to convince her that traveling to different countries and learning different cultures was the best education that we could have. He would always say that everything we saw and were exposed to, would be experienced and learned first hand, instead of reading about it from a book and what better learning than that could their be. *I truly believe the travel fever I constantly felt during my life has been instilled in me by my Father.* I've met so many flight attendants in my career that have expressed that same intense fascination with airplanes in one way or another. I think it would probably be safe to say that the *"travel perk"* of the flight attendant profession was the number one reason most of us became flight attendants. The career provided us with the ability to travel not only while we were working our trips, but on our days off as well, because another great perk this career provided for us was an enormous amount of flexibility which in turn facilitated our traveling even further. We could trip trade our trips with one another in ways that allowed us to group a substantial amount of days off together and that gave us the ability to plan what I use to call *"mini vacation trips"*. When I first began flying, I personally would go on one maybe two of these *"mini trips"* every month. I remember writing on a tablet a list of all the countries I intended to visit in order of preference when I first started out as an *American Airlines* flight attendant. Some of the countries on my list had been carefully selected many years before I even started flying. When I was a kid, I would stay up late on Saturday nights and I'd watch the old classic movies on television. There was *The Late Show,* then *The Late Late Show* and finally *The Late Late Late Show.* Most of the time, the movie storylines would take place in all these exotic places that seemed fascinating to me. I must admit my future travels were most definitely influenced by many of these movies. Every time I flew to one of the countries on my list I would always make sure that I would visit the exact same places that corresponded with a particular movie I might have seen. When I arrived at home I would proudly cross that country off my list. *Italy, Greece, Spain,*

Portugal, Brazil! This was definitely the most attractive **perk** of the flight attendant career and was what called to me. There was no way any of us could financially afford to do that kind of traveling on our own. The incredible sights and panoramic views some of us had only seen in magazines or read about in books or as in my case saw in the movies, all of a sudden became a reality for us and we were witnessing and experiencing all of it first hand and on location. That was more than just appealing to us, it was unbelievable! The flight attendant salary when I first began flying back in ***1976*** was barely livable. It was **$601.00 per month** to be exact and that amount of money or lack of, I should say, certainly didn't factor in the decision as to whether I took the job or not. I went after the profession with such zealous intensity because of the travel and benefit *"perks"* that the career offered. Those are the real reasons all flight attendants went after this profession!

As far as the pay, there were a few sizeable salary increases at the completion of certain designated years before we maximized out company salary increases, but after reaching those designated pay raise years, only ***cost of living increases*** remained. Of course, those increases were a small fraction in comparison, but let's just say that for most of us, the flight attendant salary was definitely ***not*** considered a *"perk"*. The free travel *"perk"* of this career came in the form of ***D-2 non revenue travel for airline employees and their families so besides you, that included your spouse, dependants, parents, brothers and sisters.*** At the time I started flying in 1976, all of the family members mentioned above were all ***qualifying D-2 pass holders.*** Today, it is no longer set up in that manner and your siblings are now considered ***D-3 Pass*** statuses, which means they pay a percentage of the highest coach fare. Other *"great perks"* that came with the career were ***time off, job flexibility, trip trading for days off or layovers, medical, dental and eye insurance (which by the way was completely covered by the company)*** and of course, the "elite" *status that went with the career.* Except for *the first two years that I worked for American Airlines and was based out of Dallas, Fort Worth Texas*, my home base for the majority of years as a flight attendant has been *Los Angeles* (**LAX**). There were a few years I also flew out of what the company called *co-terminals,* which were basically smaller neighboring airports such as *Orange County Airport, Long Beach Airport, Burbank Airport or Ontario Airport* to name a few. Some months I would bid to fly in and out of *Ontario Airport*, since it was a lot closer in distance to where I resided at that time than **LAX** was or any of the other ones. I, like many other flight attendants, also enjoyed the more relaxed working atmosphere that these smaller airports provided for us. Flying out of *Los Angeles International Airport* was always so much more stressful. Another *"great perk"* that was at one time provided by the company whenever we flew in and out of *Ontario Airport* in *California*, was an extra *$100.00* for every trip we flew in and out of that co-terminal; reason being that the area where that airport was located was rural and very removed from **LAX** *International* at the time, so *American* would compensate us for driving the distance and flying out of there. If you flew four three day trips out of there, which was usually the *"norm",* that was a little extra **$400.00** a month you could count on to help with the gasoline to and from, or just to pay for your everyday bills and living expenses. Flight attendants never made **exorbitant** amounts of money the way our CEO's did and still do. We were quite happy with our little *"perks"* and as far as I am concerned, we were entitled to every one of them. None of us have ever argued the fact that our flight attendant careers had some very incredible *"perks"* but by the same token, our work while on the airplanes was certainly no picnic at times either. *We had grueling tasks that had to be accomplished in record* time. **Flight attendants that have been flying as long as I have or longer,** *endured hours of inhaling second hand cigarette smoke* *from passengers* **smoking in the cabin.** *It would be twenty years before smoking would no longer be allowed on commercial airline flights and we would no longer have to be subjected to that.* *We looked at all the negative things about the career, and there were some, as minor obstacles we had to put up with in order to reap all the benefits that came with the profession, because after all, those wonderful "perks" were the reasons why we were all really doing this job and had always wanted this career in the first place.* *Our thoughts always stayed focused on the fact that if we managed to land safely at our destination, it didn't matter how harrowing the flights we worked were, because the definition of a good flight was one that always landed safely back on the ground!* There was always the possibility of any of the flights we worked to go terribly awry and could quickly turn into a harrowing experience if you were to add, oh, lets say for instance, a scenario such as your aircraft's landing gear not locking, leaving us, attempting to not only calm ourselves down, but our 200 plus passengers as well, while at the same time preparing for an emergency landing, praying the entire time for a good outcome when that aircraft came to a complete stop and *(all of the flight attendants know that at this point that's just not happening at the gate with a ramp stand approaching).* God willing, if any emergency situation did arise and we would have to evacuate the aircraft, we'd get our passengers as well as ourselves out of there safely. All of that is of course, the very glamorous and overpaid part of our careers that *American Airlines* and other commercial airlines as well, want to keep on the *down low.* Every one of us knows that the *perks* I speak of in this chapter are all but gone, if not severely hindered or diminished completely. The *D-2 travel privileges* that were once offered to our parents are now coded as *D2-P* which allows the company to make money off of us while charging us a service fee for these passes every time our parents use them and when anyone responds to me about that statement by saying that the service fee is minimal depending on where they travel, my response to them is what does that have to do with anything? It's not like any of us travel on confirmed positive space when we use our passes. We all travel on a ***stand-by basis,*** and if there is an ***empty*** seat on the plane *(**like that ever happens anymore**)*, we get on. If the seat doesn't sell and none of us are standing by for it, ***the seat goes out empty on that flight.*** Why do these greedy corporate people running this company have to make a profit off their employees? Even if it is a small service charge that we are paying, it's still money that they have absolutely no shame making off the people that work hard to help keep the airline prospering, when they can choose to easily and inexpensively show some gratitude for the hard work, time and energy we constantly give them, to help ensure the success of this company, by the simple gesture of allowing families to ***travel stand-by*** without charging us the service fees, since without them in it, the seat would go out empty anyway! There are over ***20,000 flight attendants*** alone who work for ***American Airlines,*** never mind the thousands and thousands of other employees who work for them as well, whose parents and families also travel on these types of passes. ***DO THE MATH!*** That's just the money to be made by this company off of us every time our parents utilize a ***D2- P Pass.*** Our siblings, who were also ***D2 Pass*** holders at one time, are now coded as ***D-3*** Pass holders. That translates as an even ***higher percentage*** of service fee money that is there to be made and collected off the employees. It would be one thing if they used that money they made off of us, to put back into the company and take care of our aging aircrafts for example, but it all somehow ends up as part of their inflated salaries and bonuses. We have become so complacent about everything that has to do with our jobs, that we don't even put it all together and realize that this so called ***"Pass Privilege Perk"*** is a ***perk*** that we actually pay for out of the same monies they pay us our salaries with, so in actuality, when you really think about it, some of our salary goes right back into their pockets every time our families use our so called great pass privileges. Isn't that something! When did it become acceptable for us to allow them to constantly take from us in any way they can?   I wonder if *Mr. Arpey's* parents or in-laws or siblings pay the same service fees as the rest of us *non-important* employees do whenever they utilize non-revenue pass privileges. *NOT*! I venture to take it a step further and bet that they not only travel completely free of any service charges, but they will actually deny a full fare first class passenger boarding, offering that passenger money to take the next flight, if a situation should happen to arise where *Arpey* or any one of his family members need that passenger's first class seat, and you can bank that they don't ride coach! What Am I even saying! He's paid himself so much money off our backs that he probably has his own private airplane they all travel on. That way, he doesn't have to worry about flying on one of *American Airlines safety compromised aircraft* that maybe has a hairline crack through its engine or God knows what else! Okay, so what's the next *"perk"* we went after this career for? Oh yeah, the *time off and flexibility* this career gave us. The *"time off perk"* is dependent upon whether you're a married or in a living relationship with someone who makes more money than you do, *(that's everybody)* and can carry the bills and the financial burden on his or her own because that's the only way you can afford to take any time off. If you are lucky enough to be in that position, you can take time off by dropping your trips to another flight attendant, relinquishing all ties to the money you would have made from the trip or trips you are dropping. Unfortunately, most of us are married to men that work very hard but they don't make millions of dollars, like *Mr. Arpey and his buddies.* Most of us depend on two salaries our husbands and our own to make ends meet, so we not only need to fly all of our monthly scheduled trips, but we pick up a few extra ones for the extra money to help us keep up with our mortgages and everyday bills. The *"flexibility perk"*, oh that's still there. We use it all the time to cram more trips on our already pretty crammed monthly schedules! Okay then. What are the other "perks" we haven't addressed yet? Oh yeah, the *"medical, dental, and eye care perk."* We still have that but it sure isn't covered by the company anymore, and don't even think about going out on a medical leave that keeps you from work a day over a year, even if AA is the reason why you're on medical leave in the first place, because I am here to tell you personally that the very first day after you've been off for an entire year, you can say bye bye to your medical, dental and eye insurance immediately. They send you to *Cobra,* which is their alternate insurance where the premiums you have to pay for yourself as well as your family to remain with the same coverage that you had while you were actively flying, are over $1000.00 per month! My Dear flight attendant family, I have placed much hope in all of you because I believe in you. I believe that when you are actually reading all of this it will all hit home and make you angry enough to demand the very much needed change that we are all deserving of, and you will be complacent no more. We have sat quietly and watched for so many years now, as more and more of our benefits dwindle away. We work hard and long hours for the success of this company only to have **AA** *corporate execs* personally help themselves to the money we helped to generate and create. It is time that we start doing something about that. Demonstrating to them that we stand united and unyielding will send the clear message that we are a strong entity in this company that *Does* matter and that *Will* fight! There is no doubt in my heart that your strength is there, it has always been there. If you allow it to surface, we can all **STAND!**

CHAPTER 6

THE NON-STOP HARASSMENT

There are countless times when I find myself thinking about how and when we let this employer employee relationship we all have with this company, get so out of control. As I get older in life, I work extremely hard to always look at any given situation I may find myself in, whether good or bad, and try to see what part I played in it, to allow that situation to manifest itself. As difficult as it is to admit, I can tell you with complete honesty that nine out of ten times, I contributed in one way or another to it. Much of the time that I am at work, I am listening to so many flight attendants as well as other employees from other departments within this company for that matter, sharing their horror stories or expressing their complaints about one negative thing or another that they have had to experience regarding this company's management tactics. The morale of the flight attendants out on the line today is so bad, that those with enough seniority to retire have. Others like myself that have flown for this airline for over thirty years and are close to full retirement but just can't take the bullshit anymore, even if it is only for 6 more years, look towards early retirement at the age of fifty five, knowing fully well that by doing so, *I will receive only eighty percent of the full retirement benefits I would otherwise have been entitled to receive by staying those last 6 years.* Others that have many years left to fly before they are even close to retiring are desperately trying to find other avenues that they can take which would allow them the opportunity to not have to depend on this profession for their livelihood. *I feel such incredible sadness when I stop to think about how this once elite and much sought after flight attendant career has been reduced to the job that we know today.* The career that we at one time couldn't even imagine ever giving up, is now the job we're all trying to escape from, all because of the *self serving, ego bloated corporate management executives that have been placed in the highest of positions with this company giving them the ability to make all decisions regarding this company and its employees.* The fact that they have gotten away with such deceitful and completely corrupt tactics for so many years is simply mind boggling to me. *American Airlines* employees are so upset and disheartened, not only for the simple reason that we are all so sick and tired of the manner in which this company's management from the top down, continues to blatantly disregard and disrespect us, but also because of all the lies we've been told and the promises that were made to all of us by not only the present company leaders we have, but by the past ones as well, that were never intended to be kept. They were promised in order to get us to make the concessions they wanted us to make and take huge salary cuts, which have shamefully ended up in these   corporate monger's pockets! *September 11, 2001* has been the perfect scape goat for our current greed obsessed upper management employees and CEO. What I wish all flight attendants would understand, as well as all other employees who are affected by our shameless leadership and that would be most of us, is that even though our complaints against this company are almost always legitimate, and trust me I should know, I work for them too, the problem is, that merely complaining about the injustices that are being placed upon us or the unfair tactics that are being used on us will only allow our situation to remain the same unless

81

all of us, not just some of us, take further action to put a stop to it. ***We all need to take a stand at the exact moment we are being harassed or unjustly disciplined for whatever reason and simply not allow it to continue.*** We can't just keep whining and complaining to each other about our situations the way that we do. Becoming totally dependant on our union to fight our battles for us isn't the answer either, since these days, none of us are quite sure what's happening within our ***APFA (Association of Professional Flight Attendants)*** leadership or where the hell they are when we need them! I know that personally these last years I myself have needed their assistance to help me resolve what I consider to be a very ***grave employer/employee*** dispute and I'm here to tell you that I can barely get any of the reps or union officials to return my calls, much less expect them to literally fight my battles for me! In the last few years, the leadership of the ***APFA*** has taken on what seem to me as a very ***banal*** stance towards ***American Airline's*** corporate management concerning the ***constant harassing and unjust badgering of flight attendants.*** Every flight attendant out on that line knows that these flight service managers that are assigned to us by this company, who are supposedly there to help facilitate us in whatever we may need while on or off the job to make our work flights run smoothly, are basically of no use to any one of us at any time. How many times have we heard that from each other! Whenever we need information from them pertaining to our jobs, most of them seldom, if ever, have any answers for us. Few bother to take the time to find the information out and relay it back to us. Yes, of course, there have been a handful of these supervisors that really do care about us, but in ***LAX,*** they're all gone! How many of those decent supervisors who confided in us about how horrible it was working in that office are still around? ***NONE!*** They've either left on their own to other departments in other bases, or ***had retirement forced upon***

them, as in the case of my personal supervisor, **Bertha Oaxaca,** whom after giving forty plus years of dedicated service to this ungrateful company, had company forced retirement on her! I remember getting into friendly disputes with her regarding the way this company's management handled their employees. She was always finding excuses to validate their *covert and blasé* behavior and I suppose that she felt she had no other choice but to try to defend their actions at times because she did after all belong to the management work group, but I know for a fact that she knew better simply because of the fact that when I got into altercations with certain unscrupulous management employees who were completely out of line in some way or other, she would find out the facts about the altercations, and she would stand by my actions as being understandably correct. To the bitter end though, even as she found herself being discarded like a piece of trash after all the amount of years she had put into this company, when I would call her at home to see if she was doing okay and bring up the fact that these corporate management individuals needed to be abdicated from their company positions, she would always claim that what they had done to her came about because of a few insidious management employees as well as the new *LAX* base manager who we had recently acquired, and that the new base manager just did not like her. I had been trying to warn her for quite a few years about many of these *horrible evil* people *(for lack of better words I can use to describe them)* in that office who in my opinion take much pleasure in making other people's lives miserable just because they can, and have loyalties to know one except their own self serving selves, and I would ask her how she, not being that type of human being could be around them for eight hours a day! But she would always respond to me that they were not all bad, and that I was exaggerating because *I always saw things black or white or wrong or right.* She said in her heart of hearts that she didn't want to believe that most of those people in that ***LAX Flight Service*** office were truly like the way in which I described them, and she chose to remain with her own theory of the reasons as to why her forced retirement came about. I have not spoken to ***Bertha*** since ***Halloween*** two years ago when we threw a ***Halloween*** party at my home and I invited her to come, which she did, but I am willing to bet that having had all this time gone by since her removal from her position as flight attendant supervisor at ***American Airline's LAX Flight Service,*** she has had time to ponder on the travesty that was done to her and that she has probably had a change of heart by now! My relationship with ***Bertha Oaxaca*** as flight attendant and supervisor, worked for two simple reasons. The first reason, and the most important, was the fact that ***she always treated me with the same respect I in turn always showed her.*** The second reason was that ***Bertha was once a flight attendant for a number of years, which gave her the insight and qualifications to supervise over other flight attendants.*** Most of the managers at ***LAX Flight Service*** today, come from ***Cargo or Cabins Service*** or some other position within the company that is ***totally unrelated or even similar to that of the flight attendant position therefore these people have no real qualifications or hands on knowledge about our profession!*** Yet these are the very people who have been given these managerial positions to oversee the flight attendants. Isn't that a kick! The ***LAX Flight Service*** managers these days are too busy trying to look for anything negative about the flight attendants they can find to bring to her/ his attention. I do believe that the reason for the constant vexatious attacks on flight attendants by ***LAX Flight Service management*** employees comes from the fact that ***upper management*** has given ***lower management (Flight Service)*** direct orders and free reign to behave in this ghastly manner in order so that the agenda of ***keeping the flight attendants under their constant***

thumb is always accomplished, but nonetheless, it takes a certain kind of vile person with a penchant for inflicting stress and misery to others, and those are the very kinds of people that this company finds to place in supervisory positions overseeing American's flight attendants. Even a good passenger letter written about you gets picked apart! An example of the pretty standard way in which flight attendant supervisors inform a flight attendant about a good letter that has come in on their behalf, will usually go down like this. Your supervisor or manager, whatever the hell they like to call themselves, will call you into their office *(usually on your scheduled day off)* or leave you a petty little note in your airport mailbox to remind you of the fact that even though you went above and beyond the call of your job duties, and made it possible for a passenger to have a great memorable flight ultimately making that passenger want to fly ***American Airlines*** forever, you handled the situation improperly because you broke one of ***American's*** company policy regulation. Regulation ***blah blah blah,*** per ***Federal Air Regulations (FAR)*** states that flight attendants cannot ***blah blah blah!*** Case in point: A passenger traveling on one of my flights wrote some very nice things about me and my crew in a letter and then sent the letter to ***American's Headquarters*** where it was reviewed and then passed on to my supervisor at ***LAX***. My supervisor then sent me a copy of the letter via ***Federal Express*** to my home. The letter was praising my efforts on a particular flight and day that I worked. I remember the flight and the sweet couple that wrote the letter very well because they were simply delightful people and I loved having them on board. They were an adorable older couple traveling to ***Los Angeles*** from ***New York City*** on their way to meet their brand new granddaughter for the first time who had just been born and they were beaming all over with excitement. After we completed our meal service, a couple of the flight attendants including myself, went over and chatted with them for a little while. We gave them complimentary drinks and headsets in flight and before they deplaned, we gave them a bottle of champagne and told them it was a congratulations gift from their flight crew and we wanted them to take it home and toast in celebration of the new birth with their family. They were so grateful and happy and it made us all feel good to do that for them. They made our flight as wonderful as we made theirs. It was great. Oh, but here comes the part where I get a copy of the letter and of course along with it, comes an attachment from my supervisor saying *"Dear Alicia, you did a great job on that flight but"* stating further that per *FAR* regulations; *"you shouldn't have given that couple any alcohol to take off of the airplane due to the liability for American Airlines".* Of course after reading his attachment, I was completely baffled by the B.S. that I was reading so I had no other choice but to then respond: *"Dear Brad, I received your dear Alicia you did a great job but letter in the mail today and I am a little confused. Let me see if I understand this correctly. You are worried about American Airlines being held liable by some per FAR regulation because of a flight crew giving this lovely couple an "unopened" bottle of champagne (for free) to take along with them so they could toast in celebration of the birth of their new granddaughter with their family when they arrived at their destination yet you're not worried about American Airlines being liable per some FAR regulation that I know must exist holding American liable for the passengers we allow to guzzle alcoholic beverages at (five dollars) a pop, one after another for a continuous five hour span from coast to coast until they become so inebriated that by the time we reach our destination, it takes everything they've got to muster the strength to just walk off the airplane without falling down. Then they proceed to their cars and head straight for our highways, with their driving skills so severely impairedm, that the possibly of killing other people also driving on those same highways is huge? Did I get that right? I mean, I want to understand this FAR regulation liability problem you're calling me on correctly Brad, because the last thing I want to do is create any liability problems for American Airlines by giving away an" unopened bottle" of champagne to our passengers to take home with them! So, can you please get back to me at your earliest convenience on this and let me know just exactly which part of all that it is that I am not understanding?"* That incident happened about four years ago, and needless to say, I am still waiting on him to get back to me! In fact I don't think he ever will, because he's no longer my supervisor. Basically, since they **forced retired Bertha Oaxaca,** my supervisor of twenty years, I've had so many supervisors assigned to me that it is pointless to even bother to keep track. It's not like they are useful or helpful in any way and besides, I don't like to spend my valuable time with the likes of people having such malignant dispositions and those are the only kind of supervisors I ever seem to get! Flight attendants know all too well that our current Flight Service managers, at **LAX** anyway, are all about creating chaos and drama, with my current one being the biggest *"drama queen"* of all. Most of them have nothing of real importance to do in that miserable cubicle they sit in for eight hours a day except pushing paper or running around aimlessly all day doing God knows what, because they are absolutely of no help to any of us for anything except to harass us. *I suppose they have to at least try to look as if they're doing something, anything, to justify their useless jobs for fear that the clowns in the suits upstairs that are breathing down their necks may come to realize what the rest of us have known for years!* Flight attendants who fly for *American Airlines* are an incredible breed of people. They are the most caring, committed, warm spirited, intelligent, loyal and extremely giving bunch of people I have come across in my lifetime. ***Ms. Amy Sweeney*** and the rest of the crews that lost their lives on ***September 11, 2001***, are complete and absolute proof of that. This is why it is so disturbing to me when I see how some of these flight attendants allow themselves to be put in a position where they are made to feel incompetent or unimportant and they begin to doubt and second guess themselves. ***American's*** management personnel are equipped with these sets of rules, regulations and articles that are designed to keep us in line. Don't get me wrong, as far I am concerned when it comes to any company especially one the size of ***American Airlines***, it is completely understandable that there has to be a certain amount of written guidelines for the employees as well as expectations that the company feels the employees should meet. That is just a given. If ***American*** was a company I owned, I would certainly have guidelines and expectations for my employees in place as well. However, what I am referring to in this chapter is the manner in which this company chooses to implement those rules, guidelines and expectations which simply put, is just **deplorable**. ***American Airline's Company Sick Policy is the biggest example of being the most ridiculous and insulting company policy of all company policies not to mention the high probability of its illegality***. I could certainly type it up for you the way it is written in our flight attendant manuals but why? It's not like we don't know what their absurd policy states. At one time or another each and every one of us has been harassed by our flight service managers about using our sick time*. American Airline's Sick Policy* translates for us into the following: ***DON'T GET SICK! IF YOU INSIST ON GETTING SICK WE CAN'T FORCE YOU TO COME IN TO WORK SICK SINCE AFTER ALL, THAT WOULD BE ILEGAL AND WE HAVE TO COVER OUR ASSES AT ALL TIMES. THE BOTTOM LINE FOR US IS THAT YOU ARE ABLE TO READ BETWEEN THE LINES AND UNDERSTAND THAT WE***

DON'T REALLY CARE IF YOU'RE SICK OR NOT. THE ONLY THING THAT MATTERS TO US, NOT ONLY IN THIS SITUATION BUT IN ALL SITUATIONS, IS THE ALMIGHTY DOLLAR AND WHEN YOU CALL IN SICK YOU COST THE COMPANY MONEY THAT COULD OTHERWISE BE PUT TO BETTER USE OR IN MORE IMPORTANT DEPARTMENTS SUCH AS THE ONE THAT WE HAVE ESTABLISHED TO HANDLE AND IMPLEMENT ALL THE UNNECESSARY PAYCUTS WE HAVE FORCED ON YOU AS WELL AS ALL THE BENEFITS WE ARE SLOWLY BUT SURELY DISAPPEARING THAT YOU FLIGHT ATTENDANTS DON'T REALLY NEED ANYWAY. YOU HAD BETTER UNDERSTAND THAT "INSUBORDINATION" WILL NOT BE TOLERATED. SHOULD YOU DECIDE NOT TO ADHERE TO OUR COMPANY SICK POLICY, YOU WILL BE STRONGLY DISCIPLINED. TO SAVE YOURSELF TREMENDOUS GRIEF AND AGGRAVATION SUCH DISCIPLINING WILL SURELY BRING, WE STRONGLY RECOMMEND THAT YOU DON'T CALL IN SICK! I'll try and give you an example of how that ***insouciant company policy*** is applied on an actual flight attendant sick call situation. Let's just say that you are one of the very many flight attendants that work for ***American Airlines*** who cannot be intimidated by such rhetorical nonsense ***(I am proudly one of them)*** and you went ahead and called in sick on ***June 1st*** because you had a huge operation such as a hysterectomy. You were off on ***SKLOA (sick leave of absence)*** for a total twenty nine days. ***July 1st*** rolls around and you feel healthy once again so you return to work. After returning to work and flying only two trips, you develop a severe ear infection and you are once again in the position of having to call in sick. If that second sick call with the ear infection ***which by the way is not related in any way shape or form to the first sick call with*** *the hysterectomy* happens to go over seven days in duration, the company's sick policy basically states that *your second sick call (the ear infection) will now be considered your third sick call for the year because the amount of days (twenty nine) of your first sick call (the hysterectomy), will actually be divided and tallied as two sick calls instead of one, therefore now making the second sick call (ear infection), the third sick call by their estimations, even though you know you've only called in sick twice.* Is everybody still with me? I hope so because there's more! *The first reprimand is now well on its way* and let me not forget to also mention the very important fact which is that even if you have been flying for lets say twenty years with this company and you have never once called in sick in those twenty years, your reprimand will be no less severe than it is for someone who has called in sick let's say three or four times in just one year. In fact, not calling in sick for twenty years is not only a worse case scenario for you but it also works to your disadvantage simply because of the *stupidity that management refers to as their rationale* on that very situation. You see, all those years you didn't call in sick only translates to them as; "*for twenty years you have never once called in sick and this year you have had to call in sick three times (twice really) which could only mean that you now must have some kind of an underlying problem*". They become intent on finding what that underlying problem is and if they can't find one, hell, they will just make one up for you! You'll then find a *little note* in your *little mailbox* in *Flight Service* from your *little supervisor* letting you know that you now have three occurrences (*that's the name they like to give sick calls*) on your attendance record and you need to come in to their *little office* where they will hold a *little attendance meeting* (you may bring a union rep with you) where you will be informed of how irresponsible you have all of a sudden become in your twenty years of flying, regarding your attendance record and how you leave them with no other choice but to have them place you on a *"First Written Warning"* status, making you sign the *little piece of paper* the warning is written on against your will no less since should you refuse to sign the *little piece of paper*, you will be labeled *TaDa!* You guessed it, **INSUBORDINATE.** You will quickly be   reminded that **INSUBORDINATION** will not be tolerated *(like you can forget that part)* and the drama will completely escalate to an entirely larger dimension *(termination threats)*. In order to save yourself any further aggravation, it becomes of the utmost importance that you focus on getting the hell out of their *little office* as quickly as possible, reason being that besides the fact that you already know that trying to have an intelligent and logical conversation with these people about your situation is not a possibility since they only have the mentality of the mimicking company policy puppets they have been successfully turned into by our company's top brass, you don't think you could make it through one more second of having to listen to the incredible stupidity spewing out of their mouths without spewing back some of your own momentary thoughts on the phenomenon of how they got into those company management positions with the incredible lack of intelligence they possess! Of course your *little supervisor* has to give you one last verbal warning on your way out because this is the only part of their miserable jobs that makes them feel so powerful over you, and warn you not call in sick again because if you do, you'll be finding yourself in *"Big Trouble in Little China"*! Let's say you are just having one of those years when you are catching every illness that's out there, and it necessitates you having to call in sick a fourth time *(really the third time)* in that same year. You will be placed on a *"Second Written Warning"* status so from here on out you better look out because it's down hill from there! If you think about it for a minute, the reality of it is that for flight crew members calling in sick for what is really only a third time in the span of a year (**which is more times than most flight attendants call in sick in a year** a**nyway**), is not an unimaginable scenario to envision since we are continuously exposed to an unhealthy working environment from the beginning of our trip to the very end of it. Let me give you some very viable examples because there are many. First is the aircraft all by itself which provides us with outside gas fumes along with dirty, recycled air we get to breathe for hours at a time. We work in a pressurized cabin which is terrible for your internal organs and the jet lag that never seems to go away is probably due to our trashed immune systems from the long stressful days or from the sleep deprivation that we get with our minimal rest time, non recovery layovers. Just our work environment alone make us pretty good candidates for getting sick, not to mention picking up the 200 plus germ infested items which are handed to us for trash collection by our passengers who some by the way, will happen to be sick with the flu or some other kind of contagious ailment thereby readily passing that on to us. Then there's my favorite. We have the *"company intimidated co-worker"* who makes the bad decision of coming to work sick while suffering with their own highly contagious ailment which at times is accompanied by high fever and chills and that will undoubtedly make some of the rest of us prime targets for getting sick. Those of us who are lucky enough to fly with this sick flight attendant will now undoubtedly become sick before our next trip and guess what? You guessed it. We'll be calling in sick! My big question of the day is, if the rest of us can figure out how this entire American Airlines Sick Policy is never going to work out for anybody because we are not *"super human" flight attendants* that can be exposed to anything and everything and just keep on ticking why can't they? All the intimidation and harassment they can put together to throw at us is not going to change that fact. Don't you think these egotistical dumb asses would just understand that and call it a day? Maybe they can try a new concept, one that would be completely foreign to them, but might just actually work. Maybe, they can make themselves at least seem like they care; they are already really good at treachery and deceit, and start treating us with the same respect that they are under the serious delusion that they deserve. *My career at American Airlines took a tremendous turn on September 11, 2001. I could never ever go back to the complacent attitude I once held towards it. Simply put, it is not now, or ever will be again, the same job that I signed up for thirty two years ago. These days, that old comfortable and familiar complacency could cost not only my life, but the lives of all my passengers and fellow crew members, should God forbid history repeat itself (we all know how it often does), and I should find myself in a similar catastrophic situation as the ones on that horrible day.* If you haven't figured it out by now, **INSOBORDINATION** is *American Airlines Flight Service* management's choice word for labeling those of us who speak out in protest against unfair or unjust company policies which we do not adhere to. I cannot count the number of times I personally have been disciplined in one way or another by many of this company's *insouciance managers.* I am a person who has extreme difficulty tolerating injustices of any kind being inflicted upon anyone at any time. When a situation arises within my job that necessitates my having to deal with the barrage of self righteous and predatory lower management employees whom this company insists on hiring to *"manage"* the flight attendants, I cannot willingly or otherwise, force myself to listen to the *ridiculous, folderol explanations and excuses* that these idiots come up with to justify whatever outrages, and at times even *borderline criminal company policies* they're always trying to cram down our throats while constantly holding our jobs over our heads as collateral. There is huge number of ***American Airlines*** flight attendants out on the line today, who I know for a fact are just as fed up as I am with this company's management ***tactics, cavalier attitudes and continuous imminent threats.*** Many flight attendants are always standing up for what's right and are fighting back. At times we find ourselves fighting for others who cannot find their inner strength or their voices to speak up and fight for themselves because of their ***tremendous fear of being retaliated upon*** should they complain. Those of us of us who cannot be intimidated into making decisions that we don't feel good about will not compromise our safety or that of others, for the sake of not being threatened or retaliated upon by any of this company's management employees. There is too much importance that is placed over "***safety***" these days such as cutting costs where they shouldn't or making sure their departures are "***on time***" rather than making sure their aircrafts are "***airworthy***" before sending them up in flight full of passengers and flight crewmembers. That mentality of course evolves from their uncontrollable greed. The almighty revenue is the bottom line of all bottom lines for them and nothing else comes before that, not even our "***safety!***" ***The company's lower management puppets ignominious behavior can mostly be attributed to their lacking in the valued form of self respect.*** They are the ones who are given the job of making sure that flight attendants like me are silenced as quickly as possible. They quite often take situations completely out of context or stick to company policy rhetoric whenever "***disciplining***" us, because they are very well aware of the fact that there is nowhere legitimately they can go with their accusations. This is also the way in which they maintain our personal company files, mandating that we correct these **insubordinate** behavior patterns which they claim we have, while putting us on their numerous "***advisory steps***" until at last they have enough of a falsified paper trail so that they can justify their corrective actions and prove what *disgruntled and problematic* employees we are. The real deal here however is that there is no justifying their wretched behavior and willful lying malicious acts, and of course their worthless jobs that have no justification either! We all know that many of these lower managers are completely enjoying the disgusting jobs that they do; much the same way Hitler's henchmen enjoyed theirs. Oh, our union reps are there with us protesting in vain on our behalf, but our union reps are just other flight attendants like the rest of us and are absolutely no match against the constant bullshit coming all the way down from the top! *Some flight attendants are intimidated by some of these Flight Service managers so much so, that they do not speak out against the impeding and covert actions that are being taken against them.* These flight attendants need to understand that those of us that do stand up for ourselves and at times for some of them as well, need our jobs as badly as they need theirs. We have families depending on us to put food on the table and children to put through school, just like they do. We have mortgages, car payments and other financial responsibilities just like they do! The point I am trying to make here is that regardless of the company's constant threats and retaliation against those of us that *DO* stand up for ourselves, we cannot allow that to stop us from doing what we know is right. We have all of the same if not similar responsibilities as those of us who *DO NOT* stand up for themselves for fear of that same retaliation. It is a conscious choice you are making, to cower to this company's harassment tactics when you allow them to *blind and distort your better judgment* with their continuous rhetoric. It ultimately *erodes your ability to rely on what your gut instinct is telling you to do or not to do, if and when the time becomes necessary for you to take charge of any given emergency situation.* The only thing accomplished by those of you that handle your conflicts with management in this manner, is that you personally give them permission as well as an immense power over you, in exchange for preserving your jobs. What you don't understand is that by doing that, it will not only be probable but also inevitable, that the day will most certainly arrive when it all comes back to bite you in the ass and all that I have been able to do up till now is refuse to go up in flights that I do not feel are safe and neither do you, yet you still go! As I stay behind and I watch you guys take off at times under some very compromising conditions, because you have been made to feel by this company's management that you have no other choice but to go, *I cannot begin to describe the lump that burns in my throat, as I desperately hold back my tears while I stand on that jet-bridge and take, what I hope will not be my last look at your faces as the door closes and the aircraft pushes off the gate to get ready for departure with all of you in it. As I turn to walk away, I say a prayer and ask God to please keep all of you safe in his hands and not let anything bad happen to all of you up there.* I have known and loved some of you for so many years, and my fear at that precise moment is this; should the *pre-planned destiny* that this company's management created through their complete *negligence* and *disregard* for the s*afety* of everyone involved, have its own plans to take all of you, it will become the reality I have always hoped and prayed I would never know, and that is, that *I will not emotionally fare so well from what I will know to have been an entire, needless and totally avoidable tragedy!* No one should have to come to work and find themselves being threatened into dealing with such a preposterous situation, ever! This company's leaders have the *imperative* as well as *morale obligation to maintain the maximum of safety standard for not only every single one of their employees, but the passengers who fly on this airline, as well.* Flight attendants have to begin to understand that we are not employed as separate entities, but instead as an employee group and because of that simple fact, everything that you say and do, as well as the way in which you handle yourself in these harassment type situations doesn't just affect **YOU**, it affects **ALL** of us! This company will never see us as individual people. We are thousands of employee numbers who need to be kept on short leashes as far as their concerned, for better control and efficiency! *Even though they lead us to believe that they want us to be assertive and tell us to use our gut instincts in those instances where we do not feel safe for ourselves or our passengers, and they like to blah blah blah about how we have the "right" to always feel and be safe, we quickly realize that they are talking out of both sides of their asses because the minute we try and exercise that so called "right" we have, all hell breaks loose. As all of us well know, the continuation of that scenario is that we would then be finding ourselves downstairs in Flight Service being reprimanded and threatened for the actions we had to take or the decisions we had to make.* What I want to know is what it is going to take to make every one of us understand that we should **NEVER** allow ourselves to be put in the position of having to make such decisions in the first place! Many of us are tuned in to the fact that this is an extremely dangerous mind control game that this company's corporate management chooses to engage in when dealing with their flight crewmembers, but unfortunately many of us don't get that and what that allows for, is inevitably *flight attendants second guessing themselves on every decision we are challenged with when we're dealing with situations that are safety related and can have dire consequences should they not be addresses quickly and properly.* Let us be reminded one more time of what the nature of our job is, and exactly where it is that we perform it! We are on those airplanes for the sake of keeping everyone on board, including ourselves, **SAFE!** Having an *impaired* or even *delayed* response to an emergency situation we may find ourselves in, which requires our ***swift*** and ***confident*** handling is unacceptable. We have to begin seriously addressing those company policies and tactics used by **AA** for managing their employees that are harassing in nature and are constantly used as a threat for company retaliation against us. There are a few of you out on the line that I've worked with, who have allowed this company to intimidate you into making terrible decisions out of fear, rather than your common sense, which is what should always dictate your responses as well as your actions. *I have had three different incidents where I've had to make the decision to remove myself from my trips due to the fact that I felt my safety, as well the safety of my co-workers and passengers, were being completely disregarded and unnecessarily placed at risk*! This company's management personnel failed us on all three occasions, by not taking the necessary precautions to correct the situations while we were still on the ground at the departure gate, even after all of the imploring, which we found ourselves doing on the last one of those three occasions! Almost every one of you, including the cockpit crew members, chose to take those aircrafts up, all the while knowing damn well what you knew, and feeling the same feelings as the rest of us, who would ***NOT*** take that risk. My God! Some of you guys need to wake the hell up! *Maybe the moment of truth for you is going to be when you start looking for your old pals integrity and common sense, and you suddenly realize that the reason you haven't been able to find them for such a long time, is because you sold them down the river, in order to hold on to your jobs! You've allowed yourselves to be put in a compromised situation you had no damn business being in time and time again! Is the job worth the ultimate price you could end up paying?* Up until now, you've been blessed with some incredible luck, and you have gotten to your destinations without ***incident***. *Unfortunately, we all know that luck, is not something you bank on,* *based on continuance, especially with respect to what we do for a living!* The outcome of whether we have a safe flight or not, can *NEVER* be banked on luck. *That is a given, and a no brainer at that.* It's one thing to take an aircraft up to *39,000* feet, *NOT KNOWING* that there is something wrong with it. That's just part of the risk that comes with our job description, and we handle whatever happens up there as it comes, relying on the training we have and the wits and strength of each other. But it's quite another, to allow yourself to be talked into taking and aircraft up, *KNOWING* ahead of time that there are safety issues at hand which could compromise either the flight, the aircraft itself, or both. In my guesstimation, I would call that scenario *a recipe for a possible huge catastrophe! Why would I knowingly go there? Why would any of us knowingly go there?* Many of the flight attendants who are based out of *LAX* and know me personally, are aware *(including my union reps at APFA),* that Since *September 11, 2001,* those kind of situations are just not acceptable to me. That's not to say that they ever were before, but to be perfectly honest, I don't recall ever having to battle this issue before *September 11th, 2001* as frequently as I am finding myself having to battle it in recent years. Between *September 11, 2001 and December 5, 2006* I have been forced to walk off a total of three different flights, for three entirely different *safety* issues. I might have even been momentarily inclined, to point out that maybe three times in the period of five years wasn't so bad, *although I am not quite sure what I would be comparing that to,* except that later I found out that other flight attendants in other cities and hubs were walking off aircrafts as well during the same time I was. I guess *American Airlines* was not providing *a safe working environment* for them either. The problematic situations we all seem to be finding ourselves in these days, whether they are of the harassment kind or the just the being taken advantage of financially and every other which way kind, don't just all of a sudden manifest themselves and as if by magic, poof, they're there! ***Too many of this airline's employees have nurtured their co-dependant personalities into such a submissive point, that those of us that keep fighting against that helpless victim syndrome mentality that we refuse to become a part of, truly have the fight of fights on our hands.*** Believe me there have been numerous times when I have had to take on and stand up to this enormous company's management employees which have resulted in finding myself many times being left out in the cold **(somewhat like now),** dealing with the repercussions alone, fending for myself. That is a scenario, which I have come to learn all too well and have always accepted as ***that's just how it is***, but I've got to admit not without once in a while thinking to myself ***"non co-dependant here, party of one!"*** Of course, that thought is only momentary, because I know for a fact that there are other flight attendants out there that are fighting as hard as I am and perhaps they are finding themselves alone as well. I am fully aware that there is unrest and disappointment that are among all ***American Airlines*** labor employees, not just the flight attendants. The huge difference between those of us that are out on the line today, fighting for what we know is right, fair and decent and those of you for example, that went on those three compromised flights, on those three different occasions and continue to do so on many others, is that when it comes to finding ourselves in that kind of compromised predicament, having to make those types of ludicrous decisions, there is no amount of intimidation or harassment that should make us compromise our well being or most importantly our lives, and that, is neither debatable nor is it up for discussion. I, personally, will never find myself at **39,000** feet, in any kind of stressful or panicked state that I ***ALLOWED*** myself to be placed in, knowing ahead of time that there was a possibility **(I don't care how slight it was),** where a potentially serious safety situation could arise in flight. **Are you kidding me!** Am I seriously having to even verbalize this to you guys? Isn't that a big part of our job training at the *"Charm Farm"?* How many times do we hear at our yearly recurrent training that we should always *listen to our gut instincts in any critical situation we find ourselves in, especially those having to do with the safety of ourselves and everyone we are responsible for on our airplanes.* Be safe, fly safe! That's what the instructor's at the **Farm** clearly tell us over and over again. Yet some of you have said that you'd rather just go *with the flow* of whatever the hell they want us to do, whether it is *unreasonable or unsafe,* because it's easier and much less of a hassle than having to be called in for reprimanding on your day off! *I suppose for a lot of you that includes taking an aircraft up for example, even when you know ahead of time it cannot be flown to its full capacity because of some hairline crack in the system or whatever the case may be, it's just easier right? Does the logic you are reading at the moment, which by the way happens to have come out of some of your own mouths out there, sound as intelligent to you now, as it did then, when you made your decision to go? Have you people lost your minds!* Even though I can somewhat minutely understand the reasons you gave me as to why you chose to take those aircrafts up in those compromised conditions, rather than deal with this company's threats and retaliation, but telling me that it's just easier, are you serious? *We're talking about a very bad judgment call on your part!* We're talking about how incredible beat down you are, and how every time you allow that kind of situation to happen, you're gambling with your life, and everybody else's including those passengers that don't have a clue as to what's going on and are relying on not only this company's aircrafts to get them there safely, but they are relying on *US, THE CREW!* How bad can those damn reprimands be! If the entire flight attendant crew says *NO*, we're not going unless you get us an airworthy airplane or fix the problem on this one; don't you think they are going to have no choice but to provide us with what we are asking for, or whatever it is we need? Especially when we are calling them on *SAFETY!* I need you guys to take a few minutes and think about that and tell me why then it is, that you make the decision to go ahead and be talked into going while you watch me try to take my futile *stand alone,* and then all of you continue to watch, as I am given no other alternative but to get off the airplane. You on the other hand take the compromised aircraft/flight even though all of you feel exactly the way I do and have the exact concerns as I do about the entire deplorable situation they are forcing upon us. All of you know damn well that one person out of the entire crew trying to do the right thing, does not have the opulent strength to pull the power needed to change and then rectify the ominous situation at hand, that would come from the entire crew threatening to walk off together on the principle of safety! Just say it! Out loud, so you can hear yourselves. *Company reprimands and repercussions!* Now say it again, because *that is exactly what you are cowering to, by letting me stand alone. What you have to be able to see by now, in reference to what has happened to our career, and its manipulated slow destruction, is that you're not doing yourselves or the rest of us any favors, when you don't stand up! Flight attendants, we are our own worst enemy!* I know those same reprimands and repercussions all too well. I've been living with them since **November 25, 2006**, the date of the third flight I last walked off of because *I did not feel SAFE!* As difficult as *LAX Flight Service management* has made it for me this last year, and it has been hell, we cannot give in to this kind of harassment because one of these days, it's going to cost you your *LIFE!* AA's management has a language of its own. This language is called *"Double Talk". You all know it and I know it!* They go to great lengths to cover their asses, while they are within public earshot, or when they are momentarily surrounded by a good size audience especially one made up of employees who are listening intently and they make damn sure that the **LIES** they are enshrouding everyone with, sound legitimate and are composed of all the right things that they know they need to say! We on the other hand, especially those of us that have been around for many years and are quite familiar with this company's management tactics should know by now how *unprincipled* they truly operate behind the scenes. Those of you, who chose to continue on those compromised flights, should have known better*! If you guys continue running scared for your jobs the way you do the odds are that at one time or another you are going to find yourself on an airplane, flying at a very high altitude, not making it to your destination, and you're going to be asking yourself the two big ten million dollar questions! WHY? and How could I have been so stupid?* The only excuse I can come up with to give any of you, for this kind of thoughtless behavior you keep finding necessary to display, is that you must be completely losing your God given senses! You are making choices that I know you would not ordinarily make, if you were not facing company management repercussions. For the last 32+ years of my career, I have tried to follow the guidelines, rules and regulations that have been put in place to provide me with the tools and information that I need to perform my job as an *American Airline's flight attendant* to the safest and best of my ability. This company puts the tremendous responsibility on the flight crews for the safety of all passengers we transport on our flights, as well as for our own and that of our fellow crew members and I accept that responsibility willingly, making it my first and foremost priority. We all do! But by the same token, just as this company expects me to perform my job duties to the utmost best of my ability, I expect them, in return, to run this airline to the utmost safest of their ability, and that does not mean sometimes, or once in a while, or even most of the time. That means **ALL** of the time! I cannot and will not succumb to this company's harassment policies, when they want to pick and choose at which given times they deem it necessary for us to follow their rules and regulations, especially when it comes to safety, when they in turn think that they are above any and all expectations we have of them, and feel no responsibility to provide at all times, a safe working environment for us! That is a completely unacceptable double standard mind set. Even though the ***Attendance Policy is yet another company policy that is ridiculous in its own right, by comparison, it does not hold the same emphasis, on the severity of the detriment that can come from the policies concerning safety issues***. The absurdity and nonsense that goes on in that Flight Service Management office at LAX, really has to be seen and heard to be believed. As flight attendants, we are given many duties and responsibilities, which we are expected to accomplish from the minute we sign in for whatever trips we're assigned to work, until the minute our trips are completed, and we deplane from our aircrafts at our home bases. As far as I am concerned, all of those duties and responsibilities, no doubt each having their own amount of great importance, all come secondary, to the importance that MUST be given to that of the safety responsibility, we have not only for one another, but for our passengers as well. It has been my number one priority, since I began this career on ***May 27, 1976***, and it will remain so, until the very last moment, of the very last day, I fly as an ***American Airlines Flight Attendant.*** As someone who has known and loved many of you with all my heart, for such a very long time, not just because I happen to think that you are an incredible bunch of people, who I respect and admire, but also because of the tremendous happiness and joy that knowing some of you has brought to my life, not to mention the wonderful memories I have shared with you through the years, that your friendships have made possible for me, for all of those reasons, *I am asking you to please re-evaluate your decisions, should you find yourself once again being asked by company personnel, or anyone trying to convince you to compromise yourself or your safety in any way. If you do and feel yourself leaning towards letting the fear of company retaliation make the decision for you, rather than the common sense I know you to have, please take a few moments to breathe, and think about the people that you love and left at home, the kids, who you reassured that you'd see tomorrow, and then kissed goodbye before you drove off for the airport, for work. The mom, dad, sister or the brother you have plans to go to dinner or the movies with when you get home. Please, take the time to think about all these people that mean everything to you, as well as you to them, and how important it is that you do everything "within your power", to return to these people, whose lives will be tragically devastated if you don't!* I think that most would agree these are extremely scary and stressful times, especially for those of us, who happen to be in the commercial airline profession, to be sure. The names "American Airlines" and "United Airlines" were not just coincidental names that our extreme radical Muslim friends at AlQueda, just happened to randomly pick out of a hat, as a method for selecting the weapons they would use for their big event! Those particular aircrafts bearing those names, which were used as weapons for their targets, on the devastating morning of *September 11, 2001,* were carefully selected in order to make sure that the message they were sending us did not get lost in translation! It was the icing of choice on the cake, if you will, which they methodically and diligently took many years to bake, and then frosted to complete perfection! I for one, truly believe that they are still quite busy baking these days. It goes well beyond the fact that all of us are very much aware that *Bin Laden and his merry men are still at large, vigorously planning our*

next tea party together. It's about the very grave manner, in which many Americans are finding themselves in these days, myself and family included, due to the greed of both the corporate sector **(which we unfortunately happen to know first hand),** as well as our government with both entities having been given the power, unbelievably by all of us, no less, to enable their relentless corruption to run ramped for too many years having ultimately left us all in an aftermath of much disparity and unrest within our own country which has completely spiraled out of control! As American Airlines flight attendants, regardless of the added pressures and stress that are associated with this profession, as compared to the normal, feet steady on the ground ones, most of us still remain very much in awe of what we do for a living. It remains the profession as well as the lifestyle that we have chosen. I think for the majority of us, it is in our blood, and we can't imagine doing anything else for a living. Not because we can't, but because we don't have the desire to. We have no gripes about our profession, we love that. *The gripes are about the greed driven people who are running our company and its employees into the ground!* The normal person *(non airline),* doesn't understand any of that because they only observe us on the airplanes and they have absolutely no idea of the strong bond that we have with one another. The great disservice that the corporate side of the airline industry's top level management personnel, ours being no exception, have done to the character and integrity of the flight attendant profession *(mostly women),* started years ago, through the ***demeaning*** and **sexist** advertisement they chose to solicit over the airwaves. Using such phrases as *"coffee tea or me",* or *"hi, I am Alicia, marry me and fly free",* paved the way for the complete *demoralization* and *degradation* of the flight attendant profession, ultimately causing it irrevocable damage. It sent a tremendously inaccurate and negative message to many of the passengers we transported then, which continues to ring true for many of our passengers today. In a sense, what these companies did to their flight attendant employees was give a license to the flying public to behave badly towards us at *39,000 feet.* That may have been extremely amusing and entertaining to these high powered CEO's *(mostly men),* back in those much less threatening times, but on these *September 11, 2001* days everything has changed! We have to demand from our company's so called leaders, that they respect and regard our profession, with the same importance that they respect and regard their own. *WE,* that's *YOU* and *ME,* have to stop allowing these clowns, to minimize and trivialize the dire significance of our presence on board those aircrafts, which is essential for the safety of all who are on board. They do not have the right to treat us in the abominable and disrespectful fashion in which they think that they can! Nobody does! We are not dogs and ponies that they own and display when they run their shows! We have to stop behaving in the subservient, low self-esteem manner which we keep displaying for them. That is not even close to who we are, or what we are all about! *We are moms, dads, grandmas and grandpas to people that love and look up to us for guidance.* We have to remain those same entities that we are at home, when we fly as well! All of us need to stop allowing them to continue with their constant harassment. The beating us down, the constant dangling of our jobs over our heads, the lies, manipulation, treachery, all of it, only WE have the power to stop it! It is the responsibility of each and every one of us, to elevate this profession of ours, to where it should have always been, and where it should remain, not just today but always! Returning to it, the respect it so awesomely deserves, so that one day, should our daughters, sons, grandsons or granddaughters want to follow in our footsteps, we can be proud to have been able to leave them, with the tremendous legacy that is The American Airlines Flight Attendant! A very dear non airline friend of mine, whom I love very much, Mr. Michael Lockett, happened to call me at a momentary low point in my recent life, when I was experiencing a tremendous sense of desperation and loss of hope, essentially leaving me feeling sorry for myself. He proceeded to leave me with words that I will be forever grateful to him for saying them to me, especially at the precise moment that he did, because these particular words were not only apropos, but they immediately reinforced what I have always believed in my heart to be true. As I say them to all of you now, use them, as I have, to provide you with the fortitude and wisdom you will need, not just in our careers as flight attendants, but in our every day personal lives, as well. The word itself is descriptive of a feeling we are forced to experience on a continuous basis, while we are at work. It is it's acronyms that we have to repeatedly say out loud, in order to help us keep the feelings of helplessness and desperation that the actual word itself produces, in check and under control!

F = FALSE E = EVIDENCE A= APPEARING R= REAL! American Airlines flight attendants, the time has come when we need to be united more than ever. The time has come, when we need to **STAND!**

"They like to get you in a compromising position

They like to get you there and smile in your face

They think, they're so cute when they got you in that condition

Well I think, it's a total disgrace

** (John Mellencamp Singer, Songwriter my hero)**

Passenger Commendation Letter Sent to Headquarters:

—

March 5, 2002

[signature: Alicia Lut]

Customer Relations
American Airlines Inc.
P.O. Box 619612, MD 2400
DFW, TX 75261-9612

ATTN: Greg Clark

Dear Mr. Clark,

I am writing to you to relate a wonderful experience my wife Linda and I had while flying roundtrip between Washington-Dulles and Los Angeles International on your airline. Your flight crew was so personable and charming that I thought it was important to tell the airline's management what a positive image this particular flight crew generated for the company. Let me just say that this was undoubtedly *the* best flight we have ever taken and that feeling was created by the fine members of the crew listed below.

On February 16, 2002, my wife and I boarded Flight 143 out of IAD to go to California to introduce ourselves to our new grandson, our first grandchild. About an hour and one-half outside of LAX, I got up and walked over to the galley to ask if I could have a cup of coffee so I could be fully awake when I met our grandson Matthew. Normally, the flight attendants would have merely responded with a cup of coffee in a styrofoam cup, especially since they had already worked the majority of the flight. Not this day! Instead, **Kathleen Cerrato** gave me a cup of coffee in a ceramic mug with a smile and began to ask questions about my new grandson. These were not the usual, superficial questions normally asked of new parents or grandparents, instead Kathleen showed a sincere interest in our grandchild. Moments later, **Jan Love** joined in the conversation and she, too, expressed great delight on our behalf. It was apparent to my wife and myself that these two flight attendants were genuinely interested in their passengers and were not reluctant to show it

Just before our approach into LAX, Kathleen and Jan stopped by our seats and made us feel like VIP flyers instead of the coach passengers that we were. She gave us some wine and told us to celebrate once we arrived at our grandson's home. Obviously, she did not have to go out of her way like this but the fact that she did is worthy of commendation. Shortly thereafter, the Captain announced that we were beginning our final approach and every one had to return to their seats to prepare for landing. Once we landed, in the rush of things that inevitably follows, I failed to get Kathleen and Jan's names so I could write this letter – but good fortune was on our side!

Much to our delight, when we boarded the return flight, #144 on February 24th, nearly the entire same crew was on board. As I walked to my seat, I asked Kathleen to give me the names of the flight crew when she had a chance and that is what allowed me to write this letter. Before I go any further, however, I should list the names of the crew:

Kathleen Cerrato   **Jan Love**
Alicia Lutz   **Susan McKee**
Beverly Naten   **Annette Batel**
Terri Hatchett   **Jean Richmond**
Joe DiMaria

This whole experience would have been wonderful had it stopped here, but there is more. On the way back to IAD, **Alicia Lutz** and **Susan McKee** served our area of coach and apparently had heard from Kathleen and Jan that we were new grandparents. Well, we got the same royal treatment! These two could not have been nicer, showering us with personal attention and taking the time to look at the pictures we now had of our new grandson. Alicia and Susan showed the same concern for the other passengers, providing very professional, but very personal service to all, but they made us feel special. In addition, after the meal was served and during a break in the action, Kathleen and Jan came back to ask about the baby, shared the photos with us, and, once again, made us feel very privileged to have flown on American Airlines.

And, as if that were not enough, there was still more to come! Just before the flight landed, the crew presented us with a bottle of champagne and all expressed their best wishes for the baby. Needless to say, we have never before been treated in such a personal and considerate way on any airline.

I thought it was important to let the company's managers know what wonderful, genuine people that you have working for you. I hope that you will pass a copy of this letter to each and every member of the flight crew because they need to know that there are passengers out there who really appreciate their extra efforts. They certainly made our visit to meet our grandson a most memorable event. I am certain that this story will live on in the family for many years after we are gone and everyone will remember how wonderful American Airlines was on these two days. All of the paid advertisement in the world could not improve upon the good will generated by these terrific people.

Mr. Clark, please accept my thanks for the great experience and be sure to tell the flight crew that they make the world of flying a little better by their enthusiastic and genuine approach to the work.

Sincerely,

Ronald A. Romano
47678 Loweland Terrace
Potomac Falls, VA 20165

Typical Supervisor's Reply to Commendation Letter

AmericanAirlines®

Alicia Lutz
#37668

Alicia,

Attached please find a nice letter sent in by a pax on flight from IAD-LAX 16FEB02. I appreciate the fact the letter stated you provided very professional, but very personal service to all, and that you made the passengers feel special. However, I do need to remind you that AA's liquor license does not provide for liquor to be taken off the aircraft, as stated in AA flight attendant manual, Domestic Food Service section, under liquor restrictions, p 2.1 general liabilities.

Thanks again for the positive portion of this letter. I appreciate your efforts.

If you have any questions or concerns, please give me a call.

Sincerely,

Brad Rogers
LAX-FSM

Cc:file

My Reply to my Supervisor

Brad,

You and I are going to have to <u>definitely</u> part ways as Supervisor/Flight Attendant very, very soon because I have grown quite tired of your continuous bullshit harassment! Yeap! Brad, you read that last line right, BULLSHIT! I am enclosing a copy of the wonderful and typical letter I received from you regarding a "nice letter" that was sent to Greg Clark at Customer Relations at American Airlines by one of my passengers.

Now Brad, lets dissect <u>your</u> letter here a minute. First of all, "nice letter?" I'd hate to point this out to you Brad, but a commendation letter doesn't get any better than this one. "Nice" is a little inadequate of a description on this one, don't you think?

Here's my favorite part of your letter, and the part that really set me off! HOWEVER!!! Boy, we just can't win for losing can we. You have the audacity of stating to me AA Flight Attendant Manual Domestic Food Service blah blah blah Liabilities for us giving a passenger and his wife a <u>closed</u> bottle of champagne in celebration of the birth of their "first" grandchild for them to take home; when American Airlines has us (crew) serving alcohol <u>nonstop</u> to passengers from coast to coast where there are <u>constant</u> instances of these passengers getting totally drunk into an oblivious state and then, we send them on their merry way so they can get behind the wheel of their vehicles and on the roads with the mass population. Oh, do tell me Brad, what section of the Domestic Food Section blah blah blah will I find that liability for American. Oh, but that's okay because these passengers are paying four bucks a pop and American's making their money. Isn't that what this is really all about, Brad?

You end this ridiculous letter by saying, "thanks again for the <u>positive</u> portion of this letter," like there is any <u>negative</u> part to that letter! And the thanks again part, Brad, really?! Do you think I do my job professionally and personally for <u>your</u> benefit? Seriously, no need to thank me on that one, because contrary to what you might think, I do this job professionally and personally because it's what I do for my passengers. It has absolutely nothing to do with you!!

I am sending a copy of this letter to my Union as well as a copy of the one that you sent me. I will be making arrangements to speak to Amy Carter regarding all of this as I can no longer tolerate your condescending harassment. I will be demanding a change of Supervisor because, in my opinion, you are in no way, or shape, qualified to be <u>anybody's</u> Supervisor, much less mine.

By the way, quit sending trivial correspondence to my home address. What do you send, a letter a week? That's what my mailbox in LAX operation is for. You are harassing me Brad, and I will not put up with HARASSMENT from you or anyone else. I've been with American for twenty-six years. How long have you been with them, two minutes or so? You will not harass me. I come to work, I do my job, professionally and personally at that. I do what is expected of me as a Flight Attendant, and I expect my Flight Service Supervisor to do the same.

Once again, in my opinion, people like you make life a lot harder than it should be. Do you even remember September 11th, or have you already so quickly moved on?!

Alicia

My letter to Mr. Gerald Arpey (American Airlines CEO) pleading with him to take action and stop LAX Flight Service Management from sending up safety compromised aircrafts/flights:

November 28, 2006

Dear Mr. Arpey:

I am sending you this letter in hopes that it will not be intercepted by anyone and tossed aside as junk mail. And it will reach you. I cannot believe that I am finding myself having to write to you in the first place since the only reason that I'm doing it is #1, I do not believe at your level at ARM that all information about the goings on within this company reaches you and #2, I have heard on numerous occasions that you are trying to make a difference in this company. Let me start by introducing myself. My name is Alicia Lutz-Rolow. My employee number is #37668. I have been a flight attendant for American Airlines for over 31 years and am based in Los Angeles. I have always taken much pride in my career and have done my job with the utmost professionalism. The many crews I have had the privilege of working with in those 31 years have brought me so much joy in my life that It cannot be measured. Some of those people are very close to me and my family. I have known them through marriages, children and now grandchildren. They are my second family. You se Mr. Arpey, the reason I'm even telling you all this is because I need you to understand that we are not just employee numbers, we are human beings behind those numbers. I cannot speak for bases other than my own, but I must say this, when I fly with other base crews, their feelings mirror my own.

Los Angeles Flight Service is and has been for some time now, conducting business with us through harassment and intimidation. Sean Lynch seems to make sure that situations are handled by his people in that manner and that is constant and does not waiver. Flight attendants are treated with such shameful disregard and disrespect and yet so much is expected of us. Every year at our recurrent training, we are taught that what we learn there, are guidelines and tools to help us through difficult and at times catastrophic situations we may encounter in our jobs as flight attendants. We are told year after year that we are "the eyes and ears of the cockpit," and that we are the last line of defense for the passengers we transport on our aircrafts from one state or country to another. They reiterate over and over that no matter how much training we receive, we should always assess each situation on its own merit, and TRUST our gut instincts because it is those same instincts that may one day save our lives and the lives of our passengers. "AWAYS BE SAFE," we are told.

Keeping in mind all that I have said to you sir, I have been put in a terrible and unwarranted situation by Mr. Sean Lynch and Los Angeles Flight Service. I am in the process of having to seek outside legal counsel to represent me since my union (APFA), cannot represent me due to the fact that the document that Flight Service wants me to sign (under duress), a document called "Career Decision Day Advisory" does not allow me the basic rights to counsel through the grievance process through my Union.

According to LAX Management, I will be given 3 options to deal with. Option #1: Sign the document under duress, I might add, and I can keep my job as long as I admit to having performance problems with the company and will correct those immediately. The problem with that option for me is that I do not have any performance problems that I am aware of other than the one they are saying I have which is refusing to work safety or security related compromised airplanes, and I sir, respectfully, do not see that as a performance problem but instead I see it as common sense and 31 years of good judgment under my belt. Option #2: Termination. Option #3: Termination.

I think you and I both know if I should go that route and sign this document, that the minute I should happen to find myself in a similar situation or worse in the future, and I would have to make a decision that was not pleasing to them, I would be terminated immediately without any recourse.

So you see Mr. Arpey sir, I am very sorry but these options do not seem beneficial to me in any way, and besides that they should not be anything that I should have to be dealing with because I have done nothing wrong. Mr. Lynch and his flight service people have taken my file and have twisted and turned things around so as to show my actions as irresponsible and negligent when in fact that is exactly what their actions are.

On November 25, 2006, I along with two other flight attendants did not work our trip from LAX to JFK that night because we did not feel SAFE. One of our passengers found a hostile note that spoke of bombs massacres and anti-religion. It had been intentionally left on our outbound aircraft by someone on the inbound to be found obviously in flight. That is the way we perceived it. When I went to investigate what was going on and personally read this note myself, the flight crew, ground people, including security and the agents were all on the jet-bridge, while the captain was on the phone with the SOC trying to determine the situation. During this time, the flight attendants and First Officer were extremely concerned and getting very little information and the security of the aircraft or lack there of.

The SOC along with the captain determined that the aircraft was safe to fly. This determination was accomplished through phone conversation. The reason for that determination was not made clear enough to us and at that point we pleaded with the captain and the ground personnel to run a through check on the aircraft for possible items left behind or anything suspicious. They flat out refused and said it wasn't necessary.

Three of us, myself included, made the decision to not work the flight based on what little information we were receiving and feeling very apprehensive about the aircraft. We all know that different departments, including the SOC, are people, they are not above making mistakes. September 11th is the perfect example of that. The three of us may have made a different decision had they just taken a little more time and checked the aircraft. It's easy for people in those positions who sit safely on the ground while we are at 39,000 feet to make judgments on us that are so unfair.

Mr. Arpey, just like you, I have a family I love very

much at home. September 11th has changed everything in the way flight crews assess situations these days. If I get on an airplane NOT KNOWING that something is going to go terribly wrong up there, that's one thing. Once facing that challenge, I will revert to my training and depend on that and my sense of good judgment to handle this situation so that we can get back on the ground in one piece, but when I KNOWINGLY take off on any airplane that I knew was compromised to the point where it could put myself, my crew and passengers in harms way and I strongly felt it was not SAFE, I would never forgive myself for allowing myself to be harassed or intimidated into that position.

I have been forced to watch my crew continue on these flights not because they feel differently than I do, but because they don't want to find themselves where I am now. That's why they go all the while anxious and stressed and at times fearful for their lives, not to mention the passengers on those flights who are not privy to the information that we are privy to., so as to make their own informed decision of whether to go or not. Mr. Arpey, would you sir, put yourself or any one of your family members on a flight that you felt had a compromised situation that wasn't being taken care of properly or handled seriously enough? I know with 100%

certainty that had you been scheduled on my last flight from LAX to JFK on November 25, 2006, hoops would have been jumped over by ground personnel at LAX, dogs would have been brought on to check the aircraft, and bags would have been checked, etc. etc. I am not comparing my position as an American Airlines flight attendant to your CEO status, but I am comparing mine, my crew and passenger's lives with yours and I have concluded that they are equally as important. If I am out of line here please excuse me as I mean you no disrespect. I truly believe that these situations never get up to your level in this company for reviewing and inspecting.

American Airlines have some incredible employees who have returned to work after Sept. 11th to face pay cuts and dwindling benefits making many sacrifices in order to help benefit the Company and keep it on top of it's game. I feel that it shouldn't be too much to ask that when we come to work, they provide a safe working environment for us.

In closing let me state for the record that as a whole, the majority of the time I feel American Airlines does comply with Federal Safety Regulations and does try to look out for the safety of it's crews and passengers, but there are those infrequent times when management personnel find it necessary to talk out of both sides of it's mouth, when they tell us that they would never want us to Fly an airplane when we did not feel safe on the one hand then on the other, proceed to fail us miserably by reprimanding us through harassment and intimidation when we exercise that right they claim we have.

The Christmas season is upon us. It has always been my favorite time of year. This year unfortunately instead of finding myself enjoying my family and my beautiful granddaughter, I am in the fight of my life, trying to protect my retirement and everything I have worked so hard for all my life.

Hopefully you can have this serious matter looked into for all of our sakes. Merry Christmas.

Sincerely,

Flight Attendant Alicia Lutz Rolow

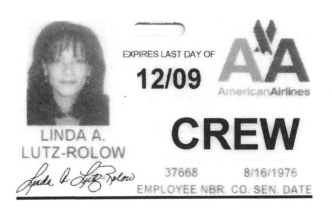

Alicia Lutz Rolow

Mr. Arpey's very concerned and heartfelt reply:

American Airlines

Gerard J. Arpey
Chairman and Chief Executive Officer

February 21, 2007

Ms. Alicia Lutz Rolow
25582 La Mirada Street
Laguna Hills, CA 92653

Dear Ms. Rolow:

Thank you for your November 28 letter, which we received early last month. I apologize for the delay in replying, but wanted to check some important information. Your description of the incident on November 25 varies considerably from the facts gathered from other people and AA departments. After reviewing the student letter left in the seat pocket, SOC contacted the student and was satisfied that it was not a threat, but his personal opinion. After other investigation, the Captain of your flight and SOC made an informed – and I believe correct – decision to continue the flight. This was communicated to you and other crew, after which you removed yourself from the trip.

I understand from Flight Service that this was the third time in two years that you have done so, and that after the immediately previous occurrence you received a sanction that was upheld in arbitration.

You make strong allegations about the management of the Flight Service base at LAX: I believe they are unwarranted and unfair. That you disagree with the actions taken does not constitute "harassment and intimidation."

Although I appreciate your taking the time to write, I am very troubled by your interpretation of the facts and your conclusions about our LAX base managers.

Sincerely yours,

ke

cc: Lauri Curtis
Frank Campagna
Sean Lynch

June 9, 2006

Alicia Lutz
EE # 037668

Dear Alicia,

It is with great pleasure that I share with you this letter that was written on your behalf. What a nice compliment to receive, and I want to thank you for all your teamwork on this flight and for making such a lasting impression to this passenger

I would like to express to you how much I appreciate everything you do. It is evident that you are proud of what you do as a flight attendant and that you truly represent American Airlines with pride.

As part of our new "Customer Service Iniative" I have entered your name into our **SPOTLIGHT AWARD** drawing. If your name is drawn you could win a 2 night hotel stay in San Diego, or a Target Gift Card or AMC Movie Tickets. This is all part of our way of saying "thank you" for providing our customers with outstanding customer service.

Thank you again for the excellent service you provided. Fly safe and keep up the great work you are doing out there, and good luck in the drawing!

Best Wishes,

Daniel A. Wickey
Administrative Service Manager
Group 30 – LAX

CC Personnel File

Commendation Letter from my LAX Supervisor Daniel Wickey informing me of his entering my name in a "Spotlight Award" drawing for Excellence in Service.

In just 8 short months I went from a "Spotlight Award" for Excellence in Service worthy employee to a "troubled interpretation employee" How does that happen?

CHAPTER 7

SEPTEMBER 9, 2001
FACE TO FACE
WITH ALQUEDA

My routine day starts at six a.m. My alarm goes off and I get out of bed and I tip toe down the stairs. I wake up to my already brewed pot of coffee. Everyone in the house is still sleeping and I wrap myself in the magnificence that the quiet holds for me for the next thirty minutes at least. I pour my very first cup of coffee and begin sipping it while I start to make my first grader's lunch for school. *I am pondering on all the details of the many errands I have to run around all day and get accomplished by six p.m. that same evening, including the meal that I have to prepare, so that I can leave my family sitting down at the table, eating dinner. I have to fly a work trip tonight and six p.m. is my cut off time for setting aside my role and responsibilities as wife, mom, and grandmother and begin stepping into my role and responsibilities as an American Airlines Flight Attendant.* I have already begun all the mental steps, without yet even leaving the kitchen. I continue to debate whether he gets a turkey, ham or a tuna sandwich for lunch that day and the turkey wins out hands down. I finish packing his lunch, place it in his *"pokeman"* back pack and then I proceed back upstairs to wake him up and get him ready for school. After I drop him off, I run around the entire rest of the morning well into the afternoon, taking care of what seems like thousands of errands that need attending to and the next thing I realize as I look down at my watch, is that it's ten minutes to three p.m. and I am racing back to his school to pick him up by three. I bring him home, help him with his little homework, and begin cooking whatever meal it is that they are going to get for dinner by six p.m. The trip I am scheduled to fly tonight is the same one I have been flying off and on for the last twenty years of my career. That very fact provides for me a comfortable and familiar feeling. As I leave my family downstairs eating at the dinner table, I go upstairs and quickly get in and out of the shower. Still wrapped up in my towel, I start repacking my suitcase with the items that I had temporarily taken out while I was home, but will once again need for my trip tonight. I blow dry my hair and put on some make up. Last but not least as I am finally throwing on my ***American Airlines*** uniform, I take a quick last look around to see if there's anything else I need to pack and whatever that might happen to be goes in my suitcase as well. I'm ready and it's only seven ten p.m. Not bad, I think to myself, since the sign in time for my trip tonight isn't until nine p.m. so I grab my uniform jacket, suitcase and tote bag and head downstairs to say my goodbyes and leave instructions with my husband Shanon for the daily routines my kids will need help with the following day in my absence. I kiss and hug everyone and tell them all how very much I love them and that I will see them tomorrow, and I head out the door. I am sharing this information on these pages in this chapter, for a very important reason. I want all ***non airline*** people to understand how crucial what you have just read on this page is, regarding my routine on the days that I leave home to fly. We ***always*** leave our homes making absolutely sure that we have told our family how much we love them because we may not get another chance. It is this same routine that the majority of flight attendants follow every time they prepare to leave their homes and families to go to work and fly their trips. *It is the very routine that Ms. Amy Sweeney and all of the other flight crewmembers who went to work on September 11th, 2001 followed. Most of us stay very focused and centered about what it is we do for a living and we have learned very early on in our careers that those loved ones we are leaving behind for what we hope will only be the short duration of our trips, are never to be taken for granted should God forbid we find ourselves at 39,000 feet, battling some sort of catastrophic situation or as in Amy's case a fatal hijacking, all the while up there, wishing we would have taken the few extra moments that it takes from our hurried and stressed out lives, to tell our families how much we love them and what they mean to us.* Working the profession of a commercial airline flight attendant is what keeps that *front and center* for all of us at all times, especially these days. The *"motto"* I have wholeheartedly adopted since the horrific events of *9/11* is: *"never put off saying those important words to your loved ones till tomorrow, when you have so many opportunities to say them today"*! I arrive at the airport at *LAX* and proceed to the *Flight Service* area where I sign in for my trip assignment. I will be flying on a *Boeing 767* this evening, which happens to be my aircraft of choice, and I am working *American Airlines Flight 10* which is my work trip of choice as well. It is a *"non stop"* all niter from *LAX* to *JFK*. The computer shows *Flight 10* departing on time at ten p.m. PST. I pull up all the necessary flight paperwork that I will need for my trip, hug a few people who I run into in the *Flight Service* sign in area that I haven't seen in a while, and hook up with the crew who will be working to *JFK* with me tonight. All of the flight attendants working *Flight 10* including me take the elevator upstairs to where the departure area is located and we proceed to the designated departure gate where our aircraft is parked. I am the number 2 flight attendant position this evening and what that means is that besides working the coach cabin galley, which is the primary area that I am responsible for, I will also be one of the four flight attendants that are responsible for the passengers in the coach cabin. After boarding our aircraft, the other flight attendants and I put our belongings in the **FAA (Federal Aviation Administration)** designated storage areas and we begin checking our emergency equipment, making sure it is all in its proper place and in working order, before I head back to the aft galley to begin my galley duties. As I am accomplishing those galley duties, the passenger boarding process commences. The fact that I am in the furthest aft section of the aircraft preparing the beverage and meal carts that we will be using in flight, does not allow me the capability of observing the passengers as they board our aircraft with much diligence, nor does it allow me to witness first hand any situations that might be transpiring at this particular time in the cabin, so the aisle flight attendants are making sure that the boarding process goes a smoothly as possible and they are addressing all ongoing situations at this time which makes me completely dependent on them and the information they continuously relay back to me, to keep me abreast of everything that is going on. After all the *"normal boarding drama"* that we usually deal with is over and everyone is now finally in their assigned seats and all their carry on bags properly stowed, I hear the words *"flight attendants prepare for departure"* over the **P.A. system (aircraft phone intercom)** coming from the cockpit. My *jump seat* as the number 2 flight attendant is located at the furthest aft left hand side of the aircraft, which is the same area in which the aircraft doors (**4LandR**) that I am responsible for arming before take-off and disarming at gate arrival are located. I arm my doors, and inform the *Purser (number 1 flight attendant)* via the *P.A.* system that my doors at **4L&R** are now *armed* and *crosschecked* and we proceed to push back from the gate and begin taxing towards the runway that has been chosen for our flight's take-off by the control tower. *I begin the same systematic routine I perform on every one of these trips that I work*. I store all the carts and other items I have out all over the galley, back into their storage locations, and make sure everything is back in its place and secured for take off. After the short safety video we play for our passengers informing them about the location of their nearest exits, how to use them, and other important safety information regarding our aircraft and flight that they need to know has been completed, I then proceed to take what flight attendants call a *"walk through"* on the entire airplane starting from the furthest aft left hand side, while at the same time performing a visual check on each passenger sitting on that side as I walk all the way forward until I reach the first class galley. Once there, I pause for a moment to speak with the *Purser* and fellow flight attendants, to make sure everything is as it should be at the front of the aircraft. After it has been indeed confirmed to me that all is well, I walk down the right hand side of the aircraft, starting from the first class cabin all the way back to the furthest aft section of the coach cabin, while once again continuously doing a visual check on the passengers sitting on that side. I am diligently checking everyone and everything, looking for anyone or anything that I might deem as suspicious. That, ladies and gentlemen is called *"profiling"* the aircraft and because of the events that took place on *September 11th, 2001*, it is a necessary systematic type of tool if you will, that I and many other *American Airlines* flight attendants use for the sole purpose of observing and detecting anything or anyone traveling with us on our aircrafts that we may feel suspicious about. I have absolutely no interest in being *"politically correct"* for anyone who would take offense with the fact that I do profile my passengers when I take to the skies. I consider myself and my co-working flight attendants the *"front lines"* of protection for our passengers on our flights should we encounter any terrorist situation up there, and as such, we are deserving of the right to choose any and all measures we deem necessary to take in order to ensure that safety. Please take note that this is not an *American Airline's* policy; but it is mine as well as the policy of many other *American* **Airline's** flight attendant's and because of the events that transpired on *9/11*, it shall remain that way for as long as I continue to work as a flight attendant! It is what is necessary these days and what quite possibly may save our lives up there should it become necessary one day. When I reach my *jump seat* at *4L* and I decide that the aircraft and passengers seem *"normal"* and *"non threatening"* as far as the all nighter goes anyway, at this stage of the game I hear the words from our Captain saying *"flight attendants, please be seated"* so I buckle myself into my *jumpseat* which faces forward on the aircraft, allowing me full visibility of all the passengers in my coach cabin as we take off. Well, this so called *"normal"* and *"non- threatening"* flight would soon prove to be otherwise! After the aircraft reached a comfortable cruising altitude where we could move about the cabin safely, we got up from our jump seats, and began readying the carts in order to take them down the aisles for our in-flight beverage and meal service. Flight attendant number 3, who was also working in the coach cabin, happened to be a long time friend of mine and we decided that we would work the cart on the left hand side of the aircraft together, while the other two flight attendants, numbers 5 and 6, worked on the right hand side. As all four of us were simultaneously pulling the beverage/meal carts up both aisles making our way up to the beginning of the coach cabin in order to begin our in-flight service, there was this man sitting on the left hand side of the aircraft (my side), who looked to be of ***Middle Eastern ethnicity (imagine that)*** and he was shouting very loud at us, as we were pulling the cart past his seat. The cabin lights were set on ***"night mode"*** because on the all nighter, most passengers just go right to sleep after boarding, and these passengers were no exception to that rule, so the aircraft was relatively dark but a number of passengers had their reading lights on throughout the cabin which helped to serve as spot lights, making it possible for the flight attendants to see everything and everyone quite clearly. This man had his reading light on as well and it was positioned directly on his face. His shouting was so loud and disruptive, that he was causing all the other passengers within ear shot of his seat to wake up from their sleep and that was making them get very upset with him. We had pulled the cart up about three or four rows past his seat, when the number 3 flight attendant and I looked at each other with sheer astonishment and we then brought our cart to a complete halt. She remained on the other side of the cart and watched in horror as I walked back to where his seat was, so I that could ask him to calm down and stop shouting, which I did. I then asked him what his problem was. By this point, he had disturbed the sleep of quite a few people who were now beginning to get a little concerned. This passenger's ***tantrum like shouting*** continued on for several minutes before I could even understand what he was saying in order to help him, but he was extremely angry and upset that there would be no possibility of speaking cordially to him simply because he would not allow it! Why he was feeling the need to shout out whatever his displeasure was in that chosen manner was anybody's guess. When I finally was able to understand him, I found his reason for engaging in that *"over the top"* scene he was displaying, to be of the most absurd kind. From the information I was able to finally gather from him, apparently one of the other flight attendants working the coach cabin had sold him a headset which he himself had requested to purchase because he wanted to watch the in flight movie. The headset rental was five dollars and he paid the flight attendant with a twenty dollar bill. When she didn't have the change for his twenty dollars at that very moment, she told him she would return with his change when she had it. Well, apparently he was convinced that I was that very same flight attendant involved in that transaction and that I was intending to keep his change from that twenty dollar bill. *I suppose all flight attendants look alike to many people out there, never mind that she was blonde and had blue eyes standing 5'10" tall while I on the other hand, have jet black hair and brown eyes and I stand 5'4" tall.* Flight attendants have a tendency to confuse passengers that way all the time. *It's a phenomenon much like every passenger having to use the vile and tiny aircraft lavatories as soon as they board the aircraft, never mind that they could have used the big clean ones out in the terminal where they had been waiting for some time to board this flight! Go figure.* Anyway, back to my story. He informed me that he was angry at the fact that I had whisked past him with the cart and he then accused me of wanting to steal his money. He said that I was passing his seat for the sole purpose of avoiding giving him his change back, and that I was hoping that he would forget I owed him money. He demanded that I give him his change back right there and then, literally screaming that direct order to me at the top of his lungs. I tried several times, in vain I might add, to explain to him that first of all, I wasn't even the flight attendant who was even involved in that monetary transaction with him and secondly, I couldn't give him back the change that he was owed because I was the galley flight attendant and up until that very moment, I had not yet been out in that cabin selling anything, therefore I hadn't collected any money to be able to make change for him and before I could finish telling him that I would find the flight attendant that had sold him the headset and that I would have her take care of it, *he called me a lying whore, among many other equally colorful words, and tried to spit in my face. Lucky for me and probably more for him, he missed his target because by that time, I was already moving away from him and heading towards the front of the aircraft to inform the Captain and the Purser about this idiotic man who was not only in an uncontrollable rage, but was in that rage for a reason I considered to be of the most ridiculous and absurd kind!* What is even more ridiculous is the fact that flight attendants have to be continuously at odds with this company's management personnel, who do not take the necessary steps that are needed, to put a stop to this type of vicious, disrespectful and at times even violent behavior that a few passengers on our flights seem to think they can direct and display towards the flight attendant crews. This company's corporate management, as well as all other airline's management personnel for that matter, has helped create this kind of unacceptable *passenger entitlement behavior problem* through the years that flight crewmembers are constantly having to deal with. Airline companies allow these problematic passengers to behave in this manner without making them face serious legal repercussions or consequences for it, simply because they are *REVENUE* for the company, thereby providing us with absolutely no protection in-flight, even though the *FAA clearly states that it is a Federal offense to interfere with flight crewmembers and their duties while in flight!* I proceeded to the front of the aircraft to inform the *Purser* and the *Captain* as to what was happening back in coach. I personally did not relay the information at hand to the **Captain** because when I told the Purser what was happening in the back, she had assured me that she would inform the **Captain** herself and then she would come back and try to talk to this irate passenger herself. I gave her what was my personal opinion, which was to let the **First Officer** come to the back *(they could do that then, since this was pre-9/11)* and speak sternly to him about correcting his abusive language as well as behavior because something was beginning to make me feel that the reason for this man's anger went way *"beyond the scope"* of just his not getting his change back. I also told her that because of his **Middle Eastern ethnicity,** I felt that he would not respond well to a female in charge telling him what to do and that her speaking to him could cause his verbal abuse and rage to quickly escalate to a more violent and dangerous level. Although this **Purser** nodded her head as a gesture of *"intelligent understanding"* what I was telling her, she chose instead to completely ignore everything I had said to her and go off of her *"lacking intelligence understanding"*. She also chose to not relay the information about this passenger to the **Captain,** which was completely unacceptable since all of us know that the **Cockpit Crew** should be made aware of situations such as this one and kept abreast of it at all times should things escalate to a more problematic and potentially dangerous level in flight. I needed to return to the coach cabin so we could begin our in-flight service so I did not find out about the way she handled the situation until later on in the flight. As we pushed the cart down the aisle and began approaching his seat, the abusive shouting resumed. The number 3 flight attendant attempted to ask him if he wanted something to drink but he ignored her question and continued his abusive rambling, this time directing it towards her. At this point, her and I had both had enough of this man's verbal abuse, and decided that it was probably best to move on with the cart and just ignore him all together because he was making it impossible to carry on any type of civilized conversation with him and quite frankly, we were not interested in doing so at this stage of the game, anyway. I was definitely beginning to get a very uneasy feeling about the entire situation as were the others; flight attendants and passengers alike. *I knew that this man had some sort of an agenda for displaying this kind of behavior but I wasn't quite sure at the time, what that could possibly be and for a* **very short** *moment, I even dismissed it as simply a Middle Eastern man, having a problem with a women telling him what to do.* As I waited for either the **Captain** or **First Officer** to come back to the rear of the aircraft (**not knowing that they did not know what was going on**) after we had completed our service, I began watching this passenger more intently and noticed that he was making eye contact with someone sitting in one of the middle seats of the aircraft, towards the right hand side aft of his seat. I was trying to pin point just exactly who he was signaling to but became abruptly interrupted at the sight of the **Purser** walking back towards his seat, with no signs of either the **Captain** or the **First Officer** behind her. I noticed she had a twenty dollar bill in her hand, and when she got to the passenger's seat, she held out that bill for him to take. Just like all the other times before when any of us tried to speak to him, he began screaming again, this time it was at her. *I have to admit, I was mildly enjoying watching the way she was cowering! He grabbed the money out of her hand with such force that he almost caused her to be knocked off balance. The more she apologized and groveled, the more it fueled his agitation as he continued shouting obscenities at her never missing a beat!* I was waiting for him to hit her at any moment and I think she must have felt that as well because she finally walked away from him in quite a hurry, and came back to the aft part of the aircraft where the rest of us were watching this event taking place as we were breaking down and stowing our carts after having completed the in-flight meal/beverage service. I was completely infuriated with this **Purser** because she had done exactly what I suggested to her she not do, and at this point, she hadn't even advised the **Captain** or the **First Officer** about the volatile and hostile situation the rest of us were dealing with regarding this passenger in the coach cabin. Had the incident escalated to a physically violent level, it might have taken all of us back there to get it under control before we could make an emergency landing and have him arrested. When she approached me, she began informing me that she had returned his initial money back to him because she had thought that if she did that, while at the same time allowing him to keep the headset for his movie viewing, her kind gesture would then pacify him. She quickly went on to say that she now realized that she had obviously misjudged the situation. *(You think)?* **It was quite apparent to the rest of us that the passenger had made her fearful and had completely rattled her. As she continued speaking to us, her voice was quivering and it looked as if she were ready to start crying at any moment.** She went on and on with her little explanation of telling us how she wasn't prepared for his hostility towards her, and that she didn't want to get involved any further, as if I had asked her to get involved in the first place! Flight attendants out there, I know there are many of you who have been in similar situations at one time or another during a flight you were working, where one or more of your flight attendant co-workers not only completely undermined your handling of a passenger misconduct situation, but they also manage to make the ordeal much worse than it originally was with their cowardly interference. Am I not correct? If you answered **yes** to my question, then I am quite sure that you can also imagine what

I wanted to do to this **Purser,** can you not? If somehow, it would have been at all possible for me to have made her stay in front of that passenger for the duration of the five hour flight we were on that night, and let him continue to verbally abuse her with the vile names he had been screaming at her when she tried to refund him his money, I would have done it in a **New York minute.** That is exactly what she deserved. Maybe the next time something like that happened on another flight, she would not even think about doing her co working flight attendants that terrible disservice again! As if she hadn't done enough damage already, she then had the incredible audacity to inform me that she didn't want to get involved in the situation any further! Sound familiar? Where do these people come from? The fact that this **Purser** did not relay the information to the **Captain** and **First Officer** about the potentially serious situation we were encountering in the back was not only completely unforgivable, but dangerous as well. Had the situation escalated to a much higher level where the entire crucial state of affairs could have turned physically violent, the cockpit crew would not have had a clue about what was going on in the back of their airplane. That is just wrong! At that point I told her to get out of the coach cabin and go back to her first class cabin and just stay there. I also told her that in my opinion, she had absolutely no business whatsoever flying the **Purser** position on any flight because that position requires the person working it, to be of an **intelligent mind** as well as **hands on** and that she possessed neither of those qualities. That **Purser** was one of the most extreme cases of flight attendants whose characters have been severely **beaten down** by **American Airlines** management that I have ever seen in my entire flying career. Unfortunately for the rest of us, we do have a few who cannot take proper charge of a difficult situation in flight, but instead just make a **bad** situation worse. She left the coach cabin, making sure she walked up the right hand side of the aircraft of course, so as to avoid coming in any contact with that passenger again. After she left the coach cabin, I personally called the cockpit crew informed them of what was happening with regards to that out of control passenger we were dealing with in the back, as well as what the Purser had just done. The **Captain** asked me if I wanted him to send back the **First Officer** to the back to get involved but I kindly replied with a polite no, and I told him that I believed the passenger was beginning to calm down.   I told him that if anything should start up again, I would let him know. He said okay, and asked me to keep him posted in case we needed him to make an unscheduled landing at the next available airport, so that we could have the authorities meet the flight and remove that passenger and have him arrested. I thanked him for his support, *(which we don't always get),* and hung up the phone feeling so much better knowing that they were standing behind us in whatever decisions we might have had to make down the road. They were watching our backs and that alone provided great comfort for us. Unlike the **Purser,** the **Captain** and the **First Officer** were willing to get involved! I decided after I hung up the phone with the crew, that I would continue observing this man closely because he was really giving me the creeps and I asked the rest of the coach flight attendants to do the same. A short while after all the main drama had **been squelched, I noticed that this man could not sit still in his seat so he got up out of his seat and began nervously pacing up and down the aisle. He was watching us and paying attention to everything we were doing.** He was also definitely communicating through eye contact with that other passenger whose exact seat location I had tried to pin point earlier but was interrupted from doing so. Now, however, *I knew exactly who it was and where he was sitting and he was of Middle*

Eastern ethnicity as well. You have to remember that September 11th doesn't happen until tomorrow, so I am not thinking along that kind of catastrophic level, but everything inside me was telling me something was very wrong, and my gut instinct of many years as a flight attendant supported that feeling! I continued watching him like a hawk. He eventually sat back down in his seat, and called the number 3 flight attendant over and asked her for a glass of water without actually screaming at her. I noticed that he popped a couple of pills in his mouth before downing the water she had brought him. I didn't know for sure what kind of pills he was taking, but I assumed they were sleeping pills of some kind because approximately ten minutes later, he was sound asleep. Now the other guy he had been eye motioning to who was sitting two rows up from the last row of coach in the G seat, decided it was time he get up from his seat and start pacing up and down his side of the aisle as he also paid close attention to **everything that we were doing.** *It seemed to us as though they were both scoping out the cabin as well as the flight attendants, while taking turns sleeping in order to be able to keep up their observance during the entire flight.* At the time, we were certainly alarmed at their behavior, but quite honestly we were more baffled than anything else. *In retrospect, looking back now after September 11th, I am today 100% sure of the fact that it was that precise activity that these two passengers of Muslim ethnicity were engaging in on that flight that evening!* A passenger's call light chimed midway through the cabin on the right hand side of the aircraft, which was precisely the side this new guy also started pacing on. As I started up the aisle, I eventually reached the area where he was standing, and I noticed he had some sort of religious book in his hands. *He could see that I needed to get around him, but made no effort to move aside and let me get by him.* I had to ask him twice to move aside before he finally did. He was intentionally staring me down as if to intimidate me the entire time I was maneuvering around him. In order for me to accomplish that, I literally had to extend my hand out towards his torso to keep his body from touching mine. As I did that, I stared right back at him the entire time. *I cannot begin to fully describe the incredibly strong sensation of pure hatred and the personification of evil I saw and felt from this man when I was face to face with him. I walked away from him towards the passenger call light, with my back feeling uncomfortably unprotected, so much so, that I found myself looking back at him several times before I got to the passenger who was calling for us.* When I got to the seat where the call light was on, I reached up to turn the light off, and looked at the lady who was in the seat. I remember her asking me if I was all right, and that question made me aware of how I must have seemed to appear a bit stunned. I smiled at her and told her that I was, as I then expressed to her my gratitude for her concern. She told me it was time for her to take a prescription pill and she needed a glass of water to do that and asked if I could please get that for her. I replied to her that of course I could, and that I would be right back with it. As I turned and started back to the aft galley, I immediately noticed that the *Muslim* passenger was no longer standing in the aisle, and I must say that I felt a tremendous sense of relief at the thought of not having to confront him in the same manner in which I found myself having to, when I was walking up to answer that lady's call light. I knew I was going to have to say something to him that he probably would not have liked if he proceeded with his rudeness towards me as I was on my way back to the galley. That relief was very short lived however. *When I reached the back galley there he was, except that now, instead of standing in the middle of the aisle making it difficult for anyone to get around him, he was on the floor sitting on his legs with his head bowed and that prayer book in front of him directly facing the 4L door of the aircraft, chanting whatever it is they chant out of that prayer book out loud as if he were chanting to the door itself.* The manner in which he was praying was very disturbing to not only me but the surrounding passengers who were sitting in the seats close to the galley area and were within ear shot when this was all happening, listening to his chanting as well. *I understood that the custom with these people of sitting in that manner while chanting is the normal stance they use when they pray in their mosques, but on an airplane cruising at 39,000 feet, to be chanting out of your prayer book in front of the aircraft door of our Being 767 well, that's was just not something that looked comforting to the rest of us!* The number 3 flight attendant, who happens to be the only one back in the Coach cabin with me at this time, was just shaking her head with disbelief as she looked up at me when I entered the galley and first saw all of this. Even though I was dreading having to get anywhere near this man due to the fact that he had totally creeped me out earlier in a very bad way. I immediately went up to him and bent down so that I could speak discreetly to him in order not to embarrass him. I spoke very quietly so that the surrounding passengers would not be able to hear anything I said to him. I asked him what exactly he was doing on the floor so close to the aircraft's door. At first he would not look up at me or even acknowledge the fact that I was speaking to him. He just kept chanting *over* my voice. I tried a few more times to communicate with him, but he was completely ignoring me continuing with his reading and chanting which was becoming louder and louder. *What happened after that still makes the hair on my arms stand on end to this very day!* I decided that I would ask him one last time, raising my voice at him this time which is what finally got him to stop chanting and sit up straight and look directly at me. *"Sir, what exactly is it that you are doing so close to this door"?* I asked him. He looked at me, and responded with; *"I am praying, what does it look like I am doing"! It was not the response he gave me that alarmed me to an extremely freighting degree. It was the way in which he used slow and deliberate body movement as he was sitting up and turned his head in my direction to look at me with this ghastly wicked grin on his face as he responded. I felt as if I were looking at some kind of vampire getting ready to strike and then feed! The very dark and almost vacant look he had in his eyes made me take a big humongous step back and immediately put me in a guarded state.* I took my eyes off of him for a minute and looked over at the number 3 flight attendant who had taken on this look of complete amazement which **resonated** that something was very wrong with this situation, even though at that time, I would have never been able to put it all together to save my life. I immediately then returned my focus back on him. *He was looking at me with such hatred and disdain that I clearly remember it sending a chill up my spine. As hard as I was trying to figure him out as well as the entire chain of events that had occurred this evening, I could not, except to say that I felt without a single doubt, that they were all somehow connected in some way. It took everything I had to calm my nerves which were frazzled by now, and I tried to look as unaffected by what had just transpired between us as possible, but quite frankly, he was scaring the hell out of me and I literally had to clasp my hands behind my back to keep him from seeing how out of control they were shaking. Something inside me kept telling me that at this very moment, I could show this man absolutely no fear whatsoever and that feat was a bit difficult to pull off since he was not taking his eyes off of me for a minute.* So, with a very stern voice that I had to reach deep down within myself to muster up, because he was freaking me out, I said to him; *"well sir, you're going to have to get up and get away from my aircraft's door and you're going to have to take yourself, along with your book back to your assigned seat where you can finish your prayers there, because in case you haven't noticed, the entire last two rows of the coach cabin are becoming increasingly uncomfortable with that prayer fest you're having back here which coincidentally happens to be taking place right in front of the aircraft door, and quite frankly, I can't tell you that I am exactly thrilled with that situation either!"* Purposely not allowing him time to respond, I quickly continued with *"I am sorry sir, but this is an airplane, not a mosque, and I can assure you that your prayers will be heard just as well at your assigned seat. I truly do not understand why you feel the need to be so incredibly close to the aircraft door anyway so, if you would sir, please return to your seat!"* I have to tell you, this man's **Bella Lugosi** eyes never veered off me the entire time he was standing up and collecting his things to go back to his seat. He was accomplishing this, very **slowly** and **deliberate** and even though my mind was thinking, what the hell is your problem buddy? I knew better than to verbally go there with him because somehow I knew the outcome of that kind of response from me could have detrimental consequences. *I had already had enough drama from that earlier nutcase passenger to last me a good while, so I just stood there quietly watching him as he slowly gathered his things, never once taking his angry eyes off of me. I knew I had to continue to stare back at him, never wavering, so that he could understand that he was in my domain, I was not in his, even though my instincts were screaming that this was so much more than it appeared.* Although we had technically left **LAX** at ten thirty p.m. (PST) on **September**

9ᵗʰ it was now about two a.m. (PST) ***September 10ᵗʰ*** making the ***September 11ᵗʰ 2001*** timeline just hours away and I was not yet privy to the horrific information, that tragic day would soon provide for me. That, sadly, would not come to manifest itself for a few more hours so I literally had nothing to compare or associate these men's behavior to, but I certainly knew it was not by any means what flight attendants would call *"normal" passenger behavior, which I must admit at times can be very strange, but never "eerie" like the behavior of these two Middle Eastern men!* As I watched him go back to his assigned seat I tried to shake it off and once again tried to dismiss it as the only thing it could possibly be. *Middle Eastern men who were extremely resentful of finding themselves in the situation of having to deal with a woman, who was not only speaking to them without having been given the permission to do so, but was ordering them around as well.* I knew that this scenario in their country was completely unacceptable. Lord knows that I was very aware then as I continue to be very aware today that in their country, I would have been *beaten or beheaded, or beaten then beheaded, and the video of the horrific event would be documented on camera and hand delivered to the homes of my Grandmother, Mom, sisters, daughters and granddaughters as a reminder of what happens to women in their country, who don't do what they are told!* Women in his part of the world have basically no human rights, and are never allowed to speak their minds, much less order any of the men around. However, I was not in his country; he was in mine and taking it a step further adding insult to injury, he was on an *American Airline's* aircraft, flying over airspace belonging to **The United States of America.** That was the way I analyzed it for myself at that time and I truly felt that whether he liked it or not was really not my problem because my job was to keep every single passenger on that *Boeing*

767 aircraft bound for *JFK* from *LAX, SAFE!* Flight attendant number 3 and I watched him walk back to his seat and sit down. I then told the *Captain* what had happened and he told us to keep an eye on both of them until we landed, which we did. That man never spoke to any of us again after that incident and neither did the other one for that matter. When we landed in *New York City* less than an hour after all that scenario had transpired, the flight attendants watched both men as they gathered their belongings, never once turning back to look at myself or the number 3 flight attendant, who were the only two flight attendants at the very back of the airplane at that point. Both men deplaned without causing any further confrontational issues or incidents. Both I and the number 3 flight attendant knew without a doubt, that both of these men had some kind of association or connection with each other, we just didn't know in what way or capacity. Except for the eye motions they had engaged in that we had noticed earlier in the flight, these two men never verbally acknowledged each other the entire time we were in flight, or in any of the flight attendant's presence including mine. We arrived at our short layover hotel at *JFK* by six thirty a.m. (EST) quickly signed in and got our respective room keys and retired to our rooms feeling exhausted from not only staying up all night but dealing with all that stress as well. As soon as I got in my own room, I stepped out of my uniform, quickly showered and stepped into my comfy pajamas. I brushed my teeth, and set my alarm for three p.m. (EST) that same afternoon finally climbing into my bed where I fell fast asleep. When my alarm went off, I got up and found that I was still tired and felt drained from dealing with the stress and *"drama"* from the night before. I poured myself a cup of coffee and turned on the t v in my room to catch up on the news for about an hour. At four p.m. (EST) I jumped in the shower and began my ritual for getting ready for my trip back to *LAX* because the designated crewmember pick up time at our hotel for our ride back to the *JFK* airport was at five p.m. (EST) we arrived at the airport a bit early so we decided to grab a bite to eat before we had to begin the boarding process for our return flight home to *LAX.* Even though most of us were still extremely exhausted at this point and weren't really looking forward to having to face a full flight of people, we eventually snapped out of that mode because we were heading home and that always cheered us up! The flight home to *Los Angeles* was scheduled to leave the evening of *September 10th, 2001* at seven pm (EST), but the inbound aircraft we would be flying home was two hours late arriving at *JFK.* It was ten p.m. (EST) before we finally took off and except for the delay caused by the late inbound aircraft, the rest of the flight went smooth and we experienced no in-flight incidents that would be considered *"out of the ordinary".* Five hours later, give or take a few minutes, we landed at *LAX* safe and sound. The time was shortly before one a.m. (PST) and the date was *"September 11th 2001"! We were the lucky ones who were able to return to our families who were waiting for us as we had promised.* By the time I got in my car and drove home to Orange County where I lived at the time and still do, it was nearly three a.m. (PST) before I crawled into my own bed on that *God forsaken morning* just hours from being awakened by *"the call" that would forever change my life, with the devastating news that would ultimately change all of our lives.* I remember being in a very deep sleep that morning. The reason I remember that specifically is because I suffer from insomnia much of the time due to the erratic sleeping patterns I have acquired during my many years employed as a flight attendant. We are exposed to constant sleep deprivation on many of our *"too short"* rest period layovers that never allow us the hours that are needed, to catch up on the proper amount of sleep that would help us recuperate. So needles to say, we're all walking around jet lagged most of the time. At first, when my phone began ringing, I didn't even know what that sound was or where it was coming from for that matter. I just remember hearing this ringing sound that just kept ringing and wouldn't stop. It went on for what seemed like forever before I realized that it was the telephone next to the bed. When I finally picked up the phone and answered it, *there was the voice of a very frantic woman coming from the other end, who seemed to be talking in between what sounded like sobbing to me.* It was very difficult to understand what she was saying because I was still trying to wake up, and at one point I wasn't very sure if that was ever going to be a possibility. I had only had three hours of sleep, if that much and was no where near ready for a telephone conversation with anybody! *At first I couldn't make out whose voice I was hearing on the other end of that phone line* so for a few moments I didn't even know who I was speaking to. I knew one thing was for sure and that was that *whoever this person was, she was crying hysterically calling out my name over and over again.* At the same time she was struggling with her words trying to talk to me, I could hear a man's voice in the background asking her *"is she okay?" "Is she okay?"* Then this woman would answer the man in the background by repeating over and over, *"yes, she's okay"* as she began hysterically crying again. I distinctly remember how I was beginning to get very irritated with these people and this call when she finally said, *"honey, wake up!"* I had already started working on doing that very task just from the fact that this troubling and very disturbing phone call was beginning to upset me. I was desperately trying to make sense of what was being said to me and who was saying it and just as she uttered those very words, the voice finally clicked in my head and in what must have been a stunned voice I said *"Marilyn?"* She started sobbing uncontrollably now and managed to respond with *"yes, it's me honey; turn your television on"* and with that, she hung up the phone as I continued to hold mine in my hand and stare at it like it was some kind of foreign object I had never seen before. It wasn't until I finally heard the sound of the dial tone that I realized I should probably hang the phone up. *Marilyn Saienz* has been my best friend for over 25 years and she worked for *United Airlines* at the time. *In all the years that I have known her, she has never once called me in that out of control manner.* I still couldn't understand it. Why did she call me just to tell me to turn on my TV? All I could think was why? *Why had she said to me "turn your television on" and then hang up?* Did she know what time it was? Was she out of her mind! *I sat there, on my bed for a moment or two and looked at my husband's face. He was sound asleep* and had never even heard the phone ring. *"Just like a man"* I thought briefly! I got up and I retrieved my robe from the edge of my bed and put it on. *All of a sudden I noticed my breathing was fast and I quickly realized that I was starting to get myself into a panicked state and at this point, I didn't even know why. I quickly ran into my little boy's room to make sure he was okay and he was sound asleep. "Just like your daddy", I whispered to him as I bent down and kissed his little cheek. As I left his room quietly closing the door behind me, that panicked feeling within me started to grow stronger, so I ran downstairs.* By this time I was wide awake and very anxious. I now begin feeling a nagging sense of intense dread mixed with worry and apprehension about what it is that I am exactly going to see when I turn on the television the way my friend Marilyn had instructed me to do. *The one day that I have regretted having this huge fifty nine inch screen television, was September 11, 2001. It was all there and so magnified for me.* The minute the television screen came to life, the first thing I saw is one of *our Boeing 767's with the name American Airlines embossed on the side of its fuselage greater than life, flying at an altitude that seemed much too low to be safe, over New York's Manhattan.* The plane was surrounded by that magnificent city's high rises as it incredibly appeared to be inching its way towards the direction of where the World Trade Towers were standing. All of a sudden my eyes start to completely fail me because what I am seeing can't be really happening. *I see an American Airlines Boeing 767 slam into what seems to be the top floors of one of the two Twin Towers and that is followed by this huge explosion of fire!* I nervously begin talking to myself which is a terrible habit that I have which only surfaces when I am facing traumatic situations that stress me out to my maximum capacity level and I am fully aware of that fact! My eyes stay fixated on that huge television screen and they are refusing to move their glance away from it; not even for a second. *"What Marilyn, what? Are they filming a movie in New York City and using an American Airlines airplane in one of the scenes? Is that what you wanted me to see?"* I felt *"lightheaded"* and *"dumbfounded."* I am trying to convince myself that this is indeed what is happening and that is all this is. *"Oh, I see. They are filming a movie and they are using an American Airline's Boeing 767 airplane for a scene in the movie, and she wanted me to see it because she knows that this is the airplane I always fly to New York in! My gut is wrenching. Why is my stomach hurting me so bad?* I now see a *United Airlines Boeing 757* aircraft flying at that same low altitude as that of *Americans* as it approaches the other Tower and, *"Oh my God!"* There is a second huge fiery explosion as that aircraft hits the second *Twin Tower!* The people in the streets below are running and screaming with overwhelming fear. Everywhere I look on that screen there is chaos and mayhem and *all of a sudden*

I feel this incredibly painful force of a great magnitude much like an electrical current going straight through my body causing it to lose its stability, finally rendering it incapacitated. My legs seem to have lost the capability of performing one of their more important functions and are now having a tough time holding the rest of my body up. They finally give out from under me and I fall to the floor. My mind is desperately racing to take this all in so that it can process what I am seeing on the television screen as having a perfectly logical explanation but it keeps refusing, and still, I sit there and I can't quite put together what is happening. All of a sudden my front door bursts open and my sister *Miriam runs through my house hysterically screaming out my name.* She reaches the room where I am sitting numb on the floor still staring at that fifty nine inch screen that is playing it all for me front and center and so damned magnified. **As I turn to look at her, I am not able to move or speak. She puts her arms around me and begins to sob uncontrollably. I cannot comfort her. I can hardly breathe.** That is the exact moment in time, where it was no longer an option for me to try and find a reasonable explanation for what I was watching on that T.V. *It was the pivotal moment that began my severe bouts with depression, helplessness, denial and the worst one of all, the tremendous guilt. I took it all on and slept it, ate it, breathe and lived it! Why wasn't I on that flight? Why was I spared the horror of being in the middle of it all by one day? If I'd been on that flight, it would have ended differently! I would have seen it coming! I would have figured out a way to stop it! We would have all stopped it in time, because I am a fighter, I have street smarts and survival skills!* This was the mental anguish I put myself through on a daily basis. I was glued to that television for what seemed like endless days and endless nights. *At times I could see actual people*

151

on the television screen choosing to jump out the windows of those Twin Towers to what had to be hundreds and thousands of feet to their "deaths" rather than to be burned up alive by the raging inferno that was set into motion from the aftermath of the aircrafts that had been used as missiles by those demonically possessed suicide bombers. All I could think about every time I saw another body jump was "how does one even begin to process the information needed, to make that kind of harrowing decision while finding themselves in that horrific circumstance? What incredible and undeniable courage that took! Shortly after that tragic day, I received a hysterical phone call at home from my fellow crew member friends who were stuck in *New York City* in the middle of all of that horror and despair. After some of the grounded flights were released to take off once again, my flight attendant piers were experiencing *"paralyzing fear"* and rightfully so, but they forced themselves to get back on the airplanes in order to try and come home to their husbands and babies and families. I specifically remember the *767* crew of flight attendants that called me at home and were giving me blow by blows on how it wasn't safe to fly yet even though our *"idiot"* president of the United States of America, **Mr. George W. Bush II** and our very own *"reliable"* and so *"protective"* **American Airlines corporate management executives and CEO Mr. Gerald Arpey** along with all the other *"dumbass"* **government officials** were telling everyone that it was. *They were all lying! I was getting the real stories from the fight attendants out on the front lines that knew better. They knew first hand "exactly" what was going on out there and knew that the flying public, as well as the entire country was being lied to by all these people that were suppose to protect us and they were NOT safe at this early stage in the game.* These flight attendants, many of whom I have know for years and love, were out there on the *"front* *lines"* and they were in a *"traumatized state."* I began to feel a serious sense of desperation come over me. I was literally coming unglued with worry for all of them because I knew that they were not **SAFE!** No one was **SAFE!** This particular crew got caught up in what was later dubbed by us as " *The Storm Troopers Flight".* A few days after the tragedy of *September 11th*, these same flight attendant, and cockpit crew were finally scheduled to work a flight home to *Los Angeles* on one of the first flights that were released back into the air by the *FAA (Federal Aviation Administration)* from *JFK.* The aircraft they would be flying home was one of our *Boeings 767*, which was the exact same type of aircraft as the one flown by the crewmembers of *American Airlines Flight 11* that was flown into one of the *Twin Towers* by the now infamous *AlQueda suicide bomber Mohammed Atta.* That fact alone carried sufficient reasons to keep this flight crew from even boarding another *767* aircraft out of fear for their safety and very lives, much less take it up to the skies! Consider the very important fact that all of the stranded flight crews as well as our passengers were trying to get back home to see and hold their families once again, and in order for that to be able to happen entailed for them having to get on another *American Airlines Boeing 767. The logic and problem solving skills that flight crews rely on everyday to perform our jobs were severely impaired during the days that followed that immense tragedy. WE found ourselves completely overwhelmed beyond our maximum capacity, but regardless of that, this courageous flight crew put their fears and anxiety aside in spite of how difficult the entire ordeal was, and they put their uniforms on and went to the JFK airport and got on that 767. Their bravery showed no bounds!* What lied ahead for this crew and their passengers would prove to be *"exasperating"* for lack of a better word. Just as these flight crews and passengers thought everything was coming under some amount of control, especially since they were being *"assured"* by their airline company execs and government officials that they were completely **"safe"** thereby allowing them to reason that they could keep it together enough to be able to make it home, there was more! When the first wave of passengers that were headed back to *Los Angeles* after being stranded in *New York City* were boarded, the flight attendants were walking up and down the aisles of the aircraft cabins doing safety checks and making sure that all the passengers were seated with their seatbelts fastened and ready to go, because the aircraft doors were now closed and armed and the aircraft was getting ready to push back from the gate. *All of a sudden the aircraft's furthest aft doors flew open in the pneumatic mode (in the armed position for take off, compressed with air for tight sealing, and can be opened by use of an override), with a tremendously loud initial pop. That was followed by a very loud hissing sound, which I can tell you from experience is a very freighting sound, especially when you are not ready for it. These men, dressed in what was described to me as "Storm Trooper"(Star Wars) jumpsuits came barreling down the aircraft aisles with armed weapons in their hands, shouting out very loud commands to everyone on the aircraft. They shouted "heads down" "hit the floor" and other such commands. Everybody on board did just exactly as they were told, but while the unfortunate incident was unraveling, the passengers as well as the entire fight crew's already severely traumatized state was now taken to a higher level. The passengers began to panic and there was unnerving loud screaming and hysterical weeping during the entire gruesome mishap. The Storm Troopers rushed specific seats that had passengers of Middle Eastern ethnicity occupying them and hauled those passengers out of those seats and off of the aircraft, never to be seen again by any* *of the flight crew or the passengers.* There was so much angst and hysteria going on, that when it was all over, the flight cancelled and everyone was stranded once again. *This information was given to me right after it happened and it was told to me step by gut wrenching step from one of the flight attendants who had been scheduled to work that trip home to Los Angeles and had personally experienced that horrific event.* Here's the big *"slap in the face"* from *American Airline's* corporate management execs that they apparently felt was necessary to bestow on all **AA** flight attendants, but especially to those *"heroic"* flight attendants that were scheduled on that traumatizing flight! When that story got out to the rest of us, **AA** officials literally *"denied"* the entire horrific event when they were asked about it and went on to claim that it *"never happened!"* I suppose this kind of *"shameful"* behavior from some of *American's* current corporate leadership individuals is somewhat along the same lines as those individuals that run amuck *"denying"* that the **Jewish Holocaust** *"never happened"* either! Can anyone out there possibly tell me how these kinds of *degenerate* people who are unfortunately in positions with a sizeable amount of power sleep at night? Can you imagine how that flight crew felt when the *company that they work* for, who is suppose to protect them, not only denies the entire mishap, but then turns their back on them by taking that contemptible stance instead? This flight crew as well as the passengers who had been boarded on that aircraft, not only had the incredible misfortune of having to personally be there witnessing the entire violent situation, but when the entire paralyzing event was over, they had to endure a slap in the face for their troubles from their so called "leaders", instead of the gratitude and respect that they all deserved and should have unquestionably received! *American Airlines* corporate management knows no boundaries when it comes to displaying shameful and unethical behavior, but then again the flight attendants have known this for quite some time now so there is no big surprise there! *Whether they know it or not or like it or not, this company's leadership has an obligation to keep its flight crews informed at all times especially when they have any beforehand knowledge of possible terrorism activity on any and all of the flights we might be working, not just the one's they pick and choose. It is that very vital firsthand information and communication we are given that will ultimately be what helps us protect ourselves and our passengers from harm. We rely on that information at all times!* Why, is it then, that this company's management people who call the important shots that affect all of our lives, do so in such a *"viperous"* manner? All the stranded fight crews and passengers affected by *September 11, 2001* eventually made their way home but definitely not without incurring more than their fair share of psychological wounds. These are very scary times when it comes to flying on commercial airliners as passengers, much less as flight attendants and what makes it even scarier is the fact that the corporate leadership that are running the commercial airlines have no real interest in our passenger's safety or even their own flight crewmembers safety! The constant threat is out there everyday. As *Americans*, we tell ourselves that we will not allow ourselves to be *galvanized* by terrorism in our own country; not by anyone or for any reason, yet in order to maintain that *vital* standing, we have to work together to insure that very outcome. When many of my fellow flight attendants find themselves in difficult and desperate situations with regards to AA management's unsavory employer tactics they pick up the phone and they call me, such as those flight attendants did after that *Storm Troopers* flight incident. This has occurred numerous times in my flying career. I somehow find myself involved in the defense of many fight attendants when the company we work for is either accusing one of them for something they did not do, or when they are being bullied with one of management's *ensnaring* tactics; even when the situation the flight attendant is being tormented about, doesn't really directly involve me. I believe the reason why my fellow flight attendant co-workers seek me out during these *incited* times they are facing against these company management individuals is that these flight attendants that know me, know that I have a tremendous problem with injustices being bestowed upon anyone, especially on so many of them who I happen to know first hand are great people. *American Airlines flight attendants are loyal and hard working employees that any company would be lucky to have working for them and quite frankly, American Airlines doesn't even deserve them*. They are very aware of the fact that if they come to me for help or if I am somehow involved indirectly in a situation they happen to be finding themselves in, where they are facing unjust and unwarranted discipline that I will fight for them, even at the risk of knowing that I could be bringing the company's discipline and wrath upon myself! During those desperate days following *September 11ᵗʰ* and its aftermath, when I received that call from the flight attendants involved in that "*Storm Troopers*" flight ordeal, I felt so *helpless* and *despondent*. I was clear across the country and so removed from them and the entire situation they were up against. Not really knowing where I could turn or who I could turn to that could help me find a way to get these people some very needed protection, I went to the media in the hopes that maybe getting the real facts out to the public about what was really happening and how *unsafe* and *unstable* things really were, would get much needed attention focused on this flight crew and passengers as well as all the others that were finding themselves in similar situations. I knew at this point that I couldn't depend on getting any kind of help from **American Airlines** or the **FAA** or any other **government entity** for that matter, because I knew that all of these organizations were working together to keep the vital information they were literally stumbling across daily, from **NOT** reaching the public or even the airline employees for fear of putting the country in a *"panicked state."* Well, *guess what?* Isn't that **EXACTLY** why *September 11ᵗʰ 2001* was able to happen in the first place. **HELLO!** If you stop and think about that for a minute, *not giving the fight crews firsthand as well as all other vital information regarding possible terrorism on any flights they might be working, is much like sending a soldier out to battle to fight for his/her country without any weapons to fight the enemy with! The flight attendants and cockpit crews are the very people who are going to be fighting "head on" with these terrorist when they are trying to hijack our airplanes in order to blow them up or use them as missiles for mass destruction the way they did on 9/11. What kind of sense does it make to keep the fight crewmembers from being completely informed of what we might be up against while in-flight!* It doesn't make sense. Believe me when I tell you that flight crews are **NOT** kept completely informed about issues having to do with security and security breaches. At least *American Airlines crewmembers* are **NOT;** *if we were, 9/ 11 would never have happened and I believe that with all of my heart.* The corporate executives and management leadership of **American Airlines** as well as **United Airlines** are no less responsible for the terrorist attacks on *9/11* than our **government officials.** That responsibility lies and always will with all of them and God help every single one of them who was too *"self involved"* in their **corporate greed agenda,** or their **over inflated egotistical power tripping,** especially when the time comes where they will have to answer for all of the lives that were unnecessarily lost on that day because of them! No one lives forever and they are certainly no exception to that rule. The reason that these corporate execs do not release the vital and important information that we all should have been privy to *before that flight occurred is that in their lame minds, keeping us in the dark is the only way of controlling the masses and averting public panic.* In their *"so intelligent"* estimation, the actions they took of not informing us, the *flight crewmembers,* of the tremendous dangers and threats that we could be possibly facing at that time, were intended for the sole purpose of keeping us, the *irresponsible hysterical flight crew* from leaking out information to the traveling population *(our passengers), thereby causing a huge response from them of complete chaos and mass hysteria!* In other words, according to corporate management, we, the crewmembers and passengers, could not handle the truth in the same *"astute"* manner in which they can, and let's face it, *our nation was under attack and according to all of them, the people of this country need to be "controlled" from not inciting a panic and they feel that they are so much more better qualified and capable of handling disasters of that magnitude than we are. It's for our own good after all. So our government leaders as well as the commercial airline companies corporate leaders took it upon themselves to keep a tremendous amount of information from all of us and what they tell themselves to justify that absurdity is that they did what they did in the name of our "Best Interest"!* Now how can we possibly doubt them? They know what's best for us right? I mean, look at how *September 11th 2001* turned out! They decided it was better to keep *firsthand information* they received from high ranking officials from other countries who were trying to warn us, to themselves, regarding the *probable terrorist attacks that were going to be attempted on The United States of America, specifically in New York City and at the*

Twin Towers to be e*xact!* Our "*much more intelligent than us*" government officials, such as the **CIA** the **FBI** the **FAA** and the **blah blah blah** were told that the terrorist who were planning this attack on the **United States of America**, would hijack our "*very own*" commercial airline companies' fully "*gassed up*" jumbo jet aircrafts, and they would fly these jumbo jets to the designated targets that they had already selected, such as the **World Trade Center** and the **U S Pentagon** for example, and they would use these aircrafts as "*missiles*" by flying them straight into these highly occupied buildings in order to **kill as many Americans (infidels) as they possibly could**. Even after possessing all of that information "*ahead of time*" (*key words there*) and so as not to panic us the "*dumb*" public *(that's us)*, not one of those amazingly "*bright*" government agencies just mentioned, ever once thought it was important enough to follow up on reports that were being called in to them by several "*flight school*" owner/operators in the United States, regarding **men of "Middle Eastern ethnicity" taking flight lessons in flight schools located in the United States of America no less, while at the same time making comments to their flight instructors about how they didn't need to learn how to land an airplane, they only needed to learn how to take off and fly it and other such "beyond" ridiculous comments that screamed "Hello, Red Flag Here. We have a problem Houston**"! These are the same "**idiots**" who are supposed to be looking out for my **SAFETY** and the rest of the people in this country? "You know what? Thanks, but no thanks. I think I'll just pass on that "*intelligent*" protection you guys are currently offering, though I do have a suggestion I'd like to leave all of you with that you might just seriously want to ponder, and soon I hope. Stop busying yourselves with trying to see whose "***hangs bigger and better***" for one thing, and start working on getting some professional help for the obsession you people seem to have with your own *"over inflated egos"* and the *"testosterone overloaded"* power tripping that you all seem to constantly be demonstrating for one another, to prove to each other who is the more *"macho"* government agency! That way, should your services be once again needed someday by your fellow countrymen like they were on *9/11,* perhaps you won't fail us as miserably as the way that you did on that God forsaken day, when every single one of you were so busy being *"arrogant",* that you completely *"dropped the ball."* As far as *American Airlines* and *United Airlines* are concerned, no one will ever be able to convince me that both of these airline's corporate management officials were not privy to firsthand information that could have changed the outcome of the horrible events that took place on *September 11ᵗʰ 2001,* had they just provided those flight crewmembers with the warnings that they deserved and had every right to be given, before they took flight. It was a conscience choice that these airline companies' corporate executives made to purposely **NOT** inform their flight crews about the possible danger that was out there with *AlQueda.* They didn't want to have to spend the time and money they needed to spend, in order to properly train and prepare their flight crewmembers for the current types of hijackings that were undoubtedly on their way! *American Airlines* and *United Airlines* corporate managements are in the business of commercial aviation travel, for God's sakes! They damn well knew who *AlQueda* was and they knew what type of terrorism that organization engaged in. *Flight Attendant's Amy Sweeney and Betty Ong,* who were both on *American Airlines Flight 11,* called *American Airlines* at two different locations from the aircraft in-flight phones literally five minutes after the hijacking and murders had begun. According to the *"9/11 Commission Report",* which is the final report of the *National Commission on Terrorist Attacks Upon the*

United States-signed into law on November 27, 2002, "Betty called American Airlines Southeastern Reservations Office in Cary, North Carolina at 8:19 and reported to a *Nadia Gonzalez* that she believed her flight had been hijacked and that the cockpit was not answering her calls. She also told *Ms. Gonzalez* that the hijackers had stabbed two flight attendants as well as a passenger in business class, and that mace had been sprayed in the cabin so they couldn't breathe! That call lasted about twenty five minutes and as *Betty calmly* and *professionally* relayed information about the events that were taking place on her airplane, *Ms. Madeline "Amy" Sweeney* was on another one of the aircraft's phones towards the back of the 767, calling *American Airlines Flight Service at Logan International Airport.* At 8:29 *Amy* was *calmly* and *professionally* relaying to her supervisor *Michael Woodward* that her airplane had been hijacked and she proceeded giving him extremely important and vital information about the hijackers that would quickly allow *American Airlines* and other government officials who were involved with this situation, to identify **exactly** who the hijackers were and what organization they belonged to. At **8:21** Ms. Gonzalez alerted the *American Airlines operations center in Fort Worth, Texas,* reaching *Craig Marquis*, who was the manager on duty. Mr. Marquis then instructed the dispatcher responsible for *flight 11* to contact the cockpit and at **8:23** the dispatcher made the attempt but was unsuccessful. *At 8:28* the air traffic controller specialist in *American's operational center* contacted the *FAA's Boston Air Traffic Control Center* about the hijacking on the flight. *The Center was already aware of the problem.* These airline and government officials were able to pull up all the information on these hijackers who had taken control of **flight 11** as quickly as they did because of *Amy's* phone conversation with *Mr. Woodward* and the particular information that she was relaying to him about the hijacker's **physical descriptions, specific seat numbers** and **weapons** that they had carried on board and used to take control of the airplane, which were simply **box cutters!** *What these two American Airline's flight attendants did on that flight is unprecedented! Theirs was the first of several occasions on 9/11 when flight attendants took action outside the scope of their training, which emphasized that in a hijacking, they were to communicate with the cockpit crew.* What does that tell you **Mr. Arpey** and the rest of you **corporate clowns** who didn't feel the need **before 9/11** to train your flight crewmembers the way we should have been and still to this day **HAVEN'T!** *Flight attendants Betty Ong and Madeline "Amy" Sweeney* were **awesome** in **spite of you,** but they are **gone because of you!** Well, you know what I say to all of the worthless corporate people at **American Airlines** who were supposed to be watching out for us? Thanks for the great **heads up** and for all of the insight and proper training you gave us in order so that we could protect ourselves and our passengers on **9/11!** Thanks for the **protection and respect** you extended to us while your flight crewmembers flew those airplanes on that day! Thanks for the **protection and respect** you extended to our passengers, who bought passage on our airline thinking that you were running our airline honorably and **SAFE** on that day! Thanks for the **protection and respect** you extended to all of those people inside and all around that **North Twin Tower** in **New York City** and the **Pentagon** in **Washington D.C.** Thanks for the **protection and respect** that you showed all those who needlessly lost their lives when you made it possible for **Mohammed Atta** and his **AlQueda** clan to hijack two of our *American Airline's Boeing 767's* and slam them into those buildings! *The way all of you handled the whole September 11th situation speaks volumes about all of you* and honestly, I think I can do a better job at taking care of my own safety than any of you ever could; I think you've proven that on more than one occasion! As far as I am concerned, you all dropped the ball on your country and *September 11th 2001* manifested itself because of all of your so called government and commercial airline corporate leadership, not to mention your incredible egos and greed*! Sit back, relax and take a good look at the current state of your country and countrymen, so you can see how well you have all performed your jobs of looking out for all of our best interests! How proud of yourselves you all must be. Hell, why don't you all just pay yourselves another bonus on that one while you're at it. Lord knows you all think you deserve it right?* Flight attendants, we may not be strong enough to take on our government officials **YET**, but we most certainly have the strength to take on *American Airlines* corporate management execs *so exactly what is it that we are waiting for?* **American Airlines Flight attendants**, the time is *NOW* and we need to **STAND!**

CHAPTER 8

The Commercial Airlines Behind Closed Doors

I think it's a fair statement for me to say that when it comes to a huge corporation, such as one the size of ***American Airlines***, it is a known fact, or there is at least a ninety nine percent certainty, that the only people who would have privy information about the situations that go on behind closed doors would naturally be the employees who work for that company. Most people's association with the commercial airline industry is merely that of choosing the most convenient airline that accommodates their necessary travel agenda in an expedient manner, regardless of whether its for business or pleasure. ***Although there are significant differences between those passengers that travel for business and those that travel for pleasure in regards to what they look for when choosing an airline, I think it would be apropos to say that safety is one of them.*** When it comes time for any passenger to actually book a flight, the airline's safety record is something that most passengers have researched, or at the very least, looked at. The business traveler fly's almost as many miles as we the crew members do, which makes them a lot savvier than the passengers who travel for pleasure. *The business traveler is quite familiar with the way in which the airlines run for the most part, and they know just exactly what it is they can expect from their flight.* Most business flyers will choose an airline that has many flights a day which allows them to get to their perspective business meetings. *They also choose an a airline for its dependability where on time departures and arrivals are concerned because making it to that meeting across the country or wherever it happens to be is of the utmost importance for them.* All that the business traveler usually requires in flight is peace and quiet, somewhere to plug in their computer and an area in or around their seat in which they can create a workspace. For the most part, he/she will only need the flight attendant who is working in the business class cabin to bring him/her an occasional beverage or cup of coffee at random times during the flight, to keep them alert and focused while they are working. *Most business class passengers are usually quite knowledgeable about the type of aircraft they are traveling on as well as all safety regulations that pertain to air travel.* The passenger who travels for pleasure on the other hand, is a completely different story. *Pleasure travelers afford the airlines a little more lenience when it comes to on time departures and arrivals, because they are on vacation and their main objective is to leave everything behind, including their worries and get to that glorious destination they've been thinking about and waiting for all year long.* They are looking for an airline that can provide them comfort and amenities to entertain themselves on their flights and aren't too terribly upset when their flight is a little delayed. *The fact that they were able to book an incredibly discounted airline fare for their   vacation flight is what is really important to the passenger that travels for pleasure. Most of them think of a delay as an opportunity to mingle at the airport bar and have a couple of drinks before their flight, just to get the party started. Most pleasure/vacation passengers are in a fun spirit mode and are just genuinely happy to be with us. They are my favorite kind of passenger.* What business and pleasure flyers don't know is that they are constantly being played by the very covert corporate management leaders of these airlines. Whenever you see them giving interviews or speaking publicly, these airline execs and officials say and do all the right things that they know they need to say in order for you to walk away feeling as if they were running their airline in a conscientious manner. These major commercial airlines executives sport huge egos, whether it is behaving or speaking publicly, or giving an interview to a writer from some *CEO Magazine* who is going to incorporate the CEO's story in one of its magazine articles and plaster that CEO's face on its cover with the captions reading *"CEO of the year",* when their mouths start running, they will not only say all of the right things, but they will say all of the things they know the flying public want to hear, making it sound as if the most important thing to them is your safety. Believe me when I tell you that it's *NOT*. The top priority on their agenda, for these so called corporate ingénues, is *REVENUE!* Don't kid yourselves; that is what you represent to them *first and foremost.* For those of you who might doubt what I am saying, all you have to do is watch the news on your television sets. Lately, there has been a massive amount of reporting being done, regarding commercial airlines and their respective aircrafts that have had safety issues such as cracks in the fuselages for example. These major airline corporate leaders have known about these aircraft problems for quite some time, and yet chose to continue flying them in that compromised and unsafe condition. This current deplorable situation in not solely contained within the boundaries of one particular airline company but many; so it's not like you can say, "well, I'll never fly *American* or *Delta* or *Southwest* or

United". Many of the U.S. major air carriers were caught with their pants around their ankles. I've known about my own airline, *American Airlines*, sending compromised aircrafts up without me I might add, for over three years! The rest of America and the traveling public is just now hearing about this inexcusable situation. Imagine that! Do you really think that what I just described to you sounds like they have your safety's best interest at heart? Flying airplanes with cracks in fuselages, or electrical problems wasn't a small insignificant mistake that they just accidentally overlooked and now think that they can make right by apologizing for it out loud to the traveling public. *A mistake constitutes an incorrect judgment. A mistake constitutes interpreting or perceiving a situation incorrectly or having fault in understanding correctly. That is not what has been happening as of late. Southwest Airlines,* for one, was told by an *FAA inspector* over a year ago that there were surface cracks found on four of their aircrafts, but wait, that's not the somber part. The deceitful, inconceivable audaciously cavalier blasé attitude on the part *Southwest Airlines Corporate management* regarding the lives of anyone traveling on those particular aircrafts is that they *knowingly kept sending those aircrafts up in that manner, with thousands of us on those flights, day after day for more than a year after being told to ground and fix them.* The fact that nothing catastrophic happened on one of those compromised aircrafts filled with hundreds of passengers, while in flight, is nothing short of a miracle. *That behavior is not just deplorable, it is criminal!* What separates those corporate management, as well as the *FAA upper management* individuals who kept looking the other way while all this was occurring, all the while instructing their safety inspectors *(through blatant* intimidation*),* to do the very same, from the hard core criminals that are serving time in a prison institution, incarcerated for murdering a single individual with a gun, or some other type of deadly weapon? The only way that I see it, not only as a flight attendant but as a commercial air traveling passenger, is that had the situation with those compromised aircrafts took a turn for the worst, and one maybe two of those aircrafts ended up crashing, taking the lives of all the unsuspecting people on board, accountability would certainly need to be sought after, starting with the top, overpaid, bonus bloated corporate company leaders and their unconscionable pajama party *FAA* buddies. It would be unquestionable that they too should then be looking at jail time for murder. Let me rephrase that, I meant to say *mass murder,* because the only difference with those two types of murderers is that one criminal murdered one person but the other criminal murdered hundreds of people. According to a news report entitled *Congress looks into "cozy relationship" between airlines and FAA by journalist Tonya Mosley of King 5 News and Associated Press, WASHINGTON D.C.* – "Federal Law makers in Washington D.C. are investigating what some call critical lapses in airline safety. The investigation comes as the *Federal Aviation Administration (FAA)* looks into four carriers, *United, Southwest, American and Delta* that have not complied with federal aviation regulations. *On Wednesday, April 2, 2008, United Airlines grounded 50 Boeing777* for safety checks amid growing questions over the nation's air safety program". A *Congressional hearing* was put together for *Thursday, April 3, 2008* to investigate the current airline crisis. Testimony was given by *FAA whistleblowers* who stated that *Southwest Airlines* continued to fly airplanes that missed inspections for up to 30 months. *Marilyn Geewax from Cox News reported Friday, April 4, 2008 – FAA inspector Charlambe "Bobby" Boutris said "The FAA has become so friendly with the airlines that it no longer acts as the public's watchdog. We are told that the airlines are our customers, but we have a more important customer, the taxpayers, who want government to ensure a safe aviation system. The chain of command has been downplaying serious safety issues to please the airline".* **Boutris,** who was assigned to the **FAA** *office in Irving, Texas,* near Southwest's headquarters in Dallas, had raised warnings about *Southwest skipping inspections since 2003.* His supervisor, who has since been reassigned, suppressed the information rather than inconvenience *Southwest Airlines!* He said *"the problems at Southwest received attention only after he contacted the Office of Special Counsel, which is a federal office that protects whistleblowers."* *Douglas Parker,* another **FAA** inspector at *Southwest Airlines* said he too *"discovered that several aircrafts had operated in unsafe conditions".* *Parker's* voice faltered as he recounted how in June of that year, while he was typing up a report about *"unethical actions" at Southwest,* he got a visit from a supervisor *(imagine that!)* The supervisor/manager began picking up photos of Parker's family and commenting on the importance of family obligations. Then Parker said that on his way out of the door, he made the following statemen*t": "You have a good job here, and your wife has a good job over at the Dallas FAA office. I'd hate to see you jeopardize yours and her careers trying to take down a couple of losers."* Parker said that despite the intimidation, *"the poor condition of the Southwest Airlines regulatory oversight was a risk that neither Boutris nor I was willing to accept."* *Committee Chairman James Oberstar, D-Minn* praised the inspectors for trying to uphold *"a culture of safety." "As long as FAA higher ups are telling inspectors to treat airline executives as customers who must be served, then that culture of safety is not going to take hold."* After the investigation, the **FAA** placed a *10.2 million dollar fine* against *Southwest* in March for the airline's failure to perform mandatory inspections. *Calvin Scovel,* the *inspector general at the Transportation Department* said: *"We found that FAA's Southwest inspection office developed an* *overly collaborative relationship with the air carrier. So instead of acting as a watchdog, the FAA allowed Southwest Airlines to "self-disclose" any safety violations without having to pay fines".* The airline placed three employees on leave and grounded 38 airplanes for new inspections. The **FAA** then called for an industry wide review of inspection practices and *American Airlines, Delta Airlines and United Airlines* and each had to cancel flights for *FAA* inspections. *Nicholas Sabatini*, the *FAA associate administrator at Southwest* said: *"I was astounded that the safety system failed so badly at Southwest".* He promised to make changes, including to end the use of the word *customer* to describe the airlines. *"We're going to recalibrate that".* It is lucky for you *Mr. Sabatini*, that those incredibly brave and admirable *whistleblowers* that your company's execs completely harassed and disrespected through company intimidation, came forward to warn the public about *Southwest's* total *disregard* for their safety, *at the risk of losing their jobs.* Thank God that there is still people *like them out there who know what they have to do in order to keep the passengers safe* from the catastrophic plane crashes that would no doubt materialize from the greed running rampant of your company's *CEO, Mr. Gary Kelly* and his stockholder buddies! is so unfathomable to me is that as serious as this situation is, *Southwest Chairman Herbert Kelleher defended his* airline by making a statement of the most *ludicrous* kind to that *Congressional Committee* about his company's actions saying that *"no Southwest passenger has ever been killed".* Well, what in tar nation *(no I'm not southern, it's just a stupid Southern expression to mimic Kelleher's stupid expression!)* does that have to do with anything in regards to the fact that *Southwest* knowingly flew aircrafts that had cracks in the fuselage? Did he actually think that he could keep flying them in that condition without eventually ever killing a *Southwest* passenger? As if that statement was not ignorant enough, he went on of course blaming the airline's *"lower food chain employees"* who he says *"made some engineering judgments they weren't entitled to make"* finishing that sentence off with *"and we have learned our lesson".* That's what he came up with as his lame apology. Sure *Judas,* oh, I mean *Mr. Kelleher,* wash your hands clean of it and blame the hard working little guys who your *order following management puppets* intimidated into keeping their mouths shut about it, when they informed you of these problems a year ago! Oh, then there's *Southwest Airlines CEO Gary Kelly's* intelligent statement that should make us all feel warm and safe. He agreed that *"better judgment should have been exercised, when the decision was made to keep flying un- inspected panes".* Better judgment? *Are you kidding me!* That statement doesn't even come close to anything viable, or buyable for that matter. I suppose he's never heard the phrase *"it's better to be thought a fool of, than to open your mouth and remove all doubt",* because he went on to say *"we will make all of the necessary changes to ensure safety will never be compromised again".* Well, hells bells, don't you think safety should have never been compromised in the first place *Mr. Kelly?* What the hell's wrong with you anyway! I mean, call me silly, but you are dealing with the lives of hundreds of human beings every day. Shouldn't they, not your cut at the end of the day, be your primary concern not just when the cameras are rolling and you are being called on the carpet, but all of the time? Don't take my bashing your bad behavior personally *Mr. Kelly and Mr. Kelleher. American Airlines CEO Gerald Arpey* and his corporate leaders are no less despicable than you. In fact I would venture to say that most commercial airline corporate CEO's come from the same dishonest and corrupted mindset. You have all proven yourselves time and time again. It's been very entertaining to say the least, watching all of you scramble for your bullshit excuses *(by*

George, that sounds like the perfect name for a board game all you airline execs can play together), since you've gotten caught with your pants down. That is the one thing I must say you're all very good at; until now that is. Lying and deceiving the commercial airline passengers into thinking that ***WE, the lower food chain employees*** who are the true hard working employees who unlike ***YOU,*** really care about our passengers and happen to be the bulk of the airlines, are the ones that are constantly trying to create chaos within the airlines by causing passenger delays and cancellations and anything else you can come up with to blame us for, in order to take the heat off of yourselves and place it on ***US,*** thereby allowing for our passengers to get angry at us when we try to take a stand against you! You are all so good at twisting and turning the truth around until you make it sound logical when it's anything but. You have the money and the power to always have the flying public thinking that you are so caring and safety conscious and that all you really want is to provide a safe and comfortable flight for them from point A to point B. ***As if!*** You purposely spend a tremendous amount of time and money for advertising so that you can clearly demonstrate to the flying public how your ***labor employees*** are so selfish and ungrateful; making us out to be these horrible people who go on strike for absolutely no valid reasons except to cause deliberate and unnecessary grief and havoc to the passengers and their flight itinerary's. You people have mastered the skill of lying and giving false information to our passengers, making them angry at ***US,*** instead of directing their anger at ***YOU,*** which is where it belongs. Somehow you very cleverly manage to convince the general public of how horrible we labor employees are, by further emphasizing to them of how it is our ***unreasonable and unbending*** employee stance and the greed of wanting to get paid more money during such difficult financial times no less ***(added drama),*** instead of ***just being grateful that we all have***

jobs unlike so many people in America today, when you, the poor company is not faring so well, with the high gas prices and aging fleets and blah blah blah! Never mind about informing them on how all of *YOU* forced *salary cutbacks on US, or about your constant diminishing our benefits in order to pay yourselves big bonuses instead of putting the money back into the company where it desperately needs to go.* So *"on and on and on it goes, and where it stops in your pockets, we know"!* The bottom line here is that it is our passenger's *flight crews and ground people,* that are the ones who are truly looking out for our passenger's safety and well being, while all of *YOU corporate execs,* are all having fancy luncheons or sitting in your big fancy offices with your breathtaking views, coloring in your *Scooby Doo's or Tom and Jerry* coloring books so you can look busy in case your secretary walks in! On *September 11th 2001,* who was looking out for those passengers on board *Flight 11* till the bitter end, *Mr. Arpey? I'll tell you who, it wasn't you!* It was *Ms. Amy Sweeney and the rest of the flight crews* that gave their lives on that day in order to save so many others. You, on the other hand *Mr. Arpey*, and all of your other corporate buddies as well as our government, knew about *AlQueda's* existence and the kind of terrorism they inflicted, long before that dreadful infamous day and you did absolutely nothing beforehand, in the way of providing any usable type of self defense training to those of us *(flight crew members to be exact)* who have a tremendous responsibility for our passenger's safety as well the huge possibility of encountering *AlQueda* in flight. Not one ounce of *viable self defense training,* that could help us combat and possibly survive that kind of terrorist attack at *39,000* feet have you provided for us to this day, and you certainly didn't do it for *Amy Sweeney* and the rest of her flight crew or for our passengers, whose lives were turned into a living hell up there on that day. Does any of that sound anything like the **LIES** you and your airline spokespeople spew out to our passengers about how your main concern in regards to them is safety, **Mr. Arpey,** sir? With all due respect, which in your particular case, I don't believe any is due, *I don't think so!* Have you spoken with *ANY* of the family members of all those who have lost their lives on *American Airlines Flight 11* lately, *Mr. Arpey?* I'm curious to know what they think when they hear your ridiculous rhetorical *safety speeches.* I know, why don't you take some time out from your current money making job and give them a call so that you can find out how they really feel about you and your corporate executives who oversee *American Airlines* and then get back to me at your earliest convenience, would you? I'd really appreciate it. *Yeah, right. I won't be holding my breath, that's for sure!* To all of the passengers I have had the pleasure of safely transporting from one place to another in this great but currently quite troubled country of ours, I say to you now, that as long as I and others like me are around still flying those incredible skies, *we will always keep our promise to you of keeping you safe to the utmost of our ability while you are in our hands.* What I ask of you is, simply, that *before you misjudge us on the basis of the slanderous lies you've been led to believe about us through the years, by the unscrupulous corporate management leaders of this otherwise incredible industry, that you take a few moments to investigate all of the allegations being made against us. Truth is just that; truth.* It's not feelings, or thoughts, or interpretation, or even perception. I' am one hundred percent certain that if you, my passengers, take those few minutes to read between the corporate lines and get past all the façade they create for you, you will find yourself exactly where you should be which is facing *The Truth.* Your flight crews need not only *your respect* to make much needed change happen in this industry of ours, but we need *your full support* as well. Please, *for the sake of all* *of your flight crewmembers as well as your own stand with us and not against us.* If you think *AlQueda* and other such terrorist groups are not watching us very closely these days as they did pre *September 11th 2001,* you better think again. *Discord and complacency* is what they hope to see in all of us. Seven years ago we learned the hard way that they are *very patient* when it comes to executing their extremist plans. *I urge and plead to all of you, the flying public once again to please stand behind your flight crews* and remember that it is *WE* not *THEY* who are *your last line of defense at 39,000 feet! I am certain that if you stand with us, together we become an impenetrable force, but if you stand against us, we all lose!* My hope is that your choice will be to **STAND** with us! *American Airlines* flight attendants, the time has come when we all need to **STAND** united and strong!

CHAPTER 9

U S FEDERAL AIR MARSHALLS GOING EXTINCT

It is truly amazing how most Americans need catastrophic scenarios that create devastation and horror all around us to make them snap out of their complacent behavior. It is really quite a problem because I happen to believe that it is that exact attitude that is going to be the fall for all of us. You would think that the horrific events that happened on *September 11, 2001* would have been horrendous enough to keep those of us who have had the luck and privilege of being born in this country as well as those that have *"legally"* chosen to live here, from staying on top of these matters keeping *9/11* front and center at all times. *The United States Federal Air Marshalls have all but disappeared these days and that is a prime example of how people in this country "move on" way too quickly around here. The Air Marshall program* overseen by the *TSA (Transportation Security Administration)* began its inception in *1970,* due to a rash of airline hijackings that occurred that year. After the terrorist attacks on *September 11th, 2001,* it was expanded significantly and specifically trained to safeguard passengers and flight crewmembers aboard crowded aircrafts. *Air Marshalls* were seen as critical components in the overall effort to secure America's commercial aviation system. *Today, the Air Marshall program is under the umbrella of the Department of*

Homeland Security, who is busy hiding behind *"National Security Law Statistics".* *CNN Television News broadcasting aired a very disturbing segment in 2008* on the **extremely important** and **very much ignored** safety situation that our country's commercial air travel and aviation industry is currently facing, regarding the quickly disappearing *US Federal Air Marshalls* that are supposed to be on board our airplanes protecting us against terrorist and keeping us *SAFE!* On *Anderson Cooper's CNN 360 "Keeping Them Honest",* correspondent *Drew Griffin* and his journalist team *Kathleen Johnston and Todd Schwarzschild,* set out to different cities and states around the country and did some investigative journalism. They spent roughly four months interviewing *US Air Marshalls* and other *commercial aviation employees* from all over the country including *Washington D.C.* and found out that the *US Federal Air Marshalls* have all but disappeared and are literally becoming extinct! The following is the information that *CNN 360 correspondent Drew Griffin and his team* consistently came up against when interviewing numerous *US Federal Air Marshalls* as well as many *commercial airline employees.*

Fact: The actual numbers of *US Federal Air Marshalls is "classified"* information, reason being; the *actual numbers are so embarrassing that if they* were to get out, it would be a *PR disaster.*

Fact: As it stands today, *ninety-nine out of one hundred* flights in The United States go up to the skies without *Federal Air Marshalls* on board.

Fact: Of approximately *28,000* commercial aircrafts that take off and land in The United States, only *one percent* of that number is protected with Federal Air Marshalls.

Fact: *Commercial airline pilots* flying in and out of New York's JFK also report that there is *less than one percent* on that particular route and further state that *six months* will go by and they *never even see a Federal Air Marshall.*

Fact: *American Airlines* does **NOT** allow *Federal Agents* to carry their firearms on board the aircraft if they are traveling in a *non revenue* capacity. Simply put, if a *Federal Agent* has a family member employed by the *American Airlines* and is traveling on a *pass,* that agent is **NOT** permitted to carry his firearm on board the airplane. *HOWEVER,* if that *Federal Agent* were to turn around and **BUY** a *full fare ticket,* then he would be allowed to carry his firearm on board! Now, I don't know how that sounds to anybody out there, but to me that's a perfect example of *American's* corporate executive *unbounded* **GREED!** Please correct me if I am wrong here but, weren't **American Airlines Flight 11** and **American Airlines Flight 77** two of our very own that were lost to terrorist attacks on *September 11th 2001,* resulting in a massive number of deaths? You would think that fact *alone* would be enough for *American's corporate* execs to be *grateful* to have an agent traveling on a *non revenue* pass offer his *protection* while flying on one of our flights.   Or how about the mere fact that we have the name *American Airlines* emblazoned on our entire aircraft fleet's fuselages, which makes us a *primo* reason to be singled out by terrorist as *targets,* the way that we probably were on *9/11!* Call me silly, but I for one would welcome and be grateful for the added *in flight protection ANYTIME* I could get it! What you have read so far, should be making you sit up straight and start paying very close attention especially if you are one of the millions of commercial airline travelers.   Even I have come to terms with having to admit that as a flight attendant for American Airlines who has been flying for over thirty years and should have known about these disturbing statistics, I myself had absolutely no idea that we have been so *poorly* protected.   One of the reasons all the *Federal Air Marshalls* that were interviewed for this *CNN* segment wanted to remain anonymous was because they *feared retribution from their employers* and believe me, *Lord knows I feel their pain*! One of the Marshalls stated that he'd rather have his employer and profession embarrassed rather than have the public find out about this shameful lack of security in some ghastly catastrophic scenario which would inevitably take many innocent lives. I believe it should be mentioned here that the government entity that is suppose to be keeping Americans and our country as safe as possible but is instead too busy doing God knows what is *The Department of Homeland Security*, which as we all remember, was put into place after and *because* of the attacks against The *United States of America* on *September 11ᵗʰ 2001*. The biggest problem with this government department is that it came together under the administration of our *intellectually challenged president George W. Bush II,* so how can anybody in their right mind think that we're safe? One *assistant special agent* working for the *TSA* stated that while the exact number of flights which *US Federal Air Marshalls* protect is *classified* because they don't want terrorist to play a mathematical guessing game based on percentage, he went on to say that the actual number of flights that *US Federal Air Marshalls* do cover, is thousands per day which he said in his estimation would be more like *five percent* which would deflate the *one percent theory*. I can personally tell you that the last couple of years that I've been out on the line flying, those *thousands* per day that he is claiming are out there covering flights must be invisible because I completely agree with the *Captain* that *CNN* interviewed who said that he never sees them because I never see them either! They stopped putting *Air Marshalls* on the *American Airlines* flight that I always work and I just assumed that the reason for not having them on board the way we use to is because I happen to fly the *LAX-JFK* all nighter, instead of a day trip, which really shouldn't make any difference. What would flying the all nighter have to do with anything! The **TSA representative** that was also interviewed by the **CNN** correspondent on that segment said that the **Federal Air Marshall Service** employs an intelligence driven and a risked based approach to *"covering flights"*. When one of the **Federal Air Marshalls** was asked what his response was to that **TSA agent's** statement, he responded that *"covering flights" was a deliberate choice of words.* He said that *Federal Air Marshalls are told by administrators internally that* commercial air flights are about *five percent covered as well, but when they get out in the field, they quickly realize that the number they are given is totally false because of how they get to that five percent. They actually count other trained armed travelers, not employed as Federal Air Marshalls to meet their "covered flights", such as airline pilots authorized to carry a gun in the cockpit for instance, or law enforcement officer (even if that officer happens to be on* vacation), **or any other type of law enforcement authorized to carry a gun.** *Airline pilots*, who were also asked the *five percent* question as well, responded that they too, have also been told that. *Captain Dave Mackett of the Airline Pilots Security Alliance took it a step further and said it was nowhere near the five percent that the TSA was claiming.* He said that as far as he was concerned: *"it was like they were whistling past the graveyard, hoping against hope that the house of cards they are calling security doesn't come crashing* **down around them!"** Furthermore, **Federal Air Marshalls** are leaving in droves and they are not being replaced. Yes, ladies and gentlemen, these are the *safe* and *secure* skies your wonderful government and the commercial airline carriers of your choice are providing for you and your flight crewmembers! Don't you think that the stakes are getting a bit high these days when you consider that all you want to do is be able to get on an airplane and get from point A to point B safely? Wouldn't it be nice to know that your *government officials* and your *airline company's corporate executives were doing all things possible to ensure your SAFETY?* We all need to stay on top of this very *malignant* situation. There are many things that we can do to make sure that the people you rely on to do their jobs properly and keep you safe while you're on a commercial airline flight, are doing just that. We all need to get it together and get this serious matter under control, starting with everyone writing our congressman and senators and anybody else we have to write to, in order to make these people accountable and start correcting these problems that affect all of us! Every single one of us matters, not just the rich, not just the powerful, but *EVERYONE* of us! *Wake up everybody! I seriously need you to wake up! This is a major National Security issue screaming for our concern and attention.* It affects you and it affects everyone who travels by air. We need to start thanking God that there are these *incredible heroic individuals* out there who are risking everything, both in their personal lives as well as their professional ones to come forward with truths about security breaches that certain despicable individuals in our corporate government, who are definitely sleeping with our commercial airlines corporate company leaders and are trying to keep us from having any access to pertinent and possible life threatening information. Everyone needs to remember an extremely crucial fact in all of this and that is that *when a commercial airplane goes down and into the ground like a dart, it takes a couple of hundred lives with it all at one time! That is a fact that all of us need to stay focused on, and regardless of whether that most unfortunate incident occurs from terrorist sabotage, security compromised flights that were not properly investigated prior to take off or compromised aircrafts having cracks in the fuselage or faulty loose wiring, whatever the reason, if we don't start holding these people accountable, who look at us as if we were mere balance sheets to help them determine what is cheaper, whether to pay the lawsuits incurred after the crash and loss of lives or fix the blatant security problems at hand, we, the air traveling public, that's you and me, are going to pay the ultimate price for their undeniable, uncontrollable and most insatiable GREED!* It's time to **STAND!**

CHAPTER 10

The American Airlines Golden Heart Award Ceremony

Those of us who work for ***American Airlines*** know all too well, that if there is one thing we can count on when it comes to management, is that the left hand never knows what the right hand is doing. Sometimes, from an employee's point of view, that's a good thing, such as in my case on ***April 2, 2008***, when I was able to temporarily shame corporate management in ***Dallas Fort Worth Texas,*** by the sheer element of surprise. I have been battling with ***LAX Flight Service*** management since ***December 2006***. They gave me no other choice but to walk off my third and final trip on ***November 26, 2006,*** because they refused to have the ***Boeing 767*** aircraft I was scheduled to work that evening to ***JFK,*** checked out more thoroughly after one of our passengers found a threatening note in their seatback pocket that the flight crew felt could be deemed as a security threat. I was called in for disciplining by my ***LAX supervisor Daniel Wickey,*** who threatened me with what else, my career, for taking such action and not working my trip even though I did not feel ***safe.*** I was labeled ***"insubordinate"*** big surprise there, and I was given three days to make up my mind whether I would sign a company piece of paper called

184

"Career Decision Day" against my will, which is a piece of paper drawn up by the company's management which basically states that I agreed with the company's opinion in that I am problem employee and I acknowledge that they are giving me one last chance to correct my *problematic behavior* before I will be *terminated!* I went home completely stressed out from that meeting as anyone could imagine, feeling incredible desperation and sadness at the fact that after giving this company thirty two years of diligent and loyal service, they could discard me in such a *vile and disrespectful* manner with this abominable letter they were trying to intimidate me into signing. I had considered what I had chosen to do when I refused to take up that compromised flight, not only to be the obviously safe thing to do, but the only right thing to do. *American Airline's LAX management* has unfortunately intimidated many of our flight attendants who find themselves in similar situations that could be life threatening, into continuously making risky decisions and taking unnecessary chances they should not be taking, to *avoid reprimand. To me, that's a lot like jumping out of an airplane, and waiting until the very last second to open your chute. Most of the time, it will open, but there eventually will be the one time that it won't, and being seconds from the ground doesn't leave you much time to think of any alternate plans. Why would flight attendants let anyone intimidate them into that disturbing scenario?* It is happening all the time! I've been personally dealing with that kind of harassment from *LAX* management at *American Airlines* for over two years now. *The unsafe and compromised way in which they have been purposely choosing to take aircrafts up to the skies, is nothing that's new for us, even though it just started to expose itself to the rest of the public, as of very recently.* Okay, so now that you have some background on why it is that I am still out on unpaid sick leave, through no choice of my own, the following is

the reason why I mentioned earlier, that the left hand never knows what the right hand is doing! *The American Airlines Golden Heart Award Ceremony,* was a façade put together, very quickly I might add, by certain corporate management employees, for the sole purpose of taking the attention away from an incident that happened on one of our flights, in which the death of one of our passengers occurred in flight. According to *CNN and The Associated Press*, **New York (AP)** – *"American Airlines defended it's staff as professional and it's equipment as sound on Monday after a swift review of a passenger's in-flight death, despite her family's claims that the crew ignored her pleas until it was too late. Carine Desir, 44, was pronounced dead Friday on a nearly full Haiti to New York Flight by a pediatrician who said he tried to use the plane's defibrillator on her as she faded, but her pulse was all ready too weak for it to work. The doctor, Joel Shulkin, was one of several medical professionals who stepped in after flight attendants asked if any (doctors) were on board. Shulkin said through his attorney, Justin Nadeau, that two emergency technicians performed CPR on Desir, a diabetic. Sitting in the 10th row, four rows back from first class, Desir had complained of not feeling well and being very thirsty after she ate a meal on the flight home from Port-au-Prince to John F. Kennedy International Airport, according to Antonio Oliver, a cousin who was traveling with her and her brother. A flight attendant brought water to her, he said. A few minutes later, Desir, herself a nurse, said she was having trouble breathing and asked for oxygen, Oliver said. But a flight attendant twice refused her request, he said. "Don't let me die," he recalled her saying. The flight attendant responded, "Ok, but we usually don't need to treat diabetes with oxygen, but let me check anyway and get back to you," "Oliver said other passengers - the 267 –seat Airbus A300 was carrying 263, the airline said – aboard Flight 896* *became agitated over the situation, and the flight attendant tried to administer oxygen from a portable tank and mask, but the tank was empty. Shulkin could not confirm whether the oxygen was flowing, his attorney said." "Oliver said he asked for the plane to "land right away so I can get her to a hospital," and the pilot agreed to devert to Miami, 45 minutes away. But during that time Desir collapsed and died, Oliver said." "Her last words were, 'I cannot breathe,' "he said."*

It was also stated in a CBS News Report Dated February 25, 2008, entitled: "**Kin: Woman Who Died On Flight Was Ignored**" that when Desir said she was having trouble breathing and asked for oxygen, Oliver said *"a flight attendant twice refused her request."* He went on to say: *"Desir was pronounced dead by one of the doctors, Joel Shulkin, and the flight continued to John F. Kennedy International Airport, without stopping in Miami. The woman's body was moved to the floor of the first-class section and covered with a blanket"* *Desir died of complications from heart disease and diabetes, said Ellen Borakove, a spokeswoman for the medical examiner's office. Shulkin, through his attorney, Justin Nadeau, declined to comment on the incident. FAA spokeswoman Alison Duquette said that agency was closed following the details of the incident."*

Now keep in mind that ***Ms. Carine Desir,*** the said passenger, who was traveling on ***American Airlines flight 896 from Port au Prince, Haiti to New York's JFK, died in flight on February 22, 2008.*** On ***February 28, 2008, just six days after*** Ms. Desir death, I received a ***"Dear Alicia"*** letter from ***Lauri L. Curtis, who is Vice President of Onboard Service at American Airlines at Corporate Headquarters in Dallas Fort Worth Texas.*** Just six days after Ms. Desir's death in flight. I'd say that was record time, wouldn't you? In this letter, Ms. Curtis informs me that I am a hero ***(meanwhile at LAX***

Flight Service, I am on pre- termination status), and there will be a ceremony held on *April 2, 2008,* in my honor, as well as other flight attendant heroes, who have used the *AED (defibrillators)* and/or *CPR* to resuscitate in-flight passengers, and save their lives. As if the timeline between the death of *Ms. Desir*, and this so called *"hero"* award, wasn't despicably obvious enough, it had been over *three years,* maybe more, since the incident happened on my flight, that necessitated my using the onboard defibrillator on one of my passengers to save his life, and until that letter from *Ms. Curtis at American Airlines Headquarters*, I had never heard a damn thing about that day, in all those years. I suppose no one at corporate, thought anyone would put all the timelines together, which allowed for making it absolutely transparent, that we were all being used by them for "damage control", and that all this so called *"Golden Heart Award Ceremony"* amounted to, was a diversion for the media and press that had been invited there by them as well, to help soften the repercussions they might have to face from the debacle that was *flight 896.* That's them all right; always thinking that they are so much cleverer than the rest of us *"lower food chain employees".* I suppose that's the reason why they justified paying themselves those enormous bonuses, with the money they helped themselves to, from the concessions the rest of us were asked to make after *September 11th 2001.* Somebody should help clarify for them that had they put that money back into the airplanes and company like they were suppose to, instead of lining their greedy self absorbed pockets with the money, maybe we wouldn't be having the financial problems we're having today! You think? Sure, corporate, just keep blaming those high gas prices *(how convenient in timing for you)*, as well as the repair costs for aircraft maintenance as the cause for our current financial woes. At this point you might as well follow that up with Pilots and Flight Attendant wages, and the salaries of the Mechanics, Cabin Service,

Ground Agents, and anything and anybody else you can think of to throw in there. Just make sure you don't point the finger at yourselves and your insatiable corporate greed, because Lord knows, that couldn't possibly have anything to do with it! By the way, *Mr. Crandall, (oops, sorry), Mr. Arpey*, I have one question for you. Well maybe two. *What in the hell did you do with all of the U.S. Government bail out money AMR received after September 11ᵗʰ 2001? Where did that go?* That was a substantial amount as I recall. Could you please remind me again, as to what you did with the millions of dollars in concessions, we, the labor employees gave you to put back into the company? You would think that with all of that money you got between the U.S. Government and employee concessions, we'd have money to spare right now in a savings account somewhere to help us get through the tough financial times we're currently facing. *What I want to know is who the hell is doing our company's bookkeeping and financial planning? That person needs to definitely be fired!* Oh yeah! Sorry, I forgot about you and your deplorable buddies' mansions and yacht money expenditures, Silly me! That's the REAL problem with our present financial woes isn't it! Flight attendants, if we want to bring the honor and the respect to ourselves that we are so deserving of, not just for the mere fact that we are all human beings which that alone should suffice, but most importantly, because our profession makes us responsible for hundreds and thousands of other human beings, while we transport them on our airplanes from one destination to another, the time has most definitely come when ALL of us, not just SOME of us, need to *STAND!*

The Plane Truth

American Airlines

Lauri L. Curtis
Vice President
Onboard Service

February 26, 2008

Linda A. Lutz-Rolow
25582 La Mirada St.
Luguna Hills, CA 92653-5319

Dear Alicia,

In celebration of the 10th anniversary for the American Airlines onboard defibrillator program, and to honor you and other flight attendant heroes who used the AED and/or CPR to resuscitate a customer in-flight, we invite you to join us for a Golden Heart Award Ceremony.

The ceremony will be held on Wednesday, April 2, 2008, from 1:00 p.m. to 4:00 p.m. at the C.R. Smith Museum in Fort Worth, Texas. A reception with light hors d'oeuvres will be held during the first hour of the event. This will provide an opportunity for you to meet other flight attendant heroes being honored and also the survivors. We expect to have media coverage for this exciting event and, therefore, request that you wear your uniform to the ceremony. Following the ceremony, transportation will be provided for your return trip to the airport.

Please RSVP by March 21, 2008, via e-mail to Leisha Dupree at leisha.dupree@aa.com. If your awarded bid line has a trip scheduled for the date of this event, you will be trip removed to attend the ceremony. You may bring a guest to this event, however, you will be responsible for your guest's travel. When you RSVP, please be sure to include your name, the airport that you would like to travel to/from, and whether or not you will bring a guest. If you have any questions please contact Leisha Dupree at 817-931-8586.

We would be delighted to have you attend!

Best regards,

cc: Frank Campagna

Dear Flight Attendant Alicia:

We are very pleased that you have accepted our invitation to attend the Golden Heart Ceremony on **April 2, 2008**. Your travel information is included in this e-mail. Please be sure to carry this itinerary along with your government issued identification and company ID for processing at the airport.

Complimentary transportation to/from DFW Airport is available.
Please proceed to the lower level, Terminal A gate 39 and catch the Total Enterprise shuttle with "Flight Academy" posted in the window. Once you arrive at the C R Smith Museum lobby, there will be greeters to meet you.

The Golden Heart Ceremony will begin at 1300 at the C R Smith Museum. Hors d'oeuvres will be served from 1300 to 1400. During this time, you will have an opportunity to meet with other flight attendant rescuers and AED survivors.

We expect to have media coverage for this exciting event and therefore, request that you wear your uniform to the ceremony.

Following the ceremony, transportation will be provided for your return trip to the airport.

We look forward to seeing you on April 2, 2008. If you have any questions, please contact Leisha Dupree at 817-931-8586 or via email at

Invitation Confirmation

American Airlines/American Eagle
GOLDEN HEART AWARDS

April 2, 2008
C.R. Smith Museum
Fort Worth, TX

Heroes at Heart

Date	Recipient	Heroes
12/28/2004	John Whitney	Jose Garcia Lisa Joy
1/30/2005	Graham Browne	Helen Hajjar
3/2/2005	Joseph Schrantz	Theresa Quinn
3/6/2005	Milagros Pascual	Susan Pittler
4/22/2005	Roger Hilliard	Ivan Vasquez Patti Hansen
5/6/2005	Raymond Todd	Jo A. Mondrous Linda Lutz-Rolow
7/30/2005	Harold Lang	Luis Lopez-Laboy
1/8/2006	Michael Reidy	Adan Medina Katherine Palma
1/17/2006	Joe C. Norval	Jean Graff Kathleen Stuart
3/20/2006	Virginia Mach	John McPherson
4/3/2006	Harold Anderson	Tracy Glassman Victor Garcia

"A hero is an ordinary individual who finds the strength to persevere and rise to the occasion. They have the power to turn impossible situations into possible miracles."

Christopher Reeves

Alicia Lutz-Rolow

Hero

CHAPTER 11

MY AMERICAN AIRLINES GOLDEN HEART AWARD CEREMONY REJECTION SPEECH APRIL 2, 2008

Good afternoon ladies and gentlemen, and members of the media press. My name is Alicia Lutz-Rolow, and I have been an American Airlines flight attendant, for almost 32 years. I have prepared this statement for those of you present, from the media that have been invited here today, by American's corporate management personnel, to cover this event. I beg your indulgence, as I will try my very best to relay all the information that I feel is imperative that all of you come away with from here, giving you the knowledge that will be invaluable to you, if and when the need should arise, where you find yourselves in a situation of having to take action personally, to protect your safety, while you are traveling, and that of your families and loved ones, should they be traveling with you, not just on American's aircrafts, but on all the other airlines aircrafts as well. Ironically, American Airlines corporate management personnel have invited me here today as well, and have even gone as far as calling me a "hero" no less, which in retrospect, is amazing to me considering the fact that I am currently engaged in an intense battle with this company's lower management personnel at

LAX Flight Service where I am based out of due to the fact that I am a flight attendant that cannot be harassed or intimidated by the disciplinary actions and repercussions this company's management insist on constantly bestowing upon me because I do not adhere to their rhetoric sometimes dangerous policies, which at times are being attempted to be crammed down my throat. If Ms. Lauri Curtis (vice president of onboard service) had done her homework thoroughly, believe me when I tell you that I would not be here today addressing all of you. Before I begin expressing to you the real reason why I know we are all here today, there are some pressing airline as well as aircraft safety issues at hand these days, that I feel are of the utmost urgency to make all of you non airline employed people aware of, since I cannot depend on either the current corporate or lower management personnel of American to not only do what I know is right, but most importantly, to do what I know is responsible. Many of the flight attendants today, including the ones in this room, are unfortunately already aware, as I am, of the current situation that is making the evening news, as well as the front pages of the newspapers as of late. Southwest Airline's corporate management who I suppose thought were not only above the law, but above human decency as well, were slapped with a $10.2 million dollar fine by the FAA on March 12, 2008 and according to the "Los Angeles Times-March 27, 2008" staff writers Martin Zimmerman and Tiffany Hsu reported that "Southwest Airlines were forced to ground 44 planes to be checked for compliance with FAA inspection rules which led inspectors to find "hairline surface cracks" on the fuselage of some of those airplanes, ultimately causing 126 flight cancellations". That report went on to state further that Southwest had been warned by the Federal Aviation Administration over a year ago, that they needed to pull in some of their fleet for maintenance and repair purposes and "they knowingly and purposely continued to fly them in this terribly compromised manner for an entire year, putting hundreds and thousands of unsuspecting passengers lives on the line, apparently having absolutely no problem with that despicable fact whatsoever! "They have since dropped their plans thank God, to move some of their "aircraft maintenance" from the U.S. to El Salvador (imagine that), after the FAA fine was announced". Further reporting by the Los Angeles Times led to information regarding "United Airlines corporate management also being held accountable for their Boeing 747's when on March 20, 2008, FAA inspectors discovered that Korean Airlines, which contracts with United to perform aircraft maintenance, had failed to calibrate an instrument used to check the jetliner's altimeters, resulting in 7 planes having to be inspected". I would love nothing better than to tell all of you that my airline, American Airlines corporate management leaders, sincerely volunteered our aircrafts up to the FAA for inspections, as it has been stated, in several reports. I know that it may appear that way, but I also know the reality of it is that they were well aware that some of our aircrafts had maintenance problems as well, and they too, "knowingly" sent those very "safety compromised airplanes" up in that manner. This is a fact I happen to know first hand because I personally refused to work on three such safety compromised airplanes/flights in a period of two years and I am currently facing company retribution for those actions! American Airline's corporate executives saw what happened to Southwest Airlines and rather than to get caught and fined in the same manner, they decided it would be a better situation for them to willingly offer up our aircrafts for FAA safety compliance checks. They wanted to come across to you, the flying public as responsible and caring regarding our passenger and flight crewmember's safety, which of course, they are not. The particular aircrafts that I was scheduled to work on all three of those occasions where I had to refuse the trips were all Boeing 767's.

On the evening of June 14, 2005, my flight was dispatched from Los Angeles International Airport by American's LAX management personnel who knew fully well that there was a hairline crack that passed through one of the engines into one of the areas that allows the air pressurization in the passenger cabins to work properly. This particular 767 we were scheduled to fly that evening had been "placard (written up by maintenance personnel) all over the place" and those, by the way, happen to be the exact words uttered by our Captain, who was to be in command of that aircraft that evening! LAX Flight Service management intimidated the rest of the flight attendants into taking the aircraft up in that compromised manner, and the Captain (JFK based) who we as flight attendants depend on to watch out for safety and always do the right and safe thing instead made the decision to go ahead and fly it to JFK that way, rather than to take a delay or deal with the less promising scenario which was that of having to take the airplane "out of service" (which is what he should have done) and hope they could find us another one at that late hour. The Captain was somehow unbelievably able to reassure the rest of my flight attendant crew with the most absurd rationale I have ever heard in all my years as a flight attendant, and that was: "because the weather was clear all the way to New York, the aircraft could be flown at 22,000 feet rather than at the normal 29 to 39,000 feet it is designed to fly at, and that as long as we didn't hit any turbulence all the way there, the aircraft would hold up okay. I decided to remove myself from my trip after speaking to the First Officer who was honest with me, and admitted to me point blank when I asked him, that "it could become a catastrophic situation, should we encounter turbulence, and have to take the aircraft to a higher altitude" and those were his exact words! Lucky for me, he was overheard saying that to me by another flight attendant who was standing near the area of where our conversation was taking place.

When that flight attendant heard the First Officer say that to me, she became extremely frightened about having to take that aircraft up in that manner but nevertheless, she went along with the rest of the flight attendants who were equally as concerned with the situation at hand as I was and flew that aircraft up in that manner! Our flight was completely oversold that night with passengers who were not privy to the condition of the aircraft they were about to take off in, therefore they were never afforded the right to make the choice for themselves as to whether they would get off should they have wanted to. I personally see that as criminal. I wrote Mr. Gerald Arpey, our current CEO a letter, telling him about the situations I considered very serious that LAX Flight Service management personnel were forcing on the flight attendants through harassment tactics, and I told him in the letter that I felt I was not being provided with a safe working environment when I reported for flight duty and instead, I was being crucified for not allowing them to intimidate me into putting my life at risk and the response I got back from him was unbelievable. He basically reprimanded me and told me that I was making some very "strong allegations" against the management of the Flight Service base at LAX. He went even further stating that he "approved and agreed with the discipline and repercussions that LAX management was making me face". He then closed his letter by saying that although he appreciated my taking the time to write, "my interpretation as well as conclusions of the facts regarding LAX Flight Service management was troubling to him". I brought a copy of that letter with me today should anyone like to see it. "Mr. Arpey, I ask you today April 2, 2008. Did you respond to the Federal Aviation Administration on March 27, 2008 in the same manner in which you responded to me on February 21, 2007 when you were forced to cancel more than 320 flights on that Wednesday due to aircraft maintenance checks that had to be performed on our MD80's because of their faulty electrical wiring? Or on March 21, when American Eagle (our commuter) had to cancel 15 of its flights? I bet NOT! Did you ever once consider using the bonus money "you" and your "top four" corporate executive buddies are paying yourselves which adds up to the tune of $17,183,270.00 with $7,695,428.00 of that total going directly to line "your own personal pockets" would have been better served to take care of the problems our aging aircrafts are facing? It's not like any of you really earned those bonuses you took off the backs of the rest of your lower food chain employees anyway. That extra cash and all other extra cash was supposed to be put back into our airline company to help save the company after September 11th remember? Has the "let's work together to keep our airline company out of bankruptcy" speech you spewed to your employees to get them to make the concessions you wanted to get from them slipped you mind? We made those concessions for you but you didn't make any concessions for us did you? None of you did! You and your buddies were much too important to this company to do that. Only the rest of us less important "lower food chain" employees did and the rest of you just helped yourselves, and took ours! You and your management personnel have shown us nothing but constant shameless behavior and it never ceases to amaze me. Just when I think corporate management has behaved as despicable as anyone possibly can, they somehow manage to sink to a lower level such as the way in which they have today. I would like to be able to tell all of you out there that American Airline's management's agenda today was honest and forthright, regarding the flight attendants and our wonderful unsuspecting passengers that are truly sincere and loyal and have come here to recognize the flight attendants as heroes with this award for what we have done for them, but sadly, I cannot just as I cannot tell those of you that are here from the media, that you just happen to be here because they simply wanted you to cover this wonderfully "sincere" event. I can tell you that the real reason that American Airline's upper management personnel has invited all of us here to this event today is for the sole purpose of acquiring some much needed "Damage Control" through the flight attendants, these wonderful passengers, and you the media, for the unfortunate incident that occurred on February 22, 2008 on one of our flights. In all the years that I have been flying for American Airlines, I have worked on quite a number of flights where medical emergency situations have arisen and I, along with my co-working flight attendant crews have had to respond to many distressed passengers some of whom were in grave and dire need. I take great pride in the fact that the outcome of every single one of those highly stressful situations was a great one for me, and I completely attribute that to the incredibly committed and hands on flight attendants that I have been privileged to be able to work alongside with. The years of seniority that I have make it possible for me to hold trips that allow me to fly with flight attendants of or around my same seniority. That very fact alone allows me the ability to count on their seasoned experience, when I need them the most, and vice versa. I don't think in these scary times, I would go up there without them. Not once, after all was said and done in those previous and at times life threatening situations, has American Airlines management personnel once commended me, other than with a typical form letter delivered straight to my mailbox in Flight Service at LAX by one of the many supervisor's I've had who really didn't give a RATS, and that's only if I am lucky! What American Airlines Management is really good at, which sadly, you the press won't get to see today because they only do it "behind closed doors", when you're not watching is harassing and intimidating flight attendants, as well as other employees for that matter, by beating us down with their continuous show of disrespect all the while holding our jobs over our heads as collateral. This is their tool of choice because they have found it to be the most effective, in getting their employees to do any and all of their underhanded bidding! Case in point! The incident I was involved in which I am "hypocritically" being honored as a "hero" for today, happened over three years ago! Can someone then, please explain to me why this award ceremony took so long in coming? I am sure it had nothing to do with that flight incident on one of our Airbus A300 that occurred on February 22, 2008. For those of you here that may not have heard about it, American Airlines Flight 896 was scheduled to fly from Port au Prince Haiti to JFK, but was diverted instead to MIA International, where it made an emergency landing due to the death of one of our passengers on board that flight, by the name of Ms. Carine Desir. Although I will not comment on any of the specifics of that particular flight, since I was not there to personally witness what exactly transpired, and I, like many of you, only know what I have read in the newspaper reports and have seen on the news, I will however, most definitely comment on the fact that this so called "flight attendant recognition ceremony" that American Airline's management personnel has dubbed the "Golden Heart Award Ceremony" which we are all in attendance here today, is nothing more than a shameless attempt on their part to exploit the press and our passenger recipients, as well as the use the flight attendants who are here to accept this award as "Damage Control". On February 26, 2008 my "American Airlines Golden Heart Award Ceremony" invitation from Lauri Curtis in headquarters was printed on the paper that was delivered to me a couple of days later via Federal Express. On February 22, 2008 Ms Carine Desir's tragic incident occurred on American Airlines flight 896 which resulted in the loss of her life. It took American's corporate management just FIVE days to put together some form of "Damage Control" that would help "exonerate" them from this terrible tragedy as well as remove all "liability". I find those corporate management actions to be most deplorable, don't you? To top that off, they flew in all these wonderful passengers who genuinely felt compelled to be here today to honor the flight attendants that had helped them get through their in flight emergency situations and for you folks, I can only hope that you can all accept my deepest apologies for the appalling behavior of the people that are in charge of running my airline. They stop at nothing to feed their own cavalier and caustic "self preservation". Except for the American's management personnel who were responsible for knowingly putting this façade event together, if I have caused any of the rest of you here today to be offended, or if I have made any of you feel uncomfortable and embarrassed by the things that I have found quite necessary to say in order to bring the "truth" here today, for that I am truly sorry. That was not my intention, when I made the extremely difficult decision of coming here today. I am humbled by the faces of my passengers that I see here today who have made this sincere journey to pay their respects to those of us that have seen them through a difficult and freighting situation in flight, and from the bottom of my heart, I thank you for being here. As for the flight attendants that I see out there, I can't even begin to put into words how I feel about all of you, except to tell you how honored I am, to be able to have been a part of the brave, caring, compassionate and most incredible entity that is you, The American Airlines Flight Attendant. The time is here and we need to STAND!

CHAPTER 12

BLOGS RESPONDING TO AMERICAN AIRLINES HEART CEREMONY REJECTION SPEECH

The blogs that you will read in the following pages are blogs that were posted on the internet and they all directly respond to my rejecting the so called *"Hero Award"* that *American Airlines wanted to bestow upon me during the luncheon ceremony held at the C.R. Smith Museum in Dallas Fort Worth Texas on April 2, 2008, to honor flight attendants who have used the on board defibrillator for the* saving of passenger lives. Here is a question for all American Airlines flight attendants out there that I need all you to ponder for a bit, before you try to answer it. *When was the last time that you can remember when American Airlines corporate management held any kind of recognition ceremony of any kind for any* one of us? They don't even provide drinks for us while we are in DFW for EPT's (Emergency Procedure Training) during those eight hours of intense training, for God's sake! **Are you kidding me!** Now, all of a sudden they are providing this banquet for us in order to show us recognition and honor us for the fact that we saved lives with the in-flight *"onboard defibrillator"*! There's just one big problem I seem to be having with

203

their so called *"bogus"* award ceremony. *It had been over three (3) years since Joanne Mondras and I had saved that passenger's life for which we were being honored that day! Until that award ceremony, we never heard a damn thing about it!* Wake up you guys, we were their pawns to be used for *"damage control"* and nothing more! You flight attendants out there are extremely bright. I should know I work with you! It is very difficult for me to believe that every single one of you who were being honored at that ceremony on that day didn't know you were being **USED!** *The sheer fact that they called the media to cover their "damage control" event should have been your first clue. When was the last time when those American Airlines corporate execs used the media to portray anything positive about any of us; on the contrary!* With the information that I have reiterated for you in this chapter, *I need you guys to really think about what I have said, and then decide for yourselves exactly what that "hero" ceremony was really all about!* I will leave you to your blogs reading and after you are finished reading all of them, ask yourselves exactly which one of those bloggers do you identify with most. *We can turn this around you guys, we can!* Flight attendants, all we have to do is **STAND!**

Source: *http://aviationblog.dallasnews.com/ archives/2008/04/aa-flight-attendant-criticizes.html*

Posted by **kmchambers** @ *5:18 PM Thu, Apr 03, 2008 Mr Smith needs to get a clue. There is no more perfect a forum to raise the BS flag on the company then at a ceremony that is pandering to the FAs without any real substantive reward for their sacrifices over the last 5 years. The company is entering the perfect storm. Sadly they will accept their stock bonuses and then act surprised at the backlash* *that will no doubt follow. And even if they do not accept the awards, they cannot undue the ill-will they have generated over the past 5 years. The employees of this company are tired of the song and dance.* Posted by **LAX FA** @ 11:47 PM Thu, Apr 03, 2008 *We love you LUTZ. We support you and I am so proud you stood up and had your say. It is criminal for the upper mgmt to take bonus when every employee for the past 5yrs has taken concessions so that AA would survive, it's pay back time AA. Get ready.* Posted by **John S** @ 12:26 AM Fri, Apr 04, 2008 *Sounds like sour grapes to me. Just another example of unprofessional behavior in inappropriate contexts. This is what you get when labor leadership sets a negative and combative tone.*

Posted by **Red** @ 7:33 AM Fri, Apr 04, 2008 *Strong words from a flight attendant on involuntary leave... I wonder what she did to deserve that...? Perhaps she's not the model FA she believe she is.* Posted by **Tired** @ 8:49 AM Fri, Apr 04, 2008 *To all the ones that are griping about managements actions: find another job or quit griping about it. Are you held at AA against your will? I think not.* Posted by **kmchambers** @ 11:26 AM Fri, Apr 04, 2008 *Tired - Unlike management the unionized employees don't have quite the same luxury of looking for another higher paying job. Yes, they can leave. But if they leave to go to another airline they go to the bottom of the seniority list which affects not only pay but quality of life. So you know what, they will stay and fight the good fight. As for our house, we will stay until the new contract is in place. If it doesn't satisfy. Then we'll walk. Meanwhile, damn straight we complain they have given us plenty to complain about. And we will fight to the bitter end* *to make our jobs worth holding on to.* Posted by **enoughalready** @ 12:08 PM Fri, Apr 04, 2008 *Unions talk tough...at the end of the day, they know that they will NEVER get a job with ANY company with similar pay and benefits. Go ahead and threaten to walk. The execs do not care. They have their money. Survival is not important to them. They'll shut it down just to show you who's in charge... it's a lost cause...take your paltry pay and consider yourself lucky that you're still working and overpaid....* Posted by **kmchambers** @ 12:52 PM Fri, Apr 04, 2008 *enough already - what are you talking about? Are you saying that unionized employees are not employable anywhere else? Is this group specific or across the board? And if the execs don't care and will shut it down, so be it. They will shut it down. If that is their attitude why shouldn't the employee groups say pay us more or shut it down. Don't you think that if AMR truly went belly up that another airline would expand and need employees to take its place. And if you think that other airline employees are satisfied with the status quo on pay then you aren't very savvy. They are all watching APFA, TWU and APA to set the bar then those other groups will be banging on their overpaid managements' doors as well. Once the economy turns around in this country there will be other opportunities. For pilots particularly there are airlines outside the US who are hiring today. That is one of the reasons AMR has lost over 200 since the first of the year.* Posted by **AA1971** @ 1:36 PM Fri, Apr 04, 2008 *To kmchambersCan you tell me the last time any union at AA was happy with their management or pay? I certainly can't remember a time in the past 20 years.*

When will it end? Will you be happy when you get a 50% raise, then AA goes bankrupt as a result, and then you have no job? What will you do with you time then? You might not have a choice and have to go work for Jetblue (gasp!).

Careful what you wish for...

Posted by **DC8 Beth** *@ 3:39 PM Fri, Apr 04, 2008* Bravo to Ms Lutz *As a former flight attendant for a major airline, also my two cousins, My Father and Uncle retired Captains, we can tell you very few airlines are REALLY maintaining their aircraft fleet, the way they did 30 years ago.*

If the Aviation Magazines, Major Newspapers, Major TV networks, had any guts, not just looking for advertising dollars from all airlines, they would do investigative journalism and write the truth.

Ms Lutz was suspended for refusing to fly on a plane with some flaws she felt may cause a problem over 18 months ago.

When the Passenger from Haiti died on an AA flight last month, AA got some bad press.

So what did they do, assemble a group for publicity. Ms Lutz's hero award was for something she did THREE years ago.

Doesn't that strike any logical person a bit fishy. They bring back a SUSPENDED flight attendant who helped save some ones life THREE years ago. A bit delayed in awarding her, don't you think.....

This was the perfect forum for addressing her complaints. She had the right to speak her mind,

I wish more flight crew, who are concerned about their jobs, (one does not get that much assistance from the union now days)would step up, but the airlines don't like that.

This country is getting shoddy in so many respects because no one wants to point out things that are wrong. AA still has not reinstated Ms Lutz. So they had some nerve bringing her back for this "photo op" She deserves better treatment.

Airline Management now days is not the same. Kudos to you Ms Lutz.all you passengers should wish cockpit crews were that concerned about the age and the condition of the planes, and voicing it.

Posted by **Suzanne Marta** *@ 3:54 PM Fri, Apr 04, 2008 Update from Suzanne: A spokesman for American Airlines confirmed yesterday that the Golden Heart awards were originally planned for November, but were postponed due to scheduling conflict.*

Since 1997, the airline has awarded Golden Heart honors three other times, the last occasion being in 2004.

Posted by **Bob** *@ 6:41 PM Fri, Apr 04, 2008 To John S. - management runs the company, not the union. Why do LUV employees seem so happy & AA employees so miserable?To Red - you should have such courage.*

To Tired - sure, just walk away after investing years of work. Be a good little girl and do what we tell you. I guess you don't support the FAA inspectors who were trying to do their jobs of overseeing LUV either...

Just be a happy idiot struggling for the legal tender... (Jackson Browne)

Bob in NJ

Posted by **VL COLLIER** *@ 9:59 PM Fri, Apr 04, 2008* UNLESS YOU'VE
WORKED FOR AA, SHUT THE F___ UP! I 'DO' WORK
FOR AA AND HAVE BEEN A F/A FOR ALMOST 20YRS!
I HAVE DONE MORE THAN MY SHARE UP "GIVING
UP CONCESSIONS" IN ORDER FOR 'OUR' COMPANY
TO SURVIVE! AND THERE ARE THOUSANDS OF MY
FELLOW COWORKERS THAT HAVE DONE THE SAME
AND CONTINUE TO DO SO! WE GIVE AND HAVE
GIVEN AND NOW ITS TIME TO REAP A "FRACTION
OF REWARD"! WALKING AWAY IS A BULL___T
MOVE! WE DESERVE TO BE RESPECTED AS LOYAL
HARD WORKING EMPLOYEES OF AMERICAN - NOT
SHARECROPPERS OF WEALTHLY LAND OWNERS! *Posted
by* **RS** *@ 12:25 PM Sat, Apr 05, 2008* Oh... I'm sorry VL COLLIER. I
*didn't know that the people who pay your salaries should have
no opinion. If you don't like people whose thoughts don't toe
the union line, why is AA's employee unions negotiating in
public? Your not going to be respected until you give a little
respect back and that includes providing thoughtful responses and
counterpoints to those opinions which you don't agree with. So...
do you care to tell all of us why you deserve a raise? What do we
get out of it?*
Posted by **Mal** *@ 2:11 PM Sat, Apr 05, 2008* If Ms. Lutz was my employee, I
would have fired her on the spot. *Posted by* **aaemp** *@ 7:11 PM Sat, Apr 05, 2008*
*I've worked with Ms Lutz and she is not a model employee. In
fact she is the epitome of the rude, bossy Flight Attendant that
is held up so often for ridicule. If she was a true professional she*

*would have voiced her opinion in an appropriate forum and not have ruined the ceremony for her fellow Flight attendants who wanted accept the award. Also her performance on MSNBC showed her lack of credibility. She basically threw her colleagues under a bus to satisfy her own persecution complex*Posted by **Corey** @ 3:23 AM Sun, Apr 06, 2008 *Did any of you see the "interview" this loser gave. She looked disheveled and had crazy written all over her face. I guarantee her favorite movie is conspiracy theory and when she gets home she puts a beer bottle on her doorknob, after guzzling the contents. In this interview she claims that AA is putting thousands of employees and passengers at risk every day. What say you LAX FA, of that? Are you one of the thousands being put at risk every day, or at least the 14-16 days a month you work. Enough about the bonuses already. We all know the story and I, along with a lot of other people believe they are completely wrong. If this wacko is correct, where is the outrage against AA for allowing thousands of people to risk their lives everyday? Perhaps the risk doesn't exist? Yeah, that's what I thought.*Posted by **dtwfa** @ 4:28 PM Sun, Apr 06, 2008 *Where is everyone getting their information about FA pay. Many FA can file, and get approved for food stamps and other government assistance.Many FA fly because they enjoy their jobs (until you put management in the picture).*

It is hard to work for a company that ask you for you to take a 43% paycut, yet management gets multi-million dollar bounus.

Posted by **Doug S** @ 11:36 PM Sun, Apr 06, 2008 *To RS: You, the passenger don't pay our salaries. the airline gives us a shred of your fare. only 11 cents an hour of your ticket price is going to each attendant* *on your airplane. on a 4 hour flight with 4 flight attendants only $1.76 of your fare went to the cabin crew. $4.00 went to the pilots (2) and $10 went to the CEO.* Posted by **Doug S** @ 11:41 PM Sun, Apr 06, 2008 *To AA emp: I have only one thing to say, : hello AA manager. your attitude is showing.* Posted by **REAL AA Emp** @ 11:46 PM Sun, Apr 06, 2008 *Ditto DC8Beth. Bravo Ms. Lutz. To All: next time you are on AA plane, look around. AMR is repairing only the minimums required by FAA to keep the planes airworthy, and then just barely. Cost savings/executive bonuses are all that's important to AMR. Passengers don't matter for squat.* Posted by **Real aa emp** @ 11:51 PM Sun, Apr 06, 2008 *Tim Smith and any other spokesperson for AAL or AMR don't tell the truth. I dare any of them to take a lie detector test while they read an official AAL quote.* Posted by **RS** @ 7:31 AM Mon, Apr 07, 2008 *Doug S., Would you like to provide a source for this information because it is contrary to all public information available. The CEO makes $650K a year according to Forbes. This doesn't include stock options. Regardless, $650K a year is roughly equal to 5 pilot salaries. You also might consider revising your statement that we (the public) don't pay your salaries. Where does the money come from? I know there is very little thinking going on over there, but really...*

Posted by **Bob** @ 8:27 AM Mon, Apr 07, 2008 *Keep in mind that this is also the FA who went on a national broadcast after 9-11 and told everyone about cockpit security protocols. I don't know why anyone would defend her, especially another AA flight attendant. Thanks to her, no one is talking about the good work the other FAs did. Their good work has been spoiled by Ms. Nutz' selfishness.*

Posted by jrp @ 3:11 PM Mon, Apr 07, 2008 *just wanted to say: good for her for speaking up about issues that she felt were of the utmost importance regardless of how crazed she may or may not be and all you folks that call her behavior unprofessional or rude are useless, middle-mgmt drones that probably live in the 'burbs because it's safer than the city and the schools are better and would like to see the good ole Us and A become a fascist state where no one ever questions authority*

there can be no democracy without dissent

Source: http://www.gadling.com/2008/04/04/honored-american-airlines-flight-attendant-rejects-award-comp/print/

Reader Comments (Page 1 of 1)

1 Apr 4th 2008 @ 4:28PM

Chuck said...

Good for her! A surprise speech is the only way her point will be heard without being squashed by the corporate controlled media. Had she stood up at a flight attendant rally, the news wouldn't have even reported it. Her issues with management are valid. The flight attendants, as all American's Workers, have sacrificed so much for the Company(keeping it out of bankruptcy) and only the executives, who gave up practically nothing(I wont waste space here on the details) are getting the million dollar bonuses. Maintenance on the airplanes is minimal. Only what is absolutely required by LAW to keep the plane flying. Ask anyone who has been on an American Plane what condition the cabin is in. This has been going on for 4 years. Executive compensation is insane. They pay the CEO $10million and the airline has *the worst statistics. it's a great job, the worse you do, the better*

you get paid. Beth is right, management doesn't care about the

customers, or their employees, just about their own paychecks.

2 Apr 6th 2008 @ 11:57AM

Lisa said...

As a 22 year flight attendant for American Airlines I am

appalled that AA management would take a second round of

million dollar bonuses when all of the employees have sacrificed

so much. Mr. Arpey, what happened to the Turnaround Plan???

What happened to working together??? The company threw all of

us some crumbs a few months ago when they awarded us all a one

time bonus of $800.00. I'd like my 80,000plus that i have given

up in the past five years. Restore our contracts!!!!

3 Apr 10th 2008 @ 4:59PM

Michelle said...

Chuck, you are sooo correct! After 15 years, I left a

(Government) job I loved because I was told to come in late, leave

early, and basically screw 700 families that were counting on me

on a daily basis. As a salary employee, it would not cost them a

cent more for me to do my job correctly.

The question is: Why would the Fed. Govt. want me to do less

than was required? Slackers are promoted. Mediocrity appears

to be what our society strives for today. I believe we should all

strive for excellence.

4 Apr 5th 2008 @ 6:50PM

mickyd said...

*I was at the awards ceremony. What you didn't hear her talk
about was the fact that she was harassed by AA for walking off an
airplane that had a crack in the fuselage. AA apparently didn't
find that important enough to take it out of service. She has
been harassed since the incident and has not flown. Every flight
attendant there knew why we had received this invitation. None
of us were thanked for the job we did until after the incident in
February. It was "damage control". You may not think it was
the right place, but any place is the right place if an airline is
dispatching unsafe aircraft. You should thank Ms. Rolow for
having the balls to speak up.*
5 Apr 6th 2008 @ 12:39PM
Chuck said...

*To Katherine: It's Called FREEDOM, something this country
used to be proud of, but has been erased by greedy corporations
and a very twisted Fascist President. Freedom of speech, freedom
to congregate, freedom to do as you please as long as it is lawful.
If you only spoke at the "Etiquette appropriate" time, women
would still not have the right to vote, Blacks would still be slaves,
and many other inequalities would still exist. You go right ahead
and speak only when your given permission to, hope to be hearing
from you soon!*
6 Apr 6th 2008 @ 3:36PM
De Sanchez said...

*I have a very special person that is in the airline industry, and
he tries to do the best job that he has been trained to do, but
management would rather have him fired, then focus in on the*

excellent customer service that he provides for his airline. All the
other agents need to learn from this person, for he knows what
is expected of him, and he goes up and beyond the service that is
expected of him.

7 Apr 9th 2008 @ 4:13AM

Beth said...

This is the ONLY time she will get heard by the airline, so
BRAVO for taking advantage of it.

I was a flight attendant back in the 60's for a major airline when
passengers were much better behaved. And we took pride in our
jobs.   I have watched the falling apart of service, maintaining
planes, managements greed, and various other things that have
made some US carriers just relics of the reputation they once
had. Even back in the 60's, if I dared suggest another way of
doing things, I was told to be very careful what I said to airline
officials. And to my Union officials also.   At least in those days,
many airline VP's, and Presidents came up in our business and
knew something about airplanes, aviation, and how the industry
functioned.It is amazing, but most airline brass don't really know
the job nowadays, know nothing about how airlines work, care
very little about working conditions or passengers rights.

They are just business school grads who flip from one job to
another, and rarely stay long at an airline, just long enough to
collect a fat payoff to leave or go onto another very high paying
position.

8 Apr 10th 2008 @ 12:32PM

onnie said...

great job!!!! its about time someone stood up and told the truth about how airlines treat their employees. AA is not the only ones who treat the employees so bad. people who don't work for the airlines can't imagine all the work laws that are violated everyday. you just can't quit. you have a family to support and you can't loose the job anymore than anyone else can. the media has their part in this. they always have horrible things to say about the employees. this causes us even more trouble with the public. the government won't even let us strike. what use is a union when you can't strike and demand better working conditions?

9 Apr 11th 2008 @ 9:27PM

Verdonna Proud said...

I applaud you for standing up for your beliefs. Greed is our problem in AMERICA. Where did pride go?

10

Apr 11th 2008 @ 6:34PM

Denise said...

This is the only way to be heard. We the employees are the small people. Honestly and sadly we have certain guidelines to meet in order to just keep our jobs and customer service isn't at the top of the list I can tell you that. In today's economic status the public and the passengers should understand this at least try. It isn't us who make the rules....we are the mere pawns who desperately need that paycheck to feed our children. Do you think we like being on a timer every time a passenger calls rushing in fear of losing our job for not keeping our "stats" within required time?

I believe most of us joined the airline to help people at least that was what I wanted to do. That has been changed....we have been changed. Most passengers I speak with are rude and mean. We get it from both ends. The upper management does not care about us as long as we continue to make the money. The customers don't care about the position we are put in all they are concerned with is that WE cancelled they're flight. Something will eventually give......I am sure by the time this happens I will be long gone. But again horary for her!!!!

11 Apr 17th 2008 @ 2:17PM

Annette said...

Hey everybody in LA, I believe what Alicia Lutz Rolow could use is your support right now, she is fighting for all of your rights as a human being as well as an AA employee, to be able to get restitution for your professions. She has put 32 years of retirement at risk because she feels that it is crucial to your safety as well as the passengers. She also feels that the Corporate management is keeping her at a distance from her co-workers in order to continue to proceed with their unacceptable behavior. Don't let them intimidate you with (FEAR) acronyms False Evidence Appearing Real...Annette ex-USAIR employee (I should know)

12 Apr 17th 2008 @ 2:18PM

Grant.Martin said...

If any of you guys know Alicia, you can get her in touch with me and I'd be happy to post her comments.

13 Apr 17th 2008 @ 2:42PM

Annette said...

Dear Grant, Martin I know Alicia Lutz Rolow, If you would like to contact her. I may be reached at 949 458-2515. Thanks Annette

14 Apr 30th 2008 @ 11:43AM

Katherine said...

I am sorry, but whatever happened to etiquette in this world? However frustrated and upset by her company this flight attendant is, an award ceremony is not the place to voice your opinion. If you do not want to accept the award, decline to attend. The example that is being set for our younger generation is that we may say and do as we feel whenever and wherever we are so moved. Perhaps that is OK with some, but it is viewed as an assault on civility and common decency by most.

15 Apr 10th 2008 @ 3:20PM

billy said...

it seems to me that you have not been screwed by your company, i work for delta and have friends who work for all the majors, sadly it is the only way to get our voices heard.

16 Jun 20th 2008 @ 3:25PM

Mr X said...

GO HER!!! It is about time someone said something. I am a flight attendant for Republic Airlines(US Airways Express) so I know all about the abuse that you get from upper mgmt that is highly overpaid while we are asked to take unpaid leaves of absence.

Other News on the Web:

Source: http://www.cnn.com/2008/TRAVEL/08/14/american.
airlines.faa/index.html?imw=Y&iref=mpstoryemail
American Airlines fined $7.1 million for safety violations
(CNN) -- Federal regulators announced $7.1 million in fines
against American Airlines on Thursday over maintenance issues
and problems with its drug- and alcohol-testing programs.
"The FAA believes the large total amount of the fine for these
violations is appropriate because American Airlines was aware
that appropriate repairs were needed, and instead deferred
maintenance," the Federal Aviation Administration said in a
statement announcing the decision. "In intentionally continuing
to fly the aircraft, the carrier did not follow important safety
regulations intended to protect passengers and crew."
American can still appeal the fines, the FAA said.
The FAA also found the airline maintained inadequate drug-
and alcohol-testing programs and failed to inspect safety lighting
on a "timely" basis.
The Fort Worth, Texas-based carrier said Thursday evening that it
disagreed with the findings and called the penalties "excessive."
"In accordance with FAA procedures for handling these matters,
we have requested to meet with the FAA after we have had
time to thoroughly review their findings, so that we may discuss
the issues," the airline said in a written statement. "Since these
matters are ongoing with the FAA, we will not have any further
comment at this time."
Don't Miss
Qantas grounds 6 planes to check maintenance files

Nearly $4.5 million of the proposed fines stem from American's continued operation of two MD-83 jetliners in December 2007 after pilots reported problems with the autopilot systems, the FAA said.

The two planes were flown a combined 58 times before the problems were corrected -- and one flew 10 times after an FAA inspector notified the airline that it had wrongly deferred needed repairs.

In one incident, the autopilot disconnected during a landing on December 21, the FAA said. "American technicians did not check for the actual problem, and instead deferred maintenance using an inappropriate MEL (minimum equipment list) item. The plane flew another 36 passenger-carrying flights during December 21-31."

The problem was later traced to a piece of radio gear separate from the autopilot, the FAA said. Meanwhile, a different MD-83 flew four flights without a fully functioning autopilot after American mechanics put off repairs. Regulators also accuse American of operating planes without timely inspections of their emergency lighting systems.

In April, American canceled more than 3,000 flights to conduct inspections of wiring bundles in wheel wells of its 300 MD-80 jets, snarling air traffic for five days.

The FAA ordered American and several other airlines to examine the wiring, which had the potential to start fires or cause landing gear to malfunction.

Source: http://www.cnn.com/2008/TRAVEL/04/10/american.
cancellations/index.html#cnnSTCText

American Airlines CEO apologizes to passengers

(CNN) -- The chief executive of American Airlines, which has grounded almost 2,500 flights over the past three days, accepted "full responsibility" Thursday for failing to meet government inspection standards.

"I am profoundly sorry that we've gotten ourselves into this situation, and I thank our customers for their patience under very difficult circumstances," American CEO Gerard Arpey said Thursday afternoon.

The airline canceled 933 flights on MD-80 jets Thursday and announced 570 would be scrapped Friday.

Potential wiring hazards in wheel wells that could cause fires or problems with landing gear prompted the action.

American canceled several hundred flights for the same reason about two weeks ago.

Earlier Thursday, American said it expected all of its MD-80 jets to be flight-worthy by Saturday night.

The airline has offered to make amends to travelers with refunds, vouchers and compensation for overnight stays.

The cancellations have delayed and stranded more than 140,000 passengers.

Roger Frizzell, an airline spokesman, said the inspections involve technical compliance as opposed to flight safety.

iReport.com: Are you fed up with flying?

Arpey said that the MD-80 has been a great plane for American Airlines and that the inspection problems should have "no impact on our long-term fleet plan."

"The FAA is stepping up their surveillance and doing their job," Arpey said. "In this case, we failed to get it right, and we're trying very hard to get it right."

He said American plans to hire an independent consultant to examine the company's inspection system.

Meanwhile, airports are doing their best to keep frustrated travelers happy.

"Getting stuck at the airport is not like a day at the beach, but we sure are trying to make passengers as comfortable as possible," said Ken Capps, vice president of public affairs for Dallas/Fort Worth International Airport in Texas.

Eateries were staying open all night, some provided free pastries and coffee, and some even handed out diapers.

The situation at American's hub at O'Hare International Airport in Chicago, Illinois, "was what you might see on a normal Thursday morning," CNN's Susan Roesgen reported. American employees handing out free coffee and granola bars found few takers.

CHAPTER 13

APFA W*ho?*

Today is Tuesday May 6, 2008 and I had been under the impression that I belong to a union. I suppose what made me think that, is the fact that I have been paying union dues since *May 27, 1976* and if my math serves me correctly, it's coming up on 32 years now that I have been making that assumption. *The APFA (Association of Professional Flight Attendants)* is the union that is suppose to *protect* and *represent* me as long as I am an *American Airlines flight attendant*, which technically I still currently am, even though *American Airlines* Management is making it very difficult for me to return to work after a medical leave of absence that they caused me to have to go on in the first place. So, *APFA* leaders, I ask you now, *where are you?* Since *November 26, 2006,* which was the date of the last flight I refused to work because it was safety compromised, I have heard nothing from any you in the way of *protection* or representation for that matter! After refusing to work that last flight for *"safety"* reasons, or lack thereof, I was reprimanded by *LAX* management for my actions and was told that I would no longer be able to work as a flight attendant for *American Airlines* unless I signed this piece of paper called *"Career Decision Day"* **against my will.** This paper basically states that I am an **"insubordinate"** employee who has *behavioral problems (because I won't fly on unsafe flights/airplanes)* and would be given one last chance to correct my behavior. If I didn't, I would be *"terminated"*. In their estimation, my signing of that piece of paper proved that I was in agreement with all that was stated in it. I was given *three days* to make my mind up as to whether I would sign it or not. Of course, I never signed the paper for the obvious reasons and was ultimately *"forced"* to go out on *medical stress leave* because *"they stressed me out!"* They were threatening my thirty plus years as an American Airline's flight attendant at the time, not to mention the fact that they put me in the horrible position of having to watch them intimidate the rest of my flight crew into going on that *"safety compromised flight"*. That deplorable act left me with tremendous fear for not only my fellow crew members, but my passengers as well. I was taken over by desperation and a tremendous feeling of helplessness because I knew that I would not be able to do anything to stop them from going. The flight attendants were all much too intimidated and afraid of the retribution they would have to face from *American Airlines LAX* management if they did not go, so they went. As far as the passengers, *they just never knew!* I, as well as two other flight attendants who did *NOT* feel the flight was safe to work, gathered our belongings and walked away from the aircraft. LAX Flight Service management proceeded to close the aircraft's door of that 767 with the rest of my crew and passengers in it, and they pushed off the gate *knowing* that the aircraft had not been properly or sufficiently inspected for a possible *bomb* which might have been left on board by an incoming flight passenger, and they sent it up to face the possibility of *"catastrophic danger"* while in flight. All I could do at that point was to say a prayer asking that they be protected from anything horrible happening to them while on their journey. *American Airlines LAX* management left me no other choice but to go out on stress leave. As far as the behavior shown to me at *LAX Flight Service* by the managers, what can I say; I've been flying for *American Airlines* for so many years now, that I have *sadly* become accustomed to dealing with these *insidious* and *deceitful* types of people. All of us know *who they are and what they are,* and that's never going to change unless we all take a **stand** and demand that these people be removed from their positions, which they really should have never been placed in them the first place! I cannot be intimidated into flying in a safety compromised manner and that's a fact, yet these Flight Service managers are constantly challenging me on that very issue. You would think that they would get a clue by now that all the harassment they funnel my way is never going to change that stand I maintain. *My two questions to my APFA leaders are this. How have you allowed certain Flight Service management employees in this company to behave in this ghastly manner towards the flight attendants and why is there even such a paper called "Career Decision Day" in existence?* You are the ones that should have stopped anything like that from ever materializing, but you did not. Where was my *union attorney* that day, when *American Airlines* Management was trying to make me sign that paper against my will, holding my job over my head? Don't you guys think that since 1976, I have I paid for an *APFA attorney's representation ten times over?* I have been informed by my union's *Vice President Brett Durkin,* that a union attorney may not be present *at* a company/employee meeting. Why is *American Airlines* corporate management allowed to get away with such deplorable, borderline *"unconstitutional"* behavior? *Even with the fact that I am having a very hard time with my Union and its lack of protection as well as representation at the present time, I have always been a strong Labor Union supporter and I completely and wholeheartedly believe that in this country of ours, Labor Unions are organizations which are very much needed, especially when it comes to big businesses and enormous size corporations that*

employ hundreds and in some cases, like American Airlines, thousands of people. The whole reason for their existence in the first place is a rather ***sad*** and ***ominous*** one, but nonetheless greatly needed. When Labor Union representatives and leaders are performing their job functions in a ***diligent, precise*** and ***forthright*** manner, most importantly keeping in tact, the ***"original moral standing"*** that was handed down by the true pioneers who brought the Unions about, what you are left with is a ***"strong non innocuous infrastructure"*** in place that is there for the representation as well as protection of the labor employees of big corporation/business. Unfortunately, for some, human nature has a tendency to go astray when it is confronted with avenues providing ways that allow for complete and abundant ***"self serving"*** greed in regards to money or unlimited power, and it is usually a combination of both. Sadly, many Labor Union leaders and representatives are not immune to this kind of ***omnipotent*** situation. They somehow forget the strong convictions they once held towards ***decency, respectability*** and a ***sense of fair play***, therefore seizing the ***opportunistic*** moment when it presents itself, never looking back to reflect on the reasons why they became involved with a Labor Union in the first place. ***APFA leaders, I feel I have to ask you; is this what has happened to some of you?*** If you research as far back to the times before Labor Unions existed, labor employees who worked for huge corporations, had absolutely no protection from the sometimes vile and unscrupulous manner in which they were treated. These employers had absolutely no regret or remorse when violating and exploiting their labor employee's basic human rights, including but not limited to, knowingly compromising their health by not providing the necessary proper equipment that would protect them. Owners of coal mines are a perfect example of such employers who had insouciance and obdurate attitude towards their labor employees, even after many of their coal miners developed what is called "black lungs" from the harmful vapors produced during mining operations. Carbon monoxide, which is at times also found in coal mines, was a particularly toxic gas. It was so toxic, that only as little as 0.35 percent could cause death within one hour. Labor employees of coal mine owners definitely needed a Labor Union to step in and force the mine owners to do everything within their power, to provide their coal miners a safe working environment while they mined, because the owners would have never chosen to do the right thing on their own. The employer/employee relationship between the coal mine owners and the coal miners is somewhat resembling and definitely correlating with the employer/employee relationship that we have with American Airlines Corporate management. They show us no regard, regret or accountability for knowingly forcing flight crews through intimidation, into taking safety compromised aircrafts up to 39,000 feet, ultimately, just like the coal mine owners, not providing us with a safe working environment. Oh, but there is a big difference in our situation with American Airlines Corporate management and that of the coal mine owners; that difference being that the huge and powerful corporation that we work for, American Airlines Inc. gets away with their criminal behavior over and over and over again. That is completely mind boggling to me, because we supposedly have a Union, and that's APFA. We, unlike the coal miners, have this Union representation that does not seem to be powerful enough, to step in and force our corporate management to cease immediately from not only sending these mechanically impaired aircrafts up to the skies, but make them accountable for the many injustices they inflict on flight attendants on a daily basis as well. They just can't seem to make American Airlines Corporate management's harassment cease, or force them to do the right thing; we all know too well that American Airlines Corporate management just like the coal mine owners will not do the right thing on their own!   I personally believe the problem lies in the fact that our flight attendant Union leaders and representatives are made up of flight attendants playing attorneys. This is the way the APFA has been set up from the start. I realize that APFA leaders contract many attorneys to counsel them on legal issues, and our Union leaders decide in what situations they may be used, when representing a flight attendants dealing with company management abuse, but I feel it is that very same fact, that makes American Airlines Management dance circles around APFA.   flight attendants are NOT attorneys, they are flight attendants, and yes I believe that American Airlines flight attendants should have the final say when it comes to negotiating our contracts, or any other representation we may need, as well as choosing the attorneys to accomplish all of that, but the bulk of our Union's body should be made up of labor attorneys who know what the hell they are doing at all times, not flight attendants! In 1869, during the depression era, the first American labor organization that was started by Philadelphia tailors was originally named the Noble Order of the Knights of Labor by its first leader, Uriah S. Stephens, and was a secret organization formed to protect its members from employers' reprisals. The platform was based on the belief in the unity of interest of all producing groups such as shopkeepers, farmers, tailors and all laborers. It proposed a system of workers' cooperatives to replace capitalism.   In 1879, the group abandoned its secrecy to further advance public knowledge of the organization, and they dropped the Noble from its title.   As the United States emerged from the depression of the 1870's, the membership of the Knights increased rapidly, reaching a peak of 700,000 by 1886. Their influence declined sharply after that year, from too frequent and violent strikes, the Haymarket Riot, which occurred in Chicago, and most importantly, in house corruption and greed, imagine that! The American Federation of Labor established in 1886, was the final blow for the Knights and it caused them to spiral into extinction. Since those days, there have been many Labor Unions formed for the protection of many different industries and large corporation labor employees, but none in comparison to the Teamsters Union, which was formed in 1903 and became the nation's largest and most powerful Labor Union by 1940. In 1950 it had more than 1,000,000 members. Once again, like in the case of all the rest, the Teamster's Union leadership was romanced by the incredible greed and corruption just waiting to be had, and that romantic interlude ended in their expulsion from the American Federation of Labor-Congress of Industrial Organizations (AFL-CIO) in 1957. It also played a part in the passage of the Labor Act (Landrum-Griffith Act), which brought many internal union matters, such as fund usage, under government regulation. That same year, three of its presidents- Dave Beck, Jimmy Hoffa and Roy Williams, were convicted of various criminal charges and sentenced to prison terms. Jimmy Hoffa had clear links to organized crime. In 1987, they were readmitted to the AFL-CIO. A civil racketeering suit was filed against the Union, but the suit was settled out of court in 1989. What does all this information tell you, about what happens to decent well meaning people, who start out getting involved with Unions because of genuine concern for the protection of labor employees who work for big business/corporation, and instead, these so called Union leaders and representatives end up on either nice yachts, heading for the Cayman Islands with the words "With Your Dues Money" painted on the side of their vessel, as its name, or in prison, because they got caught playing their own Monopoly game with each other and our dues! When I started flying in 1976, the Union who represented American Airlines flight attendants was the TWU (Transport Workers Union). Now, I am not saying that they are who I would like representing me in my battles against American Airlines Corporate management these days, but I have to say that the major accomplishments and battles fought and won for the rights of the flight attendant profession, in the way of needed change coming about, from the ridiculous, sexist and bottom line unconstitutional policies that were implemented back then, happened while under the Union leadership of the TWU. They are responsible for helping us get a tremendous amount of change to happen, regarding bad company policies.

1968 - The mandatory retirement at the "age 32 rule" eliminated.

1968 - The mandatory "no marriage" rule was eliminated

1971- The mandatory "no pregnancy rule" was challenged and court papers were filed to convert pregnancy to LOA (Leave of Absence).

1972 - Federal Government renames "Stewardess/Steward" to Flight Attendant.

1972 - American Airlines hires first male Flight Attendant.

1978 - Final maternity class action suit settled (started by TWU in 1971).

*APFA replaced the TWU in 1977 and became the certified bargaining agent for all American Airlines flight attendants. APFA is also responsible for some notable changes that have happened as far as American Airlines Flight attendants are concerned, but in my personal opinion, those changes have been mild in comparison to the changes made while we were under the TWU. If you were to ask me today if I thought the APFA could make the changes come about that the TWU made happen while they were our Union, my honest answer would have to be no. Maybe when they first started representing us they might have done it, because I have personally experienced the

APFA fighting for my rights and protection in a much more aggressive manner during the beginning years, when they represented me in 1980, then they have as of late. They were a much stronger entity back then, leaving me with a very strong sense of being truly protected. The APFA President was a flight attendant named Pat Gibbs, who managed to find ways to intimidate our CEO, Robert Crandall, at that time. But quite honestly, I have not had that sense of having a strong Union representation as well as protection for quite some time. In fact, I as well as many other American Airlines flight attendants have questioned the behavior and ethics of some of the APFA leaders in the last few years, which have left quite a number of us doubting as well as wondering if the best interest of the American Airlines flight attendant is what they are truly keeping in the forefront when negotiating with American Airlines corporate management regarding our contracts. At times, it sure doesn't feel like it. As for me, to be perfectly honest, my interpretation of why I have not been contacted by any representative or leader of the APFA after so much time has gone by is that, either they have allowed this deplorable situation I am finding myself in with American Airlines LAX Management to go on for as long as it has, because they just simply do not have the power to stop them, or they have just washed their hands of me and sold me down the river for the right price! At this point, I am really not sure which one it is, but I'll tell you what; I am a survivor, and have dealt with many hardships in my life. I will stand for what I know is right, no matter how difficult it may be, and like I always say; "you may be able to keep me down for a little while, but when I do finally come up, I will always come up swinging". American Airlines Corporate management will never intimidate me into taking risks with my life or that of my fellow crew members and my passengers. I will stand by those words whether I have the support of the APFA or not! Flight attendants, it's time to STAND!

Association of Professional Flight Attendants

*Proudly Representing the **Flight Attendants** of American Airlines*

Office of the President

April 1, 2008

Mr. Gerard Arpey, Chairman, President and CEO
Mr. Daniel Garton, Executive Vice-President, Marketing
Mr. Thomas Horton, Executive Vice-President, Finance
Mr. Robert Reding, Executive Vice-President, Operations
Mr. Gary Kennedy, Senior Vice-President, General Counsel
American Airlines, Incorporated
4333 Amon Carter Boulevard, Building 1
Fort Worth, Texas 76155

Gentlemen:

In March of 2003, the leadership of APFA, APA, and TWU responded to the call of senior management to restructure our contracts to avoid imminent bankruptcy. Collectively, our members agreed to concessions worth 1.6 billion dollars annually. At the time, AA's Senior Vice President of Human Resources forwarded a letter to all AA employees stating that this was "a time for shared sacrifice(s), and management will continue to do its part." Shortly thereafter, Mr. Arpey wrote a letter to all AA employees stating, "My strongest hope and expectation is that everyone will share in the rewards that our ongoing efforts will produce in the future." Five years later, American's employees continue to sacrifice while management, under your leadership, has rewarded itself year after year with bonuses worth millions of dollars. In the last three years, the bonuses have been worth in excess of $340 million.

As the newly elected President of the Association of Professional Flight Attendants, I expect senior management to keep the promises they made to the front line employees of American Airlines in 2003. Failing to do so further erodes the trust our membership has in American's senior management team. Especially now when we are about to begin bargaining, that trust is vital to a successful conclusion of our negotiations. I am therefore urging you to forgo your April 2008 bonus until your promise of "sharing in the rewards" has been kept, and all three labor unions have reached agreements that their members have ratified.

I would urge you not to further compromise your ability to lead this airline but instead to take a significant and critical step in restoring the employees' trust in your management. Should you make the wrong choice and accept a bonus, I would have to ask that you resign your positions as executive officers of AMR and American Airlines. Please let me know by April 15, 2008, if you intend to accept or decline your bonus.

Sincerely,

Laura R Glading

Laura R. Glading

1004 West Euless Blvd. • Euless, Texas 76040
Tel: (817) 540-0108 • Fax: (817) 540-2077

APFA President Letter to Gerald Arpey asking him to decline corporate bonuses or resign:

American Airlines

Sent via Fax as well as US mail

April 16, 2008

Jeff Brundage
Senior Vice President
Human Resources

Ms. Laura Glading
President
Association of Professional Flight Attendants
1004 West Euless Blvd.
Euless, Texas 76040

Dear Laura,

I am writing on behalf of the executive team in response to your letter of April 1.

There is no doubt that the numerous contributions of American employees were critically important, alongside all the many changes and savings we made as a company, to address the seismic industry changes still underway.

Looking forward and on to new challenges, we will succeed only to the extent that we keep our focus on the rapid evolution of the industry and what is right for American Airlines over the long term. That is the focus of our executive team.

As you know, since 2003 we have provided the unions with comprehensive financial briefings and operational information, including information about executive compensation as established by the Compensation Committee of the AMR Board of Directors.

The Board has set a compensation structure for AA's leadership team that targets our executive's compensation to the average of their peer group at 32 similarly sized corporations. The Board believes the current pay structure is appropriate and market-competitive.

I wish you all the best as you begin your term as President of the APFA, and am happy to meet with you at your convenience to answer any further questions you have.

Sincerely,

Jeff Brundage

Mail Code 5604, P. O. Box 619616, Dallas/Fort Worth Int'l Airport, Texas 75261-9616
(817) 967-1752, Fax (817) 967-3553, Email Jeff.Brundage@aa.com

Gerald Arpey's reply to that request via spokesperson:

Association of Professional Flight Attendants
1004 W. Euless Boulevard
Euless, Texas 76040

PHONE: (817) 540-0108 FAX: (817) 540-2077

April 16, 2008
FOR IMMEDIATE RELEASE

Contact: **Leslie Mayo**
(949-510-7272)
Anne Loew
(203-919-9636)

Flight Attendant Union President Calls for Membership Action
Calls for Senior Execs to resign for failure to decline bonuses

Euless, TX (April 16, 2008) -

In a campaign begun two weeks ago APFA, the Union representing 19,000 American Airlines Flight Attendants, demanded that the top five executives of American Airlines refuse their annual bonuses until the Flight Attendants had a ratified Contract. Members have been sporting tags imprinted with the word, DECLINE on one side and RESIGN on the other side.

Today, APFA learned that these five corporate officers – Gerard Arpey, Tom Horton, Dan Garton, Robert Reding and Gary Kennedy – will not decline their bonuses. "By taking these bonuses they have broken their promise, destroyed their credibility and lost their ability to effectively lead this airline. So today, the 19,000 Flight Attendants represented by APFA will turn their tags over to the side that says RESIGN," Glading said.

"Our customers are without pillows or food, a dependable flight schedule, and on-time departures. Shareholders have lost 75% of their stock value in just one year. And workers are struggling to make ends meet after sacrificing 33% in wages and benefits."

"Even assuming these officers were willing to turn their back on their commitment to American's employees, customers and shareholders, the debacle of 3600 flight cancellations in a single week, and today's reported $328 million quarterly loss, should have compelled Mr. Arpey and company to refuse their bonuses. Unfortunately, neither integrity nor shame could convince them to make the right choice."

Glading closed by adding, "if the five officers do not tender their resignations APFA plans to expand its campaign to AMR's Board of Directors to demonstrate to the Board that these executives simply lack the kind of judgment required of corporate leaders."

APFA is the nation's largest independent flight attendant union representing only American Airlines Flight Attendants.
www.apfa.org

Release upon receipt of reply:

CHAPTER 14

HEY, WHERE IS EVERYBODY?

Hey Flight Attendants,

Has there ever been a time in your lives when you were absolutely certain that you were being viewed by the other flight attendants with whom you work with, as if you had suddenly developed some kind of highly contagious disease? I am presently experiencing that very feeling. Don't get me wrong, it's not like I am baffled about why it is that I am presently being scrutinized, and then forsaken and abandoned by my fellow co-workers, and what is even worse yet, is that those of you whom I have brought into my personal and private life, and have loved no differently than as if you were part of my own immediate family, no longer seem to cross my path as you once did. I can only say to those few that although my heart is currently broken, you need not worry yourselves, because in knowing me, you are very aware of the fact that I am a survivor, and I will fully recover. I have not taken any of it personally, nor do I ever feel anger towards any of you for keeping your distances from me. I completely understand your newfound critical contemplation of my character, as well your quickness in summing it up and labeling it as detrimental to your well being. Basically, what I have been observing from many of you for quite sometime now, is the tremendous FEAR that is presently engulfing your lives. F=alse E=vidence A=ppearing R=eal. Those are the acronyms you are allowing to not only dictate the way you live your lives, but to consume it as well. For those of you that are at this moment becoming bent out of shape after reading that about yourselves, stop being defensive and instead do yourselves a favor and think about that for a minute. Even though most of you are in complete agreement with me in regards to the way I see the contemptible and disdainfully deplorable situations that are currently transpiring at work, the FEAR of the company's powerful retaliation should you choose to take a stand against them, is so overwhelming that it paralyzes you. Your mind immediately focuses on the depressed, dilapidated and completely unstable condition in which this country of ours is currently finding itself in, such as the failing economy, loss of jobs and unemployment on the rise as well as home foreclosures, etc. etc. and it completely magnifies this FEAR for you and provides perfect opportunity for them. It makes you easy targets for them to get you to do irresponsible things that under normal circumstances you would never do, such as flying in unsafe situations or taking up aircrafts to the skies that you know damn well should be in the hangers being repaired instead! Your FEAR of the loss of your much needed jobs. You FEAR the loss of your much needed medical insurance and benefits for your families. You FEAR the potential loss of your hard earned retirement, resulting from the many years you have invested in this company. Your FEAR unfortunately is endless. It just goes on and on. There was a time not so long ago, when I also felt this FEAR you carry with you at all times, because I too, not being any different from you, need all of those benefits as well as my job, but after a while, even that tremendous FEAR, could no longer keep me in that state of silence in which so many of you continue to live in, because these days, that terrible FEAR may cost me my LIFE! In regards to my profession and the industry that it belongs to, the current wretched, and gradual destructive manner with which it has been managed, for quite some time now I might add, has currently escalated to such colossal proportions, that it has become not only completely unacceptable for me to continue working my profession under those tyrannical conditions, but impossible as well, and because of the stance American Airlines Corporate management has forced me to take against them, regarding this issue, I have no other alternative but to STAND! When I reflect on this incredibly unfair and critical state of affairs I am currently finding myself in, I can't help but think back to a time long passed, but still frightfully relative, and although you might find the analogy of it, a bit off kilter, the resemblance as well as relevance of the dynamics, should hit close to home. I know most of you remember how insecure and vulnerable we were about everything and everybody, especially ourselves, when we were in high school. We wanted everybody to like us, and we wanted to hang out and be seen among the "popular" crowd because that precise idiocy was what mattered and was most important to us back then. We saw what happened to those that weren't as fortunate (for lack of a better word) enough to be as self absorbed or ostentatious, as those of us who were overflowing with "popularity". Sometimes, when I get together with friends, we reflect on those times and it seems like we always start out happily reminiscing about how great those days were and all the wonderful times we shared, but then it quickly turns in to a reality check down memory lane. The things that today, seem so unimportant to us were unrealistically magnified in high school. When I was in high school, the winning ticket was our school team football games on Friday nights. Everybody who was anybody attended those games, not so much because we really cared about the game itself, though some of us did of course, but it was because we always knew that there was going to be a party at somebody's house afterwards. Maps and directions to these parties would be inconspicuously passed around amongst ourselves, always carefully making sure that not one of them ended up in the wrong hands, because that would have been disastrous. None of us would have ever been allowed to go to one of these parties, and we knew that, so why even bother to ask for permission, right? All of a sudden, everybody was spending the night at somebody's house, or we would come up with other lame excuses for our parents on why we couldn't go home after the game. Telling them where we were really going wasn't an option. While continuing to reminisce, we recalled the wild and fun times spent at all the school dances we had attended, and there were so many. Inevitably though, our walks down memory lane almost always end with analysis by dissection; separating fiction from the sometimes ugly truth, piece by piece until we finally reach a plateau of honesty that sheds true light on the realities of high school. Reality, is the part few people want to remember, much less talk about, because the truth of the matter is, that yes, we all experienced some special memorable moments here and there, but for the most part, high school was probably the first big stress out of many more stress outs to come, that most of us would have to experience in our future lives. Back then, our FEAR was about what everybody thought about us. Pier pressure ruled our lives, so much so that the FEAR of retaliation kept us from allowing ourselves to show what we were really thinking and feeling, much less verbalize it, especially if it went against the grain of the "popular" flow. We just followed wherever the flow took us, and agreed with whatever the flow did, or commanded us to do, even to the point where we would look the other way when members of our little "popular" social group would say or do unkind things to those others that were not considered part of the "in crowd". We never allowed ourselves the quiet reflective time we needed, to find out who we really were and what was really important to us. That came much much later. I think that period in our lives created the beginning stages of our co-dependant personalities we display today. We began rationalizing way back then, that it was just easier to go with the flow, even when we knew that some things weren't right, because the repercussions we would undoubtedly face from our "popular" piers, should we choose to stand against them in any particular situation, or protest against one of their cruel and insensitive demonstrations towards another "unpopular" student, would leave us ultimately standing alone, and in high school, that's just not how you wanted to be left standing! Doesn't reading about the way many of us behaved in high school, just sound utterly ridiculous now? At the time though, you don't even realize or understand completely, what it is that's happening to you, or how the very core of who you are is being negatively affected by all of this, although, in all honesty, I must say, that in those moments of our display of shameful behavior, there was an apprehensive and perturbed feeling that came over you, that left you with a strong sense of disgrace as well as dishonor. At least for me it did. I had the complete understanding of the very important fact that just because I was not the one personally inflicting the physical or mental suffering, upon whichever person had been chosen on that given day, to endure the humiliation these "cool" people I was hanging out with, were dishing out, my simple gesture of just looking away, for the sake of not feeling uncomfortable by it (which I did anyway), would not lessen the degree of my cowardly behavior, nor would it qualify me for any medals of moral principles or virtuous integrity, to be bestowed upon me. The day finally came for me when I realized that I had stopped looking away during these daily despicable episodes, because I was having tremendous trouble justifying and then dismissing my behavior to myself as acceptable, which deep down in my soul I knew it was anything but, and that I was just as guilty as they were by association. I remember the very day that I found myself verbally lashing out at the very same people whose company I had reveled in up until that very day, and who I had proudly called my friends. They were giving their daily dose of humiliation to some poor kid, and all of a sudden it didn't matter whether these particular "popular" people were in my life or not, and I began to see just how repugnant and contemptible they really were, and I was disappointed in myself at how I could have allowed any kind of involvement between myself and these worthless wannabes to have materialize. I began working hard on ridding myself of this indifferent apathetic behavior I had acquired at some point, by stepping in and speaking up in the defense of these kids that had done absolutely nothing to deserve this kind of lurid and ghastly treatment, instead of looking away and pretending I wasn't a part of that. For me, that small simple change in my behavior had a huge affect on my life, even though I couldn't tell you in all honesty that I knew it was that big of a deal at the time. I just knew that it felt very right, and it developed within me a tremendous sense of non tolerance for injustices of any kind that is to this day pretty unshakeable, but I must tell you that it has, more times than not, including then, left me standing alone. That unfortunately, just goes with the territory, and if there is something that is vital to your sense of self, that necessitates your taking action in a manner that will ultimately leave you in that capacity, like it did me, you have to find a way to not only accept that very difficult part of it, but become accustomed to it as well. There was a statement I once heard a long time ago, and I don't even know who said it, or why it was said, but the words have remained in my head throughout my entire adult life, the words in that statement said: "the only difficulty in change is your resistance to it"! Those words are so few, but carry so much truth. Many people carry a listless and passive apathy with them throughout their personal and professional lives, that creates for them a path of affable and self satisfied complacency, and although that path can be a formidable one in some cases, when it comes to handling the un pleasantries our lives sometimes stumble across, it is a detrimental one, at best. Flight attendants are not exempt from that. The huge problem at hand that exists with flight attendants developing this type of aloof and detachable persona is that when it comes to the enormous responsibility and obligation attached to the flight attendant profession, with regards to our passengers, there is no room for apathy. Yet, it is that very same apathy that we are constantly displaying, not only for American Airlines corporate management, but our passengers and for each other as well. When did that start? All of you must remember very clearly, because I know I do, when there was a time not so long ago, when all American Airline's flight attendants knew that no matter how bad the battles we had to fight this company got , we always had each other to lean on and turn to for strength. How did we lose that? We all have experienced numerous times when there's been an unpleasant situation in flight, such as a passenger demonstrating unwarranted and out of control verbal abuse when he/she is communicating with a fellow co-working flight attendant. Ask yourselves honestly, how many times in your careers lately, have you found yourselves walking past them, simply looking the other way pretending you don't see or hear anything, because we have become so detached from each other, that you don't want to get involved in any way with that confrontation, instead of showing support and solidarity and aiding in your fellow flight attendant's defense? I can't tell you how many times I personally have been left out to hang by some of you out there on the line, when I have found myself in similar situations, and you know who you are. If honesty was the manner with which you were looking at yourself at this very moment, you know for a fact that for some of you the numbers of times you are guilty of that exact behavior, is shameful at best. What happened to the days when we could count on the fact that we always watched out for one another? I've got to admit that I really wish I could blame American Airline's Corporate management for that as well, but I can't, because that cowardly behavior is one that some flight attendants have chosen to embrace, for the benefit of their own self preservation. I wish to ask this of you now. Does that road you are choosing to travel, still preserve for you the integrity I knew you to once have? Does it allow for you to feel good about who you are the way you live your life, the way I know you once did? Is it easier to live that way rather than to change instead the present mindset within ourselves, and begin fighting the battles together as the "one entity" that we are which will ultimately bring about what benefits all of our preservations! Although I try hard not to judge you, because I too have been guilty of that self serving mindset in my high school days, that was a lifetime ago, and I no longer understand, or want to understand it. The fact that I will always STAND for all of you, despite the very real fact that there are some of you that will not STAND for me, will not change. It is not because I look at myself as being a better person than any of you in one respect or another, because I don't. I STAND for you because maybe I am in a stronger place within myself, than you are within yourself at the present time in our lives. I STAND for you because my memory still holds vividly, the images of the camaraderie we all once shared with one another, and the hope that we can share it once again, remains with me. I STAND for you because I knew you when our profession was not at risk, or seemed hopeless as it does today. We were not disillusioned and heartbroken from the corruption and greed that threatens our very livelihoods and the career that we so once loved, leaving us divided and in despair. I STAND for you because in my thirty plus years flying career, I have had the honor as well as the great privilege of having been given the opportunity to be able to work alongside some of the finest human beings I have ever known. I STAND for you because in the end, when everything has been said and done in our lives, the most important and lasting legacy we can leave our children and grandchildren, is the integrity with which we lived, and the courage that we displayed while we were here; and finally, I STAND for you because I am proud to be included in the incredible entity that you honorably represent each and every day, which is that of The American Airlines Flight Attendant. The time has come when we have to STAND for what we represent!

CHAPTER 15

LET'S NOT WAIT UNTIL IT'S TOO LATE

Before "we the people" of this country are placed once again in another needless catastrophic situation such as that of September 11, 2001, where we were forced to endure tremendous loss of life at the hands of our arrogant, indifferent and negligent leaders, we need to not only pay serious attention to what is currently going on within the commercial airlines and the entire aviation industry, but to speak up loud and clear as well. As crazy as this might sound, running a major airline carrier, such as American Airlines, for example, isn't as difficult as one would think, or as the commercial airline carrier's CEO's would have you believe. If the certain individuals who are positioned at the top levels in their respective airline company, and are responsible for all decision making in respect to that company, would keep their main focus constant and unwavering on what is in the company's best interest, to ensure its survival and meet the needs of its passengers and its employees, instead of obsessively focusing on their own bloated salaries and huge bonuses, it would have taken much more than high fuel prices or competitive low fares, to run our industry into the ground, the way these so called corporate leaders are presently doing. What we needed immediately after the tragedy of September 11th 2001, was a financially responsible and lucrative plan to be put together, that would allow for a partial but substantial amount of the millions of dollars the airlines received from the U S Government bail out, to be placed in an interest accruing type account, set up as an "emergency fund" to be used exactly for that reason and that reason alone! The 1.6 billion more that American Airlines alone, has been receiving annually, from the labor contract restructures and labor employee concessions since March of 2003 which is over and above the bail out monies, should have been added to that "emergency fund" as well, especially because of the fact that the financial sacrifices that were made by all Labor employees in order to produce that 1.6 billion annual amount, has taken its toll on our personal lives, and more importantly, those concessions were given by us, for the sole purpose of putting the monies collected, back into the company, in order to ensure its survival and keep it out of bankruptcy courts. It was not given, nor was it ever intended for our dishonest and corrupt corporate management leaders to use for the purpose of rewarding themselves year after year with millions and millions of dollars, which they have. With all the talk that is going on out there in the media and every other place, about the way in which the Commercial Airline Industry is in so much financial trouble these days, no one ever brings up the very quietly kept little fact that millions and even billions of dollars have been paid out as salaries and bonuses to these companies corporate CEO's and their little stockholder buddies in the last 35 years instead of being returned into the companies to keep them flying strong and profitable. That, amazingly enough, never gets any kind of newsworthy attention and is exactly where the real trouble is coming from with respect to the problems the airlines are facing today! In the last three years alone, our very own American Airlines CEO and his corporate clowns have paid themselves bonuses worth in excess of $340 million dollars! That's just our corporate big wigs ALONE! Do the math for roughly 35 years! It's not a pretty picture. Had the commercial airline companies been properly run by business execs whose interest was in the long standing and wellbeing of the company they managed as well as its employees, there would have been enough money to get them through this difficult time because the monies would have been allotted for those times. That would have required they not have the insatiable greed they posses, which of course they do and that is the reason we are currently not only witnessing but experiencing the complete discombobulating and annihilation of the commercial airline travel experience! That's where so much of these companies' monies have disappeared to, and it has been disappearing in a steady pace for quite some time now. American Airlines corporate big dogs are justifying their actions, all the while knowing first hand, the company's many financial responsibilities, regarding but not limited to safety, that have been requiring immediate attention for quite some time now, but have instead been purposely ignored, such as our aging aircraft fleet (second oldest in the U S) for example, which has been in dire need of either being completely overhauled or simply replaced. It is my personal opinion, that these so called corporate leaders who are in charge of running our country's major commercial airlines, (which happens to be the most widely used type of transportation whereby people travel from one state or country to another) offer very little regard for the safety of our lives. If it were not so, we would not have witnessed what we did a few weeks ago, which was commercial airline aircrafts being continuously flown in a safety compromised manner, with hundreds of unbeknownst passengers on them, as well as the crewmembers, with the complete blessings, I might add, of not only the commercial airline's CEO's, but with some upper management FAA Supervisors as well! By the way, can anyone out there bring me up to speed as to what is being done to these corporate commercial airline leaders and their corrupt FAA friends who were allowing this criminal behavior to go on for years? Anyone? The answer to that very question is an unfortunate and unequivocal NO! It is a rhetorical question which I am posing for you in order to hopefully get you to stop and give it some much needed thought, because for me personally, the answer to that question not only presented itself a while back, but also resonated crystal clear leaving no room for any doubt. This country's leaders as well as the leaders of these huge corporations, such as the one I work for, American Airlines for example, are presently operating under their own governance and interrelationships, completely unrestrained and uninfluenced by public opinion. Simply put, they are operating under any or all of the following mindset modes: "above the law" "above reproach" "above shame" "above remorse" "above accountability", and the list just goes on and on, take your pick! There is too much power that has been placed in the hands of extremely corrupt people in this country, and if there is anyone out there who would dare to dispute that very fact, I say to them, take a good hard look at what is happening to our country, The United States of America. If you are under the very misguided impression, that because you live in this great country of ours, which is all powerful and protective of its people, that your involvement in keeping it in that safeguarded manner is minimal, and you see the majority of that enormous responsibility as belonging to our so called elected leaders, let me warn you that it will be that very same "entitlement attitude" and complacency, that will help create the path that will allow for our country to end up in the wrong hands. We need to wake up, and then STAND up together, as a strong people of a strong nation, against all those who shrug off the incredible privilege they posses, which is that of being able to live and work in this country, and instead, use the freedoms its Constitution provides for us, to exploit and barren it for the purpose of their own personal power and profit! This incredible and magnificent country, that I was born in and will die for, most certainly can be lost. It's happening already! Don't kid yourselves into thinking that all who lives within Her domain, respects the Freedom and all that she stands for. There are many, some who were even born here, who would be wholeheartedly willing to sell her down the river, for the right amount of money or the right amount of power! Unfortunately for all of us, there are more of them already in this country than we can count, and that is frightening! We are the country everybody criticizes, yet everyone wants to emulate. We, as a country, have been and must continue to be, the true definition of "success". Not just for ourselves, but for the entire world! Every single one of us has to get involved and remain involved in any and all decision making, when it comes to our country and its leadership, and we have to scream loudly at those elected leaders when they are not doing what we elect them to do, but instead dictate to us what they will do! Those types of elected leaders need to be reminded as they are being ousted, that the game is played like this; we live in the "Free World", not in Cuba or Saigon, therefore "we the people" inform them "the elected leaders" of the way in which we want things to run in our country, and the way in which we want to live. That's the way our Forefathers' set it up, and that is the way we want it to stay, not the other way around, which is the way this country has been managed for the last 7 ½ years! The Imperialist/Dictatorship type government which has been ruling over all of us, is almost at the end of its term, somehow miraculously leaving us still standing. It is imperative that we learn from all the harrowing events that have been forced upon us from this current God forsaken administration, and use that knowledge to make sure we never again allow ourselves to be decimated by any future Presidential Administration, in the same manner by which we have permitted ourselves to be, in this current one. In my own way, I suppose, by writing this book, I am trying to take on that same responsibility, even though it is on a much smaller scale in comparison to my government, of course, but nonetheless as fatiguing and wearily exhausting, by holding accountable the commercial airline that I work for and represent, every time I put on the uniform that is embellished with the American Airline's logo, and demand they place passenger and crewmember safety first and foremost above all else. That is, after all, what I was hired to do. There are several definite factors that contribute to the hardships that have fallen on the commercial airline industry as of late, such as outrages fuel prices, unrealistic airfare ticket pricing, and of course, the aftermath of September 11th 2001, which can truly be considered a legitimate hardship, although it was one that was completely avoidable, and should never have happened. On the other hand, there are those unnecessary hardships that the airline industry has been forced to endure, that come from the enormously colossal and guaranteed amounts of money that have been paid out in salaries and bonuses, to these airline's higher monarchy employees and CEOs' over the years. Of course, that fact is seldom mentioned or brought up in the media reports or articles written for "corporate financial minded" CEO of the year type magazines, that are constantly rattling off monetary statistics, always placing the blame of the commercial airlines current financial woes on what I like to refer to as "the three E's". "Everyone, Everything and Everywhere" else, except where the blame really lies, which is in their own insatiably greedy hands! The salaries of Pilots, Flight Attendants, Engineers, Mechanics, Maintenance and Cabin Service have never been outrages and obscene, such as those of corporate; on the contrary. These salaries have always been on the somewhat humble side, an are even more so today due to all the concessions we have been forced to make in order to keep the airlines from going into bankruptcy, the way so many of them have. All of these Labor salaries mentioned are not legitimate hardships on any of the commercial airlines, on any level. We make a "living wage", not the "bloated salaries and bonuses" that the so called "Upper Crust" employees and the CEO's of these airlines make! Airline Labor employees are, and always have been the backbone of the industry and are the ones who are looking out for the passenger's safety, while at the same time making the idiots in suits upstairs look good. All of us are aware that these times are indeed of the most challenging kind, but, unlike what these airline CEO's would like you to believe, there is, and always has been a definite solution to this current economic problem regarding these airlines, and their ability to sustain themselves through difficult and challenging times. How I have come to that very conclusion is all there for you to read in the following pages of the next chapter entitled "Making Air Travel Safer" by Annette Garcia. Annette, my sister, who is currently attending Saddleback College, was required to write a paper for her speech class. The thesis had to contain researched information on the subject matter of the topic of her choosing. She was prompted to write her dissertation on commercial airline safety, or I should say, the lack of, because of the current serious and alarming issues surrounding the airline industry, and their safety compromised aircrafts, in the last few weeks. She was previously employed by US Air, and worked as a Gate Agent for that airline for over fifteen years. She felt she had valuable hands on information that she would be able to use and contribute to the content of her thesis. After the completion of her paper, it was really quite clear that the number one reason for the present commercial airline debacle and the problematic situations that the commercial airline industry faces today is pure and simple Corporate management Greed! I am one of those people which carry the belief that all problems have a solution, and part of the solution for this particular industry's problems (once you start breaking all of it down), is to do away with the present airline companies' "corporate" leadership, and put the commercial airlines back into the hands of the employees who work them. They are the people who know the ins and out of how the industry runs. In the next chapter, Annette gives us her insight on how positive change can most certainly come about in regards to the safety as well as all other aspects of the commercial airline industry, by simply giving its management a completely thorough and much needed overhaul. After reading it, ask yourselves if her simple theories hold their tremendous weight in truth. It is definitely something to consider, since we know first hand what the alternative has been, and what it is leading to, should it be allowed to continue in its present manner. Just as it has with our Government, our time of simple idling complacency has run out! We stand to lose everything if we don't fight! Regardless of whatever changes, if any, transpire from the terrible and blatant mismanagement of the airlines that we have all been subjected to for quite some time now, flight attendants, the time is definitely here and we need to STAND!

CHAPTER 16

MAKING AIR TRAVEL SAFER BY ANNETTE GARCIA

Specific Purpose: When you buy an airline ticket to go from point A to point B, you want to be assured that making it to your destination is not something you have to worry about. It is the responsibility of the Airline you're traveling on to provide you with not only FAA compliant safe equipment, but all other safety related issues as well.

Central Idea: There has to be some changes made in the way
airlines arc managed today

The CEO's that the airlines have currently employed to oversee the organizations, are of the corporate mindset, and in this particular industry that mindset is not viable. The airlines cannot successfully conduct its operational system without prioritizing. The human element has to be placed above the balance sheets and safety has to be placed above all else.

INTRODUCTION

Proposition of Policy

I.   <u>Attention</u>:   The FAA is the police of the skies. All airline policies are written to conform to the Federal Regulations set forth by the FAA. FAA interprets company policies and procedures, to ensure airlines are in compliance with Federal Regulations. All commercial airlines are required to report to this government agency, any and all maintenance issues regarding the aircrafts, when being inspected. Because of the current situation, where the airlines are being managed by corporate mindset, the avenue is being cleared for a revenue based liaison between airline CEO's, airline stockholders and certain high officials employed by the FAA, thereby allowing a mutual self serving monetary interest. If this present situation continues, the catastrophic possibilities concerning the safety of passenger transportation will become a certainty.

II.   <u>Credibility</u>:   From 1938 to 1978, interstate airlines were one of the most regulated industries in the U.S. Almost every aspect of interstate air travel was controlled by the federal government. Each airline was required to obtain approval from the Civil Aeronautics Board (CAB) for each route it intended to travel, city it would serve, and ticket price it would charge. Air safety was regulated by the FAA, which is a separate federal agency. In essence, regulation had created high prices for travelers which hurt consumers rather than protect their interest. Financial pressures caused by increased competition encouraged airlines to cut costs by cutting corners on maintenance. This steadily increases the risk in flying and the chances of accidents in the future. (The Economic Effects of Airline Deregulation) Steven Morrison 1986.

The first round of audits, conducted over a two week span last month, checked 10 airworthiness directives that apply to each carrier's fleet. Under the second phase, which runs through June 30, individual inspectors will check a random sampling of 10 percent of the orders that apply to each airline's fleet. For a large carrier like American that operates many different aircraft, that could be several hundred directives.

III.   Relevance: The FAA mandatory inspections that have been imposed on the major air carriers have caused a detrimental impact on the flying public. Taking one airline for example American Airlines estimated more than 100,000 travelers were booked on the cancelled flights, although the airline had already scrubbed 460 flights, the federal inspectors found problems with wiring work done on the MD-80 aircrafts which had improperly bundled wires. Another example is United Airlines keeping batteries that power the Boeing 777 emergency slides for years beyond their approved life span, causing cancellations. After several meetings of addressing the underlying safety risk the airline took no action. Continental Airlines found more than 4000 aircraft life vest had been improperly overhauled. FAA management allowed airline to continue operating with compromised vests. (Orange County Register, 4-10-08) Paul Beaty the Associated Press. The bottom line here is that it effects the general public because many things are transported by air including but not limited to hospitals needing organs for transplants, businessmen missing crucial meetings involving million dollar deals, extraditing prisoners from one state to another etc. etc. the domino effect is endless.

IV.

V. <u>Purpose</u>: Airline safety should not be left in the hands of the corporate sector; it should be managed by knowledgeable individuals that have had extensive experience with the airline industry, since that industry functions in a non typical business manner. It should be overseen by VP's or Presidents that are selected by a board of collective seasoned employees with a qualified expertise within their airline position.

<u>Preview</u>: I will explain the problems with the current managing of the airlines in the aviation industry. I will explain how taking it out of the corporate sector and placing it back in the hands of qualified employees, overseen by elected VP's / Presidents who are knowledgeable in every aspect of the airline industry, will benefit both airlines and the general public.

Body

Transition: Let's start with the problem.

I. Need:

    A. The current way in which the airlines are conducting business is not working.

    1. The corporate sector, which is in control of managing today's major air carriers is mostly responsible

for the recent problems that the industry is facing today.

a. In the early 60's to mid 70's the airlines where overseen by VP's or Presidents, who viewed the entire aviation industry in a different business mindset. These individuals had a tremendous respect for aviation and love of the industry.

b.

c. They would eventually retire, relinquishing power to a new type of business mindset, presently known as corporate.

d.

e. In retrospect, had the VP's and Presidents of that era, had the foresight of things to come, the process regarding that transfer of power, would have been researched more extensively.

B. The commercial airlines corporate management practices today, continue to
deteriorate the airlines previous high quality standards, regarding their economic, customer service, employee relations and most importantly safety structure.

1. If the commercial airlines corporate leaders continue to prioritize revenue and all other forms of monetary gain, including government

bail outs over safety, there will be irrevocable damage, and the industry will not completely recover.

a. After the terrorist attacks of Sept. 11, 2001, American Airlines and United Airlines were compensated by the U.S. Government with funds to help diffuse the revenue loss from the necessary grounding of aircrafts for a number of days. Those funds were given to help sustain the companies through the temporary financial hardships they would incur.

b. Shortly after that government bail out, American Airlines corporate leaders requested from their employees that they make temporary monetary concessions, achieved through pay cuts as well as other employee benefit cutbacks, in order to keep the company out of bankruptcy and allowing it to get back on its feet.

That concession money, which was given to them for that very purpose, was intended to be placed back into the company, for any and all necessary use, including the maintenance of all of its aircraft.

2.   Top corporate leaders at American Airlines decided among themselves that the money received from employee concessions would be better served lining their own pockets via bonuses, to the tune of 19,183,270.000

> a. With the airlines recent high profile maintenance issues regarding mandatory FAA inspections on almost half of its fleet, the safety situation has become quite dire. Taking the proper steps to ensure that all safety requirements are met; obviously cannot be left up to the airlines corporate management.
>
> b. Safety issues have become so unstable, two FAA inspectors Bobby Boutris and Douglas Parker stated that they had complained to their superiors last year about airline safety issues being ignored and their warning went unheeded as the airline continued to fly planes that had not been properly checked for cracks in the fuselage. Mr.Boutris further stated that his supervisor suppressed information rather than inconvenience the airlines. FAA's oversight in this case appears to allow, rather than mitigate, recurring safety violations. (Los Angeles Times Mar.27,2008) staff writers Martin Zimmerman and Tiffany Hsu.

3.   The flurry of maintenance issues has also focused attention on outsourcing of aircrafts maintenance.

          a.   United Airlines 747's maintenance has been outsourced to Korean Airlines. FAA inspectors discovered that an instrument used to calibrate the altimeters on the jetliners had failed. Southwest had plans to move some of its aircraft maintenance from the U.S. to a third world country. (El Salvador)

Transition: Now that I have given you a glimpse of this tremendous safety problem, I will give you my ideas on what can be done to begin restoring the integrity of this industry as well as keeping the public safe.

Alternative Plan:

1. Corporate management, as well as current stockholders have to be removed from the position of hiring company CEOs.

     a. A committee must be formed having one representative from every department within the airline, for the purpose of hiring CEOs. The individuals applying for that position must go through a rigorous screening process, ensuring that their qualifications meet the demanding industry's criteria.

     b. As it stands today, corporate CEOs that are currently overseeing the airlines, have come in with explicit contracts allowing for high salaries, overblown bonuses and tremendous company stock options, regardless of job performance (Golden

Parachute); most of them having very limited knowledge concerning the aviation industry and its dynamics, as well as lacking in the human safety element, not only necessary but vital, as well, in this industry.

2. A case study reported by: Explicit vs. Implicit Contracts: Evidence from CEO Employment Agreements *Stuart L. Gillan/Arizona State University-Jay Hartzwell/ University of Austin Texas/Robert Parrino-Current Draft: March 17, 2005. Explains in details the nature of the employment relationship between the firms and their CEOs which has long been the focus of scrutiny by academics, practitioners and regulators alike.

1. Once we were able to implement this new structure of hiring and we have the appropriate network of individuals overseeing the airlines, we will begin to re-establish the integrity as well as the customer service and most importantly the safety the industry has been known for in the past.

2. Opening an emergency account for placing funds collected by government help or bail outs, as well as temporary employee monetary concessions, to be assessed on a monthly basis, and withdrawn only for unexpected or unforeseen emergency situations, such as fuel increases and unfortunate disasters.

3. A separate fund, made up of a percentage of revenue should also be established   to b used for automatic replacement of aging fleets.

Transition: Now that I have explained the plan for making air travel safe once again, let me explain how this very plan will benefit us all.

II.   Visualization: Under this new structure, excessive and unnecessary lower management could be greatly curtailed, saving the companies millions of dollars.

Along with safety we will have better customer service. For instance, the substantial amount of bonus money CEOs are paid, which is above and beyond their already bloated salaries, can be better used for aircraft maintenance. Employees will feel a sense of recognition, which will lead to better productivity and overall morale, which will thereby allow the rest of us the ability to experience quality customer care.

Under this alternative plan, better maintained aircrafts lead to more frequent on-time departures and arrivals in turn making it a pleasant transition from one destination to another, and most importantly, the aging aircrafts will be replaced with newer ones, more often, assuring us of arriving at our destination safely.

Conclusion:

Summary of Main Points: In conclusion, I have explained the problems with the current airline safety issues. I have discussed how removing Corporate management as well as current stockholders from the position of hiring CEOs, and placing it back in the hands of qualified employees, overseen by elected VP's and Presidents who are knowledgeable in every aspect of the industry, will benefit both the airlines as well as the general flying public.   Action: If we are going to make a difference in this current irreprehensible and well as incomprehensible lack of concern for the safety of the American public, we need to react quickly and speak out against it, before our luck runs out. This is just the tip of the iceberg. We can begin by writing our Congressmen and demanding that a deeper investigation continues to exist, and that we take every precautionary steps available to ensure and re-instate the safety of our skies.

I would like to very quickly share a situation involving my sister who is currently employed and on leave from her 32 year employment with American Airlines. She was recently awarded and recognized for her bravery in saving a passenger's life. Unfortunately, she was forced to use that very forum, to express her regret of accepting the award, due to the fact that she did not consider herself a hero, and was more troubled about the fact that the current dire safety situation was the reason she went on leave in the first place since she would not allow her company, to intimidate her into flying safety compromised flights and or aircrafts, one of which had a crack in part of one of the engines that controlled the pressurization of the aircraft cabins, that American Airlines LAX Management allowed to take off in that manner, filled with unsuspecting passengers. I have to say that I was very proud of her for taking on a corporation, especially one the size of her airlines, in spite of the retribution she is currently facing. The following day after the award ceremony where she refused to accept her award, she was broadcast live from MSNBC in New York, via satellite from their Burbank studio in Los Angeles, where she expressed her concerns. I wanted to share that story with you with the hopes that you take part in your own safety and become involved in making extreme changes that need to be addressed immediately.

Washington-Senators charged that the public's safety is at risk because of lax airline oversight by Federal Aviation Association

Regulators. "The aviation system may be operating on borrowed time before there is another major accident", Senator Jay Rockefeller, D-W. VA., warned a top official of the Federal Aviation Administration at a Senate hearing. (Courier-Journal.com) a report by James R. Carroll (April 11th 2008).

Tie Back: If you intend to fly in the future and want to live to see your grandkids or just live, I suggest you get involved and do it as soon as you possibly can

CHAPTER 17

DEAR MR. GEORGE W. BUSH II

Dear Mr. George W. Bush II,

Although I am very well aware of the fact, that at the time I find myself writing this letter, you hold the title of that of President of The United States of America or Commander in Chief; take your pick. Unfortunately, I cannot, in all good conscience, bring myself to address you by either of those titles for the simple reason that I strongly believe that you are not deserving of either one of them. If the people of this nation would have looked up the definition as well as the description of the functions, responsibilities, duties and ultimate power and authority, that is given to the person who holds the title of The President of The United States of America, you sir, would not be residing at The White House in Washington D. C. for the last 7 ½ years, but rather, you would have remained back at "The Ranch" in Texas, which is exactly where you belong! It is inconceivable to me, as I am sure it is to many Americans, how someone, such as yourself, could end up as President of the United States. The only somewhat rational explanation that I can attribute your winning the presidential election to, that would allow for me to be able to find some level of understanding, no matter how minute, of how something so incredulous and tragic could possibly happen (because I know I didn't vote for you), is that when you were running for office, the people of this country, who did in fact vote for you, were in some kind of temporary mental comatose state at the time, and definitely didn't know anything about you! What is even more baffling is the fact that you held a term in that office, for not only the first four God forsaken years, but the last four as well! In the first four miserable years, you've managed to inflict such incredible damage to this country and its people in that relatively short amount of time through your ignorant and arrogant reign, but it's the last four you somehow managed to get re-elected which gave you the opportunity to come back and finish us off by means of complete annihilation! Can you even begin to grasp the severity of injury and harm that this country, my country, has sustained because of your egoism and that of your ridiculous administration? I don't think you're even bright enough to wrap your head around that! Every single person in it has proven themselves to be unworthy of any consideration for future positions having to do with any critical decision making, in regards to this country and its people? I am under the understanding, that you are a person who considers himself a "Christ"ian (spelled in that manner on purpose). Do you get through your head the undeniable knowledge that none of us live forever, and if you believe in God, as you supposedly say you do, then you know that we will all inevitably come face to face with that TRUE POWER one day, and we will be judged by that POWER for the manner in which we lived our lives, and the things that we did while we were here? The only thing that I can say to you, and I'll say it as simple as possible so that you can understand it completely is; you are in "Big Trouble in Little China"! I also believe in God, and I know that when my time on this earth is over and I find myself face to face with Him, I too will have to answer for a few things, but whoa! Nothing like you! Not even close! You have sent the sons and daughters of thousands and thousands of American people, to their deaths, and the ones you haven't killed yet, by the grace of God, you have placed in harms way. My heart hurts tremendously for the losses of the mothers. Every time I see the faces of those young people who have lost heir lives at war on the television, I say a prayer for your soul sir. I am a mother of two sons. From the moment they came out of my body, I have loved those boys, more than life itself. They are an incredible gift given to me from the heavens to honor and cherish, and I have lived my life working very hard every single day to teach them by example, not by rhetoric, how to be great men, and live their lives to the best of their ability. As far as I am concerned, you sir, know nothing of that. How nice for you, that you can give orders for other people's children to go and fight your war of a thousand lies, because that is exactly what this war has been about; LIES! Yet you have two daughters that are of the age where they too could be fighting your "Oil War" in the Middle East, but instead get to stay behind and drink and party (chips off the old block), then have big weddings! How nice for you and Mrs. Bush, really. To never have to feel that gut wrenching pain that comes from losing a child, especially in such a horrific and most unnecessary manner. The parents of those incredible and courage's young men and women that you have sent out to die will NEVER get the chance to give their children a wedding! What ever happened to the rules of engagement set up by our Founding Fathers during this country's formative years, when the great First President of the United States, President George Washington, actually led his troops into battle, placing himself front and center when he declared WAR. No, that's not what you do is it? What you do instead is run around from country to country, making a complete fool of yourself every time you open your mouth and then, after you're done humiliating yourself as well as the people of this country who you are supposedly representing, you retreat to your cowboy ranch in Texas, in between your useless ranting stops. We need to bring the rule back, where it is mandatory for the Commander in Chief and his offspring to lead his troops into battle when he declares war on another country. Maybe then and only then, will people like you, who unfortunately hold the power to declare the ultimate atrocity on mankind, will certainly think twice before going there. I am sure if that were the case, and you had to lead our troops into this current battle you've got us "stuck on stupid" in, you would have paid closer attention and you would not have missed or purposely ignored the way you chose to do, the very important FACT that September 11th 2001, had ABSOLUTELY NOTHING to do with Saddam Hussein and

Iraq. You, sir, took incredible advantage of your position as leader of the Free World, and you intentionally dropped the ball on the good people of this country. As an American Airlines Flight Attendant, which I am, I can tell you without any hesitation whatsoever, sir, that I resent your stupidity, your arrogance, and your complete indifference. I hold you, as well as the prior administrations that had been warned this was coming and also chose to ignore it, and all of those other idiots holding court around you, for the tragic events that were allowed to transpire on that horrific day! On that morning, when I, along with the rest of this country and world, had to watch my airline's Boeing 767 aircraft, with my company's name "American Airlines" on its fuselage, go into that World Trade Tower, as well as The Pentagon, like some kind of deployed missiles, carrying my co-working "Hero" crew member friends and my passengers inside them, I wanted to die! I like all Americans and people all over the world, for that matter, wanted justice! We wanted the people responsible for planning and executing this blatant attack on our country and our very lives, to be served up on a silver platter. That was your big CUE, to be the formidable leader of the free world, and go after the TRUE perpetrators responsible for this abomination and dastardly crimes, and you knew damn well that it wasn't Saddam Hussein and Iraq. Almost every single one of the hijackers were Saudi's and you knew AlQueda, who was operating under the direction of their despicable leader, Bin Laden, was completely responsible, because he had even warned you as well as the previous administration that he was intending to do this. He not only OWNED it, he REVELED in it; as if spitting in our faces. So what do you and your highly intelligent administration do with all of that? You declare your BS war on Saddam Hussein and Iraq all the while, letting Bin Laden get away! Some president you've been! You took advantage of our mourning nation, knowing how angry, frustrated and helpless we felt, and how we all wanted to go and fight in order to restore our sense of self as well as honor, which we felt we had been robbed of, and then make them accountable for what they had done to us! You and your administration lied to your countrymen, while we were in our darkest hour, leading us to believe that Saddam Hussein was responsible for September 11th 2001, when you all knew damn well that he was not! I shed no tears for the fact that Saddam Hussein, along with his satanic sons and every one of his vile and ruthless henchmen that took pleasure in following the inhumane orders that were given to them are all dead, good riddance! But that doesn't change or excuse the fact Mr. Bush, that you led this country and its people down a very misinformed path; sacrificing hundreds and thousands of lives, worth much more than yours will ever be, as far as I am concerned, and in the process, you've made it possible for Bin Laden and his Murderous Merry Men to regroup and remain out there "lying in wait" for the perfect moment when they will strike again, which they surely will! Thanks so much for that, Mr. Leader of the Free World! Hopefully, you'll be out of that White House when that chain of events come around and someone else will have stepped into the mess that you and your administration circus will leave behind to

271

*be cleaned up by the next administration. I can only hope and
pray that whomever it is that ends up in The White House for the
next four years after you're out of there, has a bigger love for their
country than they do for their own over inflated egos, and that
unlike you, he will possess the fortitude and humility that will
enable a formulated plan to come about which will not only lead
us in the right direction, but restore once again, the strength and
power this nation has always been known for, as well as the world
wide respect that our country has always commanded, that is, up
until the last 7 ½ years now, and counting. There is one last
thing I need to make you aware of, that I am amazed no one in
that entourage of yours has brought to your attention. As the
leader of the Free World and the people of this great nation of
ours, every time you step up on a podium to speak, representing
The United States of America, and all who live in her, you should
be exuding eloquence and dignity and fortitude, speaking in a
manner which demonstrates much intelligence and elocution,
correct? Unfortunately for us though, you exude or resemble
nothing of the kind and here's the huge problem I am having
with being represented by someone such as you. It mortifies me,
as I am sure it does most Americans as well, to think that people
all over the world who are also watching and listening to you,
believe that the rest of us are as stupid and illiterate as you.
Besides the fact that there isn't any possible way for anyone to
actually take you, or anything you say seriously, because they can't
get past that ridiculously inappropriate cartoon like grin you
constantly have plastered on your face, you also have a tendency to*

make one futile attempt after another, to incorporate these complex words into your very limited vocabulary range, and it's quite obvious that you have absolutely no clue of their meaning much less their proper pronunciation. Stop it! It's not cute. You're not cute, you're embarrassing! You come across as this unread and badly educated person that I have no doubt that you are, but please! When the cameras are rolling, and the whole world is watching you and listening to you speak, please, say as little as possible, or better yet, don't speak at all, and let someone else in your administration, who sounds more educated and presidential than you, do the talking for you! You owe the great people of this nation at least that much, for having to endure the last 7 ½ years of watching you trying to pass yourself off as a United States President, as if! Do us all a favor. Until you move out of that White House and go back to your rootin tootin cowboy wannabe Texas ranch, where you do belong; please, for the love of God man, don't touch anything, or sign anything, or do anything else on your way out. You've done enough damage! By the way, in case you were wondering, I don't think you have anything to worry about concerning the presidential legacy you leave behind for the history books. You can rest assured that you are going to go down in history as the most intellectually challenged president The United States of America has ever had. Congratulations! Thanks for letting me get all of that off my chest. I feel so much better now that you know how most of us out here feel about you. It brings my soul PEACE! Good bye and good riddance, Mr. George W. Bush II and your entourage of clowns.

As respectful as possible,

American Airlines Flight Attendant

Alicia Lutz-Rolow

P.S. Please sir, if you have to make another trip to the Middle East anytime between now and the time you're out of the White House, try to keep your mouth shut and stop ranting your illiterate and embarrassing comments regarding Senators Obama, Clinton or any other Representative from The United States, to the ENEMIES of this country who wish us death! The world already thinks you a fool; no need to keep proving it! The less you say the better off the rest of us will be.

** *Well we're dropping our bombs*

In the southern hemisphere

And people are starving

That live right here

And they're tearing down walls

In the name of peace

And they're killing each other

In the middle east

Chorus:

But love and happiness

Have forgotten our names

And there's no value left

In love and happiness

They raise the price of oil

And they censor our mouths

If you are a young couple today

Forget buying a house

And we wage our wars

In the neighborhoods

We kill the young to feed the old

And men that ain't no good

So if you sell arms

Or if you run dope

You got respect

And you got hope

But the rest of us die

On your battle fields

With wounds that fester and bleed

But never heal

(John Mellencamp Singer, Songwriter my hero)

CHAPTER 18

MY DEAREST PASSENGERS

This is by far the most difficult and challenging chapter that I will have written in this book, simply because of the enormous weight and responsibility it carries with it, in providing you the necessary information that will hopefully give you the ability you will need, in order to form a reasoned judgment concerning the fact that each and every one of you play a very important role regarding the Aviation Industry's commercial airlines, not just in the past and present, but it is with a certainty that you will in the future as well. The commercial airlines are here to stay due to the fact that it is currently the fastest form of passenger travel to get us from point A to point B. That is a given, and is not what is in peril at this point. What is most certainly in peril however is the "quality" of the commercial airline companies' infrastructure, which has held the highest of operational standards in the past, but as of late, those standards have been caused to be all but diminished. The basic framework of these airline industry organizations are systematically breaking down in almost every possible capacity, especially the system of bases that pertain to you, the flying public. To put it simply, every aspect of the negative experience you now undergo every time you travel on *ANY* commercial airline company, whether you travel for business or pleasure, comes from the *domino effect* that began occurring in the early *1970's*, when the airline company leaders at that time, began abdicating their high powered positions to a new type of leadership, for lack of a better word, and that leadership's type of disparity and company/employee depleting system of work ethics, has now almost reached its final phase. It has been a long and very slow process thereby making the demise of the commercial airline companies almost impossible to have been   detected early on.   It is not until approximately the last 15 years, where the clarity of this industry's ongoing destruction from the severe corruption and greed that is burrowed deep within this industry's higher monarchy walls, has been seen or felt.   At first, it was primarily the airline companies' labor employees who were feeling the affects of the injurious detriment that is now expanding at an alarming rate.   That is the timeline when many of us who could see what was happening, began protesting against the manner in which these corporate leaders were managing the airline companies.   That, in fact, was what led to the ***American Airlines flight attendant strike*** that occurred back on ***November 18, 1993*** over the ***Thanksgiving*** holidays, during the reign of then ***American's CEO, Mr. Robert Crandall.***   That flight attendant strike that the majority of us engaged in and was led by our ***APFA*** union leaders, was the pivotal moment in time when we were no longer able to pretend or talk ourselves out of the obvious fact that our company benefits, salaries and sheer work environment was well on its way to the deteriorated and ravished condition we find them in today.   We were left with no other alternative but to publicly strike against ***American Airlines*** because ***Mr. Robert Crandall*** was determined ***NOT*** to return to the flight attendant contract bargaining table with our ***APFA*** union leaders, to discuss the much needed revamping of our ***expired*** contract which we were still working under for well into a year, because of the fact that he was too busy enjoying the fruits of our labor! The flight attendant strike was successful because of two very important strategies used by our savvy **APFA** leadership, who was under the direction of flight attendant and president **Denise Hedges** at the time. The first of those two strategies was that the **APFA** proposed to the flight attendant body, that the strike would only be in effect for **eleven days** because the union leadership had researched the timeline that was necessary in order to protect the flight attendants who were engaging in the strike, from being legally replaced by **SCAB** employees who would be hired by **American Airlines** management for that very purpose. The **FAA (Federal Aviation Administration)** mandates the training for the flight attendant profession, and the information that is required to be learned and retained by individuals who train for the course of that profession, takes approximately **eight weeks** to thoroughly complete in their judgment. **American Airline's then CEO Mr. Robert Crandall** felt differently and thought that the already intense at **eight weeks** training could be crammed down to eleven days. He quickly realized though, that his plan of hiring **SCAB** employees to take over all of our jobs was an impossibility that was just not going to ever materialize for him. **Yesiree! Eleven was truly the "magic number"** and because we figured how to play that out, we weren't winning any popularity contests as far as **Crandall** was concerned. **If he hated us before, which we all new he did, he sure hated us now!** He was hell bent on **SCABS** replacing years and years of flight attendant seniority and experience, as well as taking his big shot at possibly busting our **UNION** while he was at it, and that was something that all of us knew he lived for. Try to imagine what kind of aviation catastrophes the flying public as well as this country would have had to endure, had the **APFA** leadership not done their homework, and the flight attendants strike would have extended past those eleven days. You would have been exposed to the inexperience of **SCABS** that would have been used to replace years and years of flight attendant seniority knowledge and experience, and that very situation was not one I would wish on anybody, especially our passengers traveling at ***39,000 feet!*** We managed to foil his despicable plans though, and that was like music to all of our ears because by the time that strike rolled around, we had grown quite tired of all his carrot dangling and continuous ***LIES!*** We hated him as much as he hated us, probably more! The second ingenious strategy was involving the ***President of the United States of America***, who at that time was ***President Bill Clinton,*** and asking him, for the sake of our traveling public, our country's economy and ourselves, to put a stop to the back and forth bantering that was going on between us, and ***American Airlines*** corporate management, and force ***Mr. Robert Crandall*** back to the ***APFA*** flight attendant contract bargaining table, which they had been refusing to do, prior to ***President Clinton's*** intervention. By the way ***Mr. Bill Clinton,*** I don't know if any one of us ever thanked you for what you did for all of the ***American Airline's*** flight attendants and all of our passengers with that intervention, so I shall take this very opportunity I have right now, to tell you how grateful we all were, and still are, and how very lucky we felt to have had an ***intelligent Democratic President in the White House as opposed to the stupid one we presently have,*** during that extremely crucial time in our profession. You responded when called upon, in a fair and forthright manner, and that was all we were asking for. ***We thank you from the bottom of our hearts for STANDING for us.*** Those two key strategies were what cause the newspapers and television media to dub us as ***"The little airline flight attendants that could"!*** During the first few days of the actual strike, the flight attendants, as well as all other labor employees, not only witnessed but unfortunately came to know all too well, the tremendous sanctimonious and deceptive skills and tactics used against us by ***American Airlines***, the company that we were all once so proud to be associated with, and work for. They were now blatantly *LYING* to you, our passengers, directing you to get in your cars and come down to the airports, even though the flight attendants strike was in full force. They led you to believe that they had employees who were flying as our replacements, and that flight operations had been minimally affected by our strike stance. Maliciously and reprehensibly, they went on to inform you that flights were going out on time, without experiencing major delays, therefore, the chances were more that great that your flight was not adversely affected by our strike! *LIES, LIES and more LIES!* What had become undeniably apparent for all of us out on that strike line during those first few days of the strike, was the fact that we had made the enormous mistake of believing in the false promises that had come from our company's *CEO Robert Crandall,* of shared prosperity that we would eventually come about, from the *"supposedly temporary"* years of sacrificing accomplished through our many labor concessions, in order to allow American to grow as a company, and become more competitive with the other major air carriers by expanding its international routes. Well, there eventually was much prosperity from all our concessions all right, except that the only salaries and compensations that flourished from all of it, was *Crandall's and Corporate!* We trusted his word, which was worthless, and had allowed ourselves to be manipulated by them, for what was way too many years, thereby giving up too much of our own salaries, benefits and perks, which to this very day, we have never been able to regain all of them back! Knowing the information that was *privy* to only the company employees on the inside, as well as witnessing first hand what was really going on at the airports, made us painfully aware of the fact that the shameless way in which they were *"Lying"* to *all of YOU*, was the exact shameless way that they had be *"Lying"* to *US! American's* corporate spokespeople had convinced you to go out to the airports for your flights in vain! Well, I've got to tell you; *Mr.*

Robert Crandall, who was infuriated with the flight attendants strong show of solidarity at this point ***(90% of us were out on the strike lines),*** and had never minced any words about just how little of an opinion he had regarding the flight attendants, had given his sanctimonious order to his corrupt corporate management incumbent clowns (who welcome the opportunity of engaging in unethical practices, just like their leader), that was derived from the little devious plan he had come up with, consisting of using YOU, our passengers, as a means of getting back at US, the flight attendants, by getting you out to the airports, only to find that American Airline's flight operations, had been virtually shut down and completely paralyzed by our strike! Our Pilots, who were in complete support of our necessary strike, but whose jobs were being held over their heads should they refuse to follow Corporate orders, were forced to take off and land with completely "EMPTY" aircrafts, thereby, making that very   process, which was facilitated through the news media for your viewing pleasure on your television sets, as if American Airline's flights were departing and landing as scheduled, without any disruption whatsoever from our strike. Crandall's sole purpose and intent for sending out that despicable LIE out to you, was to infuriate all of you enough, from the inconvenience you were having to encounter and deal with, when you finally did arrive at the airports during what was the busiest flying season of all, Thanksgiving, and then realize that you were not going anywhere! Crandall not only knew, but he banked on the fact that the tremendous anger and frustration that all of you would then feel from that very situation "HE" had created for "YOU", would then cause you to completely direct that at US, the flight attendants, instead of where it rightfully belonged, which was on Mr. Crandall himself, and the rest of his greedy, horrid, despicable, capricious, and greedy Corporate buddies! Did I say greedy twice? Oh well, anyway, the bottom line was, Corporate was once again able to divert their unethical business practices on the flight attendants! What else was new! Mr. Crandall's ingenious plan had worked exactly the way he thought it would, and all of you were "played" exactly in the manner in which he knew he could "play" you, because all of those vile adjectives that I used in the previous paragraph describing the behavior of Crandall and Corporate, was the very same influx of lurid name calling, You, our passengers, showered Us, your flight attendants with! Believe it or not, there were even a couple of you who actually took it even a step further than the name calling, and literally SPIT on us, not once ever seeing a problem whatsoever with your outrages and incredibly hurtful behavior! I am happy to report though, that WE got the last word, didn't we Mr. Robert Crandall? Although it was all relatively short lived, with all due respect, we un metaphorically and with absolutely no amount of exaggeration, did kick your "not so mighty ass" didn't we Mr. Crandall, sir? And that alone, made the "HELL" you put us through with respect to our passengers, bearable! Unfortunately though, for us the flight attendants, it was too little too late, because much damage had already been allowed to transpire, and there was so much more that we knew was already inevitably on its way. It hasn't been until the last couple of years that you, the flying public have begun feeling the aftermath of the Commercial Airline leadership's corruption and insatiable greed that the Aviation Industry's Labor employees have been feeling for what has been now so many years! You are feeling it in the diminishing customer service, no pillows, no blankets, no food, less and less on time departures and arrivals, higher ticket pricing, less allowable "free" baggage, tax charge, surcharges for this, surcharges for that, etc. etc. and of course, the most dangerous and unacceptable airline company cutback of all, your SAFETY. Well, let me provide you with a little "inside" perspective on the true reasons as to why all the above mentioned amenities and perks that were once provided for you with the price of your ticket, are now a thing of the past. The Commercial Airline companies are using higher fuel prices, forced competitive ticket pricing, Labor costs, the country's economy and anything else they can throw in there, as scapegoats for all of the financial problems they are currently facing, with of course September 11th 2001 as their "scapegoat" of scapegoats, when the reality of it is that the Commercial Airline companies current financial woes, stem straight from the 32+ years that airline companies greedy corporate CEO's and their greedy incumbents, have seen fit to reward themselves in salaries and bonuses with the billions and billions of dollars taken from the excess revenue of these companies, as well as from the Labor Employee salaries and benefit cutbacks and concessions! That, is the #1 reason for our Aviation Industry's Commercial Airline companies current rapidly deteriorating status, that no one seems to be addressing aggressively enough, probably due to the fact that the "immense power", that the Corporate entities who have been engaging in such corrupt, vile, morally vacant and borderline criminal behavior, with respect to the inefficient managing of these very companies for so many years, is powerful enough to keep the focus from being placed where it should be, which is directly on them and their greed, and circumventing that focus instead, to all of the other reasons, which although less in priority, still definitely factor into the equation, of enabling the entire situation to manifest itself, into the enormously monstrous airline debacle, we are left to deal with today! These Corporate individuals, will do anything and everything within their power, to make sure that YOU, the flying public, will NEVER, EVER see any type of thorough and completely enlightening investigative reporting done, regarding this very issue, and the fact that it is precisely because of that Corporate insatiable greed, that a domino effect has been created from so many years of Corporate airline company ravaging, ultimately leaving all of us with the appalling Commercial Airline companies we enjoy today! You, the Commercial Airline passengers, are not looked upon by your Flight Crews as merely revenue or the bottom line dollar amounts on balance sheets, which is exactly the way these companies CEOs and corporate leaders see you, but rather, you are viewed by US, as the main figures involved in a reciprocal type relationship, having mutual interaction with your flight attendant crews. It is imperative, not only for our safety and well being, but for yours as well, that you begin the process of readdressing your current perception of the flight attendants that are working any and all Commercial Airline flights you may be traveling on, and together, we must immediately begin to work on construing a path that will provide for all of us, a complete and equally respectful open line of communication free from any form of discord. That type of interaction can only be achieved through the mutual regard and consideration we show one another. If any of us, passengers and flight attendants alike, should find ourselves at some point during our travels together, in a dire, or even worse; a possible catastrophic situation at 39,000 feet where we are fighting for our very lives, you need to remember the very important fact that it will not be the corrupt corporate leaders and CEO's of the Commercial Airline companies, who will be the ones experiencing the horror and desperation that will have transpired from that type of situation up there, but rather, it will be You and Us! That, my friends, is the bottom line. I pray with God's almighty help that I will be able to convey to all of you, just how important it is that you understand that, because every single flight attendant out on the line, including myself, need to know that you STAND behind us and not against us, and that we have your complete support as we try to regain some amount of control over our airline company, American Airlines, from these corrupt corporate leaders, especially when it comes to issues dealing with safety. At the moment, it's all about the revenue (your corporate board room name) and the balance sheets, and when it comes to our safety, it is being severely compromised and neglected every single day. If, after reading this chapter, and the information in it that I will have hopefully enlightened you with, or at the very least provoked thought from you, you still do not come away with a much clearer understanding of our profession and the enormous responsibility that comes with it, regarding our involvement in your safety; and if the current defamatory stigma that has been attached to the flight attendant profession for such a long time, does NOT then become unacceptable to you making absolutely NO difference in the way in which you view us, then sadly, I will have not only failed all of you miserably, but I will have also failed every single flight attendant, from every existing commercial airline, including myself. I have complete confidence that you will come to understand, that the disrespectful and mean spirited manner in which many of you have chosen at times to communicate with us for so many years, does not come from your own personal observations of us, although some of you may have convinced yourselves that it does. Trust me, it doesn't. For many years, the commercial airline companies gave the flying public the green light for demonstrating temper tantrums, or using impertinent dialogue when speaking to any of us. In fact at one point, these companies actually encouraged the public's bad behavior to continue by apologizing to you for the inconvenience that we, "the passenger abused employee's" might have caused you, thereby enabling you to find further justification for resuming that same rude behavior you may have displayed towards us in the past, now in your future travels as well. You have been officially accorded by the "big kahunas" of American Airlines, to come on board our flights and use the flight attendants to absorb any and all of your frustrations and feelings of hostility from the bad day you might be having. If I didn't know any better, it's almost as if the airline companies provided you with your own personal punching bags (flight attendants) when you boarded, to use for relieving your stress! Even though I know that at times you feel that this negative treatment you provide us with is exactly what we deserve because of our reactions to your actions, believe me when I tell you that we do not deserve that. No one does! One of the reasons almost every flight attendant that I have ever worked with or came across in my extensive flying career, including myself, sought out this profession, was because of the enjoyment we found in helping others, as well as interacting with other people. At times, the customer service portion of this profession can be unbelievably rewarding for us. I personally, have had some of the most incredibly warm and happy memories that I will always treasure and carry with me forever, which so many of you have helped create with your kindness, your humor and your warmth. You have honored us by allowing us into your lives while traveling on our flights from coast to coast, sharing your wedding and honeymoon stories, on flights going to or coming from the exotic and exciting destinations we've either dropped you off at, or picked you up from. We've experienced alongside many of you, the complete joy you have felt and could barely contain for the duration of our five hour trans-con flights, from the excitement of the knowledge that you had now become grandparents, and were on your way to the hospital in Los Angeles to meet your beautiful brand new baby granddaughter for the very first time! Or those of you that allowed us to fly you to that huge 50th wedding anniversary bash that your kids put together, and were giving in your honor. Besides flying you to your happy destinations and sharing in all your blessed times, you've allowed us into your lives during some of your darkest hours as well. We have flown you to destinations that you have anticipated with much apprehension because it was there that the funeral of a loved one would be held, and having to face that was more than you thought you could bear. The tremendous loss of a parent or a child or best friend made you inconsolable and you needed words of encouragement, or even a hug or two from us that helped provide for you some amount of comfort and strength, even if just for a little while, because that was all we could do on a five hour flight. So we listened and shared and mourned with you wholeheartedly. The times we have put our hearts together with yours are endless! Most have been happy ones, but some have been terribly sad. For me personally, those events have came and gone for over 32 years of my flying career, and I know without a single doubt, that when the day comes when I leave this profession and lifestyle that I have so dearly loved and still do, and I have flown my very last flight as an American Airlines Flight Attendant, I will take all of the memories of so many of you with me, and I will keep them close to my heart, as many flight attendants will, for the rest of my life. It has been so very unfortunate, not only for us but for those few of you as well, who have made it your unrelenting quest to treat us with such contemptible disrespect, as if flight attendants were some kind of non-human species, serving no real purpose for anyone. For those very few of you who happen to fall in this category, I now ask that you would please try to recognize that it is precisely that very reason which has caused us to put up the walls you immediately now see when you come on board our aircrafts. You leave us no other choice but to do that for our own protection. Other than the main reason that fuels the considerable amount of disdain that some of you seem to feel towards us, which I believe is the false consciousness that has been purposely planted in your heads, I truly don't know why it is, that some of you feel such animosity towards us; and to be perfectly honest, I don't think you do either! Perhaps it is because those of you who behave in this vile way, posses lives that are joyless, therefore you bring your misery on board our flights, and begin your rituals of trying to take the joy out of our jobs, so we can be as miserable as you are, and unfortunately, there are many times when you succeed. The flight attendants you sometimes experience on some of your flights that seem bitter and confrontational at times, have not become that way of their own choosing. It is the regrettable alternative that many of us have been left with, which comes from our much too frequent dealings with passenger misconduct, time after time after time. Even comediennes in the entertainment industry, such as Jay Leno, David Letterman and Joan Rivers to name a few, have taken their pot-shots at us, with their famous lines ending something about "having to put your flight attendants in their upright position". To be perfectly honest, most of us find the skits those comediennes do on us, to be pretty funny. Many of us, including myself, have actually had those particular three comediennes on our flights and have spent some really fun and memorable times with them, especially Joan Rivers, we love her, she's a kick! Flight attendants don't take the jokes made about us from those entertainers as some personal attack on our profession, because we are intelligent enough to know that they are just trying to make people laugh, which they do, and thank God for that, because as difficult as life can sometimes be, we could all use the laughs! I do not believe they mean us any intentional harm from it, nor do I believe they are purposely trying to encourage negative behavior or passenger misconduct to come from it either. Fortunately, most passengers are intelligent and savvy enough, and they get that, but there are those few of you who take what those comediennes say when they joke about us as scripture, and it unfortunately helps to fuel your unkind behavior towards us. Believe it or not, even after everything that I've just shared with all of you, I honestly still do not completely blame those of you who choose to behave so badly, simply because I feel you have been led to believe for years, that your behavior is in fact acceptable. Well, I am here to tell you that it is not. Please don't misunderstand me for a New York minute, and think that I am in any way trying to keep you from owning the negative attitude some of you hold towards us, and that I am in someway trying to take the accountability for your actions away from you, and find someone else to place it on, because the bad behavior after all, is coming from you. But on your behalf, and in somewhat of a defense, I must say that most of the blame for the way in which some of you perceive your flight attendants, lies with the people who oversee and manage the Aviation Industry's Commercial Airlines companies. They have always gone to great lengths to preconceive and conveniently package for you, the intentionally gross misinformation and misrepresentation of us, and then intensely and cleverly propagandize the detrimental information that comes from that process, over and over again, abundantly providing and reinforcing for you, its negative resonance, year after year for what seems like nearly a decade, ultimately leaving you with the end result of not only the severely "devalued" view of the Flight Attendant Profession that unfortunately some of you currently posses, but also the unwarranted opinions you have formed of us from that very information, which is; that commercial airline flight attendants are nothing more than "glorified waitresses in the sky", unworthy of commanding or deserving the same respect that all of you command and believe to be deserving of yourselves. How many of you have found yourselves shamefully making that very statement? Sadly, that opinion has been passed on from one generation to another. I write this chapter with much hope and the virtuous expectation, that I will somehow be able to find and formulate the proper words that will completely clarify for you, any and all incorrect assumptions or ungracious judgments, that you may have unfairly opinionated about us. Hopefully, you may be able to rethink those very negative opinions, and together we can begin forming a desperately needed bond between you the passenger, and us the flight attendants, that is not only strong and unshakable, but also creates a kind of invisible "safety net", if you will, needed in these current difficult and very uncertain times in the Aviation Industry's Commercial Airlines. That bond will give us the ability to rely on one another with complete confidence, when it comes to watching out for each other's safety. If together, we can somehow successfully achieve that goal, it will certainly be an invaluable as well as an impervious and unbeatable force that we will have created for ourselves, for securing the protection that may even one day ultimately save our lives! My reliance and state of trust for that very outcome is based upon my confidence in YOU, as well as my confidence in US. So, let's get this party started. The recognition as well as merit, for the unessential, promiscuous and inarticulate manner in which flight attendants have almost always been marketed and portrayed as to the flying public, belongs to the Commercial Airline Companies' corporate leaders, and is attributed through their slanderous advertising campaigns, and their countless choices of offensive slogans used in the early 1970's. Those offensive slogans gave birth to such sexist phrases as "coffee tea or me", "marry me fly free" or "we'll move our tails for you", which are just three examples of so many that were used in that era, for the sole purpose of representing the commercial airline flight attendants in a morally and intellectually vacant light. The 1970's era also provided the flying public with visual sexist commercial advertising that everyone could watch on their television sets as well. How many of you out there remember the television commercial where they had a flight attendant dressed in her very skimpy and inappropriate uniform, consisting of a miniskirt of miniscule proportion, barely covering her "ass"ets, and the four sizes too small blouse she had on, giving her breasts that "overfilled water balloons" look, completing her pole dancer; sorry, did I say pole dancer out loud? Sorry, I meant flight attendant ensemble with matching bright and shiny pat and leather "go go" boots. Now I ask you, seriously, what kind of profession would require you to wear that type of attire to work? Do you remember how that very same flight attendant, in that very same commercial shimmied down the aisle of the aircraft carrying a tray full of drinks and pausing ever so hospitably when she came upon the row where those three male passengers sat side by side? Do you also remember how she then bent over them as she reached across the furthest one of the three who was of course sitting by the window as she handed him his drink, while the other two watched this whole process in motion with lustful grins plastered all over their faces? How many of you out there recall that commercial? Well, the problem with that type of advertising is that it promotes sexual misconduct as an "allowed commodity" for the passenger when communicating with the flight attendant who is working the flight he happens to be on. What that particular airline carrier who ran that television commercial ad, as well as many others similar to it, clearly meant to imply as well as intentionally depict of the flight attendant profession with that type of advertising to you, the public, was that she was nothing more than a sexual object provided by the airline for the entertainment of its male passengers and she was included in the price of his airline ticket! That, of course, was exactly the way we were perceived by the traveling public and treated by many of the male passengers. During the 1970's, when the majority of the flight attendant Profession was made up of mostly young beautiful women, we were having to deal with what seemed like non stop (no pun intended) sexual harassment from male passengers. The wives or women of these men, who sometimes happened to be traveling with them, were also a horror story all in their own right! More times than not, flight attendants would choose to deal with the sexually harassing male passengers front and center, which was an extremely difficult enough task, since most of the time these men boarded our flights already drunk and belligerent, and there was, and still is, no possible rationalizing with that kind of behavior. But as troublesome as that situation was at times, we would always choose that path over the alternative, which was that of having to subject ourselves to the wrath that the women traveling with these men would have in store for us, which was usually ten times worse than the sexually harassing belligerent passenger himself! The raging jealousy and the state of fear that was involved with these women, regarding any flight attendant who happened to be caught in this ridiculous triangle, provoked in them a sense of threat or challenge to their possession and caused a "one sided" rivalry to manifest itself. Adding insult to injury, the public humiliation and lack of respect these men showed the women they traveled with, fueled these women's already enormous appetite for the vindication they felt they had to achieve against the culprit flight attendant involved, in order to redeem their respectability, especially in front of not only their mates, but the rest of the passengers in their surrounding area, who unfortunately had to witness this very common circus that went on quite frequently. The distorted view of these sadly pitiful co-dependant women was what enabled them to arrive to the absurd conclusion that it was the flight attendants who were sexually harassing their husbands and boyfriends and not the other way around. As if! Most of us had our own husbands and boyfriends, and those of us that didn't, had no problem finding our own. We certainly didn't need theirs! We would be left with no other alternative but to become confrontational with these people, and demand that they refrain from the disrespectful behavior that they were engaging in and displaying towards us. These women passengers were under the delusional impression that their alcoholic, testosterone overloaded husbands and boyfriends, were men that these young and beautiful flight attendants lusted after. Please! Give us all a break! These out of control women were constantly threatening us with their so unoriginal and infamous line which was always: "what is your name? I will have your job"! For those of you out there that remember spewing that absurd statement to any of us at any time during your travels with us, maybe you could answer the following questions for me because I have always been curious as to why you would say something that vicious to anyone! Did it make you feel powerful and superior to us in some way? Did it allow you to walk away from us feeling happy and fulfilled thinking that you could really make that happen? For those of you who have communicated with us in this manner, I suppose the question of all questions I have for you is; did blurting out that sinister statement to us, help validate in any way for you, who you are and abolish any and all responsibility as well as accountability for yours, and your husband/boyfriend's abhorrent behavior towards us? As if finding ourselves up against that kind of "passenger created chaos" and ridiculous turmoil unworthy of any reasonable consideration wasn't enough, your unwarranted letters of complaints to American Airlines Corporate Headquarters, although not powerful enough to materialize the end result that your threat carried and you wanted so badly, were sufficiently damaging enough to provide the ramifications of the unfair discipline shown to us by our company's Flight Service Managers! The on and on complaining you provided in your passenger complaint forms, was always of the horrible treatment and the rude behavior you received from the flight attendants working your flight, and of course never once was the fact mentioned, that the flight attendants you wrote about in that complaint form, became rude and defiant towards you and your husband/boyfriend, only after we were put in the horrendous position of having to thwart off his sexual misconduct in the middle of the in-flight service, while at the same time trying to desperately hang on to our dignity and composure as we attempted to proceed with our service, and continue to take care of the rest of our passengers, seeming unaffected by the colorful words you were choosing to belittle and berate us with. Do you have any idea just how difficult it was and is for us? I can personally tell you that accomplishing the extremely difficult task of always seeming to be in control is quite a feat! In the 1970's 80's and even well into the 90's, all the Commercial Airline companies alike, adopted the ridiculous policy that basically stated that "the passenger was always right", and they continuously rewarded passengers for their bad behavior. These companies didn't want to acknowledge the problems with the passengers, because after all they didn't want to upset the "revenue" that was coming in and lose the business to another carrier. As far as the corporate attitude was concerned, the passenger was not replaceable but the flight attendant was. These type of ridiculous company mindset, is part of what has come back to bite them in the ass! The problem is, we're the one's having to undo all the damage that has been done for years. Those complaint letters sent to American Airline's Corporate Headquarters would then trickle down through the system, until it reached the flight attendant's Flight Service supervisor at her home base, who was never by the way, in the slightest bit interested about hearing her version of what really happened on that flight. It was never and has never been about standing behind the flight attendant. Heaven Forbid! That's wasn't the American Airlines way. There was always some form of disciplinary action taken against the flight attendant instead of on the sexually harassing and belligerent passengers, and their out of control wife/girlfriends, who were the ones that really deserved it! The whole dynamics of that type of absurd situation from beginning to end has always been mind boggling to me. Unless you had a decent and forthright supervisor, the kind who did not allow upper management to intimidate them into subjecting unwarranted and immoral discipline on the flight attendants that were in their group (those type supervisors wouldn't last in that job very long), harassment was the drill you came to know, understand, and expect over and over again. Don't get me wrong and think me so naive as to believe that there are no flight attendants out on the line that resemble the "coffee tea or me" remark, as well as emulate that form of negative behavior while on the job. I know for a fact that there are. I don't know why these people behave that way or much less care, but what I do know is that the only thing accomplished with that inappropriate behavior by any flight attendant is the degradation of the entire profession. The majority of flight attendants do not behave in that manner therefore they are not deserving of that bad rap! Even though I know that common sense is not something that is so common, when it is present, it clearly dictates that every profession out there, whether it's corporate managers, Politicians, Judges, Police Officers, Teachers etc. etc. and yes, even the commercial airline flight attendant, has its share of people behaving badly, but that doesn't mean that the entire profession should be made to suffer or be humiliated for what a handful of lost souls do. That self disrespecting type behavior can indeed sometimes be found in the workplace, among the most diversified and even the most elite professions in existence and that is unfortunate, but we simply cannot begin to corral everyone belonging to a certain profession and then brand that profession, with a specific stereotype because of a few people who choose to use poor judgment when representing themselves or their profession. Doing so, would only demonstrate an enormous amount of ignorance on the part of the person doing the stereotyping. Unbelievable as it may seem, even to me at times, most of my 32 years in this career have rarely left me wanting to do anything else for a living, and on those very rare occasions when it did, it was not because of the profession itself, but rather because of the disrespect and disregard shown to us by Corporate management, both upper and lower! The flight attendant profession is not just a job or a career, but a way of life for most of us. There have been times, including the present, when I have certainly wanted American Airlines to rid itself of the egotistical and deplorable management people and corporate leaders that currently run this company, and instead find honest, decent and forthright replacements that can find the necessary ways in which to stand this once elite company back up on its feet, and restore the magnificence it once held, which is after all, the reason that made all of us so proud to work for American Airlines in the first place, at one time not very long ago. My co-working flight attendants, as well as the majority of the passengers, whom I have had the privilege of transporting from one coast to another all these years, are the reason why I wouldn't trade this career for any other career out there. Flight attendants, just like passengers, respond accordingly to the manner in which we have been addressed. Contrary to popular belief, flight attendants are not people who enjoy upsetting passengers on our flights for no apparent reason! That could not be any further from the truth. We do not belong to some secret society that teaches us the art of pissing passengers off just for the hell of it! None of us want to commence our flights with our passengers feeling angry or upset towards us for whatever reason. I realize that it is difficult at times for people to calm themselves down when they have experienced situations that cause them to become irate, or they have those kinds of days when one thing after another seems to go as wrong as it possibly can. I've been there; we all have. But if those of you who come on board our aircrafts, already in that frazzled state just stop to take a breath for a moment and regroup, instead of immediately lashing out at the flight attendants, because of the anger someone else caused you, you will find that most of us will go out of our way to try to help you with whatever it is that caused your anger in the first place. When you are on one our flights, I, along with the rest of my co-workers always try to make your flights fun and memorable, or at least we start out with that premise, but sometimes there are some of you that come on our flights, that are already furiously angry with something or someone in the boarding area, outside of our aircrafts, and the first one of us you see wearing the American Airlines uniform, which of course is representing of the company, gets your wrath! We can't control the many cutbacks of amenities and frills that American Airlines and other airline companies see fit to make; we unfortunately don't own this airline company but only work for them, therefore we have no say when it comes to the sometimes unscrupulous manner in which the people who are responsible for running the operations of American Airlines choose. Flight attendants, as well as most of all the other employees, Labor or otherwise for that matter, that work for American Airlines do not feel that everything American Airlines Corporate management does is acceptable! At the present time, as I am writing this very book you are reading, I am in what is probably the biggest battle of my life, facing American Airlines Corporate management's unbelievable repercussions for the simple reason that I have chosen to STAND up against them, not allowing myself to be intimidated into taking aircrafts/flights that are safety or security compromised in some way, completely oversold with many of you on them, as well as my co working crews, up to the skies in that manner! I have 32 years of seniority with American Airlines on the line, because I am CHOOSING to keep YOU, my passengers, as well as myself and co-workers, SAFE! That is my job! You depend on me, and other flight attendants to always do our utmost to keep you as safe as we possibly can at 39,000 feet! Ironically enough, I am being retaliated against, by the very company I have given allegiance to for 32 years of my life, American Airlines, for doing the very job I was hired to do, because today's airline companies primary agenda is about the REVENUE, which is quite different from the agenda that existed back in 1976, when I was hired and originally trained, which was primarily that of SAFETY! By the time this book is published and you are reading it, American Airlines will have terminated my employment with them because I have chosen to uphold my integrity and the integrity of my much loved profession, and do what I know is right. The fact that I speak out when American Airlines Corporate management allows the flying public, that's you, my passengers, to be placed in harms way by allowing aircrafts to be sent up to the skies that have mechanical issues that need to be addressed, or flights that have security issues that are not checked out properly or thoroughly enough, will be the real reason I have been terminated. That is just WRONG! There is no amount of REVENUE absolutely none, that makes that inexcusably greedy and corrupt corporate behavior anything but what it is; and that's CRIMINAL! If, what I am choosing to do at this point in my life, which is putting everything that I have worked so hard for in the last 32 years of my life on the line, for YOU, my passengers, in order to call enough attention and public awareness to the way American Airlines, as well as some others, are sending some of our compromised aircrafts/ flights up, and if it stops, or at minimal, slows the process down considerably, of the dire manner in which these companies' so called leaders, are presently running the Aviation Industry's Commercial Airlines into the ground by their greedy quest to line their own despicable pockets, and if my choosing to STAND for YOU, as well as for US, taking all the apparently necessary hits I am currently taking on all of our behalf, in order to force American Airlines management to make all the necessary changes that need to be made, to ensure that we all remain SAFE when we take to the skies, if all of that does not convince every single one of you out there that it is indeed your flight attendants that are, and will always be your LAST LINE OF DEFENSE while up in the skies, then I truly don't know what else I can say or do in order to make you understand that it is US who are watching YOUR backs, not THEM! We need your help and your support, so that we can work together to make change happen. Flight attendants need to know that you, our passengers, have complete understanding of what has been, and is still to this day truly happening in this industry, and that you can now see clearly through the very cleverly disguised and ambitious corporate smoke screen, that has been provided for you by these Corporate entities to look through for all these years. Flight attendants everywhere need to know that you believe that what I am telling you in this book is the truth, and that you will take that very TRUTH and STAND behind us with it, staying supportive of us, and of what we are trying to accomplish for all of you, as well as for our profession and company's restitution. We need to make sure that these so called Commercial Airline Company leaders that have so seriously devastated this Aviation Industry, are held accountable for their malfeasance, and we know that the only way we can be truly successful in accomplishing that very huge and incredibly difficult, and for some, that seemingly impossible task, is with you and your complete support! We need you so very much. This Industry needs you so very much! Until now, I had never quite understood why some people had such a tremendous fear of flying because, I have always been nothing but completely fascinated by every aspect of aviation, and have had a consistent and undying love affair with flying, all of my life. I've traveled the world over, and have taken my children and family with me on numerous times when I've gone off on my very many adventures. I have advocated to many of my passengers on more that one occasion, about how safe traveling by air was because I truly believed that once, and that is exactly how I have felt. Once in awhile, I would come across a passenger in-flight who would show signs of extreme anxiety at the sheer fact of having to be on board an airplane. The all consuming fear of flying would actually cause him/her to start sobbing hysterically out of control (and this was sometimes before take off), making it necessary for me, or any one of us, to take a few minutes and sit in the seat next to them in order to try and calm them down. I discovered that I could always convince them of how safe air travel really was, by simply using the amount of years that I had been flying as a flight attendant for American Airlines as an example. That analogy would give them more times than not, some amount of comfort as it then allowed them to rationalize that if I had been up in the skies flying for so many years on a continuous basis, and I was still around, the odds were better than just fairly good, that it was indeed a safe way to travel.   The unfortunate problem I am currently facing though, as an employee on the inside privy to observations of too many unacceptable aircraft/safety violations being purposely ignored by American Airlines Management, is that I cannot in all good conscience give my passengers that same sense of things being "safe" up there that I once could, because I myself have seen first hand how we were all being exposed, crewmembers and passengers alike, to possible danger, by boarding flights, or in the flight attendants case, working flights that were less than stable, and that situation caused for me to no longer be able to be provided with that sense of safety! American Airlines will tell you that because I am currently not an active flight status, due to the fact that I have been on sick leave since December of 2006 due to unnecessary stress (that they will conveniently forget to mention they were the cause of), I am no longer privy to all of the inside scoops that previously kept me informed on the safety, or the lack of I should say, when it comes to the flight operations of the company. What they are so arrogantly failing to understand though, is the fact that there are plenty of American Airline flight attendants, who are on active flight status, and are keeping me posted on what is going on within company walls, while I remain on the outside of those walls, and besides their overlooking that very fact, I am capable of reading, and I've been able to read in every major newspaper in the country, just like the rest of you, about the 900 flights that the FAA forced American Airlines to ground (that's just in one day), in order for our aircrafts to be inspected for missed or conveniently "ignored" and "deferred" safety maintenance issues, and those 900 flights aren't even inclusive of the many other aircrafts that were also later grounded, including the McDonnell Douglas DC9's (Super 80's), which when inspected, were consequently found to have electrical wiring problems that had needed immediate attention. Of course, nothing was ever mentioned about the fact that those very same aircrafts were knowingly allowed to be continuously flown in that compromised manner, much the same way that Southwest Airlines had knowingly continued flying their aircrafts which were found to have hairline cracks on their fuselage. The very big difference here though, is that when Southwest Airlines got caught, and then got slapped by the FAA with a $40 million dollar fine, they publicly owned up to their disgraceful behavior, and gave their somewhat tepid apology to the flying public. American Airlines Corporate on the other hand, quickly went on to make sure it was publicly noted, that they were not "busted" like Southwest Airlines was, and wanted it to be perfectly clear to everyone that they "willingly" offered our aircrafts up to the FAA for similar inspections, thereby coming across to the public as if they were of a forthright nature, and completely caring about our safety, and of course, had absolutely no possible idea, not even an inkling, as to the FACT that our aging McDonnell Douglas DC9 (Super80) aircraft fleet, was experiencing electrical wiring problems. Well, I have to give credit, where credit is due, and I have to say, you're pretty fast on your feet Mr. Arpey. The amazing public display of heartfelt concern you managed to muster up not only for our passengers, but your for your "lower food chain employees" as well (and we all know how you really feel about us), when you almost got caught with your pants down like Southwest did, almost made me think you really cared. You're good! That innocent appearing "oh my gosh we had no idea" face, as well as the old reliable song and dance routine you presented to all of our passengers and the rest of the flying public, was truly a "brilliant" and "inspirational" move on your part, and as convincing as always, because it was what completely saved your corporate asses from a possible huge FAA fine similar to that of Southwest Airlines, and that after all, is what all of you were really concerned about; money, money, and more money! American Airlines Labor employees have been working under the constant menacing orders of our Corporate "Heil Hitler Gestapo" management, for what seems like an eternity, and we have all learned to read between your corporate lines unmistakably well. American Airlines Corporate management can deny everything that you have just read in this book, until the cows come home for all I care, and it is with certainty that they will. But all their denial is still not going to change the FACTS as they stand, and FACTS don't LIE! They are of the exact same concept as that of the TRUTH. The FACTS are just that. It is not opinion that can be interpreted in different ways by different people. They are FACTS! One day you and your friends are going to have to answer to a much higher power than yourself, and that sir, is a FACT! I will say a little prayer for you. A few months ago, many of you were lucky enough to be home and not traveling during the inexcusable airline companies self created chaos, when those very FACTS materialized in the form of hundreds of FAA mandated

Commercial Airline aircraft inspection groundings, for possible safety violations committed by none other than the previously mentioned airline companies corporate leaders, and you, the flying public, were able to witness it all for yourselves, while in the comfort of your own homes on your television sets, as it was all being filmed LIVE, and played on every news channel in the country. The rest of our passengers, who did have air travel plans and reservations, found themselves caught right square in the middle of those unfortunate FAA mandatory aircraft groundings, which caused massive, delays that succumbed to hundred of flight cancellations, all   causing unnecessary and unjustifiable travel disruption as well as inconvenience, to our passengers. If by chance I missed reading any of the details in the newspapers, all I had to do was turn on my own t v, and I could watch the news media reporting for hours on end, of the current compromised safety of commercial airlines. American Airlines had some groundings of their own. The "unsafe" and "unethical" manner in which my company has been operating under, for quite some time now, and the very abandoned and run down condition in which my airline currently finds itself in, are both issues that I have been protesting against for a few years now. I am presently facing company retribution over those very issues that have obviously gotten so blatant and out of control, that it no longer could be kept hidden from you, the flying public. The entire corporate created nightmare has finally begun to unravel right in front of the corporate faces who responsible for it all! What irony! I suppose all of you seeing that on your own television sets, or reading it in your newspapers somewhat validates for me, what I have known for some time now, and have been reporting and complaining about for a few years now to American Airlines LAX management, as well as to our self proclaimed top banana, CEO Mr. Gerald Arpey himself. I actually took the time to personally write a letter to him immediately after I refused to fly a trip for the third time in a period of two years because I did not feel safe, and in that letter I wrote to him, I literally begged him to please investigate LAX Flight Service Management, for their unbridled and beyond reproach attitude towards flight attendants protesting against compromised aircrafts/flights not being checked out thoroughly enough before being taken up to the skies, but his response a couple of months later, basically stated that I was making some "serious accusations" about LAX Management, and that he agreed that they were justified in the disciplinary actions taken against me for not following company rule # 7 which states that "insubordination" will not be tolerated, and blah, blah, blah, and that as an American Airlines employee, I must blah, blah, blah and furthermore, blah, blah, blah! In closing, he warned me that I better get a handle on my "insubordinate" attitude and stop challenging LAX Flight Service and start doing what I was told! Well, my, my, my, Mr. Arpey, sir. A year and a half after having the honor of being ostracized by your "worshipness" in that response letter you sent me for doing MY JOB, you and the rest of your corporate clowns got busted by no other than the FAA for failure to maintain our aircrafts in a SAFE and AIRWORTHY flying condition. Imagine that! Karma, you think? Tell me, Mr. Arpey, sir, did you tell the FAA inspectors that they too were making some "serious accusations", when they informed you that we had some McDonald Douglas DC9's that were experiencing electrical wiring problem? Did you also suggest to them sir, that they get a handle on their "insubordinate" attitudes as well? I am just curious! My dear passengers, when American Airlines Corporate management decides to terminate my 32 year employment for going public with this information, and they will, believe me, if they haven't done it already before you even read this book, it is going to be real interesting what reason they are going to give for my termination. Stay tuned, I'll let you know. All I know is that they better start thinking of some excuse to use other than the usual corporate choice of "disgruntled employee" as the reason for the termination, because I really don't think that particular excuse is going to "fly" (pun intended) very well for them. On April 2, 2008, I was christened a "lean mean defibrillator using life saving hero machine" remember? American Airlines flew me to Corporate Headquarters in DFW, and put on that flight attendant award ceremony in our honor, remember? So my question is; who in their right mind would desecrate the honor of a full fledged American Airlines flight attendant life saving hero, by later calling them a "disgruntled employee"? Besides that being a totally ridiculous contradiction, I haven't returned to work since December of 2006 so how could I have gotten disgruntled from home? I am sure that they will try to come up with something they can accuse me of, to be deserving of my employment termination from American Airlines, they always do! To ensure that every single one of you out there, who use air travel as a means of transportation, stay completely informed at all times about the safety and the security of the flights you will be taking on board American Airlines, I know for a fact that there are many others like myself, who are employed, not only by this company, but by this entire industry, who are just as concerned, and will always try to somehow communicate the facts to you in some way or another, so that the information you should have at hand, will permit you to make the correct and informed decisions with regards to your air travel, your safety and that of your loved ones. It definitely seems as if the underhanded and deceitful manner in which American Airlines greedy CEO Mr. Gerald Arpey, and his corporate entourage have been running our airline, is beginning to finally catch up with him, from what I can see all over the news media. The corporate airline leadership which took over the Aviation Industry in the early 1970's, and has concurrently managed the airline companies up until, and including the present time, have systematically annihilated this once magniloquent airline company that I work for (by the time you're reading this, probably "worked" for), as well as the entire Aviation Industry. That movement was led by Eastern and Continental Airlines CEO, Mr. Lorenzo, and sadly, our very own American Airlines CEO, Mr. Robert Crandall, to name just a couple. These people, along with the help of their many greedy associates, are responsible for the demise of the upscale social class and eloquence that were once associated with the Aviation Industry, and was the standard staple that could be found on every commercial airline flight. At one time, traveling on a commercial airline was a huge event that was not at all common, and so was working for one. It was during the last bit of that golden era of aviation that I was fortunate enough to have stepped in and experience the nuance of my profession. Sadly, the kids today who are employed by American Airlines as flight attendants will never have an instance of that direct knowledge those of us who have been around for a while possess. The unfortunate running of the commercial airline companies into the ground is destroying the lives of the many loyal and hard working employees. It has taken all of us; the Pilots, Flight Attendants, Mechanics, Cabin Service, Gate Agents etc. etc to build up American Airlines to the huge airline company you know today. We did it with our sweat, diligence, hard work, loyalty and most importantly, our hearts. We are the ones who stand to lose everything, up to and including our retirement. They on the other hand, already have their "golden parachute" money they have literally stolen from us, and drained from our company. Unlike the rest of us, they're financially set for a couple of lifetimes, whether our company goes under or not, and they do not care about this company the way the rest of us do. We see it as the company that houses the many years we have given it, and sacrificed for its well being and success. They, on the other hand see it and YOU, the passenger, as REVENUE, REVENUE, and REVENUE! That is the true story. Much damage has indeed been done, folks, but here's the thing. I believe with all my heart, that if all of us together, Labor employees and passengers, begin focusing on finding ways to begin the restitution of this incredible Aviation Industry's Commercial Airline Companies, starting with lobbying Congress to immediately begin implementing laws that would prevent individuals, such as the corrupt ones that are presently running some of our airlines, from making monetary self serving decisions, that directly affect the well being and SAFETY of the greater flying public, we can shake things up and make much needed change happen! Commercial air travel is not going to disappear altogether. That is a fact! It is the number one form as well as the fastest way of travel for the business as well as the pleasure flyers. No one, especially big business and Government officials, are going to all of a sudden start thinking; "Hey, you know what"? "I'll just take a train across the country to that other coast for that really important meeting I need to get to in a few days, or the Presidential Campaign Tour, so I guess that means that I'll just have to leave five days earlier than planned" to make sure I get where I need to be"! Yeah! Right! Like that's ever going to happen! Believe me, the Commercial Airlines are here to stay; certainly not all of them, but some of them. The questions are though, which ones, at whose expense, at what kind of quality and most importantly how SAFE? Which airline companies are going to be able to be the ones that survive all of the on going corporate corruption and greed, and be left over for the rest of us, and will we even want to fly on that garbage? (It will no doubt be expensive garbage to boot) because that is exactly what will be left over for us; garbage disguised and a Commercial Airline company, and isn't that what we're almost experiencing already? Presently, American Airlines and all others as well, are trying to tell us through the media air waves, that the reason the airline companies are in such financial trouble is because of the high fuel costs, therefore, they have no other choice but to start charging you, the flying consumer, for everything they can think of to charge you for, when you travel on their airline, and they are already warning the you about how the prices of air fare are going to sky rocket, all the while letting you know how very sorry they all are, but that the situation cannot be helped because it is the cost of fuel that is the culprit, after all, and surely you cannot hold them responsible for something that is out of their control. Isn't that the jest of what you are listening to on the news as well as shows such as Larry King Live, by the ATA guest he had on the other night? Well, let me tell you that these corporate leaders are plenty responsible for what seems to be the inevitable demolition that is on its way, which will cause the extinction of many of the current airline companies that are barely hanging on to existence by a thread, because Lords knows that the ones they have already disappeared aren't enough for them! Airline companies corporate management executives have paid themselves billions and billions of dollars in salaries, perks, bonuses, benefits etc. etc. in the 32 + years that I've been around, and I am sure that if you were to combine all of those billions and billions of dollars from every airline company out there, and then add them all up, the dollar amount that would come up as total would be beyond astronomical! Hey, maybe that's exactly what someone needs to do, because that way, we would all be able to actually experience the art of being "blown away" together, by the actual dollar amount we would see on paper! These people have been taking and taking and taking from these airline companies until they have finally sucked them dry, with absolutely no accountability or responsibility to be shown by any one of them, for the devastation they have caused to this industry and all of its great, hard working and loyal employees! Let's take a trip down memory lane and count together the number of airline companies this great type of leadership has managed to obliterate into virtual non existence, shall we? We won't name all of them though okay, only a few of the big ones, so that way, I don't end up with so many names, that it would necessitate my having to write an entire chapter on Commercial Airline companies that have plummeted into non existence by greed and corruption, entitled: "The Corporate Demolition of Commercial Airline Companies for Dummies Manual", and you won't be forced to have to read it! Ready? Braniff Airways, Eastern Airlines, Pan American Airlines (Pan Am), Trans World Airlines (TWA), Western Air Lines ("the only way to fly") Air Cal, Pacific Southwest Airlines (PSA), Continental Airlines ("we really move our tails for you" version), and that's just to name a few. Do we truly understand the severity of what is going on here? The defalcation of funds, the grotesque travesty of employee trust, the embodiment of greed and self gratification, the many years of incendiary incompetence used for leading a company towards a slow but spiraling downward direction, right into the ground like a dart, and lest not we forget, the reprehensible, blatant insensibility and cavalier attitude, continuously shown to "lower food chain" company employees as well as the flying public (that's YOU), especially when it comes to our SAFETY, are all appropriate, more than well deserving and "on point" descriptive of the corporate leadership managing that is presently in progress in the Aviation Industry's Commercial Airline companies in the United States of America! The detriment and devastation that these self empowered, self rewarding egotistically emblazoned airline company CEOs and their counterparts have been allowed to commit for so many years now, can no longer be ignored or be allowed to continue, and we can no longer afford to tolerate such criminal behavior, if we want this Industry's Commercial Airlines, that we are all so very dependant on (like we are on oil), as our most important form of travel for business as well as pleasure, to remain as safe as it once was. The safety of the flying public, while traveling on any Commercial Airline Company, is the ultimate responsibility of the company we are traveling on, as well as the Federal Aviation Administration (FAA), whose entity exist for the sole purpose of policing the skies of the United States, as well as making sure that ALL Commercial Airline companies are following mandated FAA regulations, and the Federal Bureau of Investigation (FBI), who have the responsibility to uphold and enforce both civil and criminal prosecution of infractions against Federal Aviation Laws (FARS) that affect All Commercial Airline Crew Members, as well as the flying public traveling on them.   Unfortunately at the present time, neither the Corporate Leadership of the Commercial Airline Companies, nor the U.S. Government entities who are overseeing the airline companies, are doing the jobs that they are responsible for, which is that of ensuring our safety. Besides the fact that the once # 1 priority level of "Public and Flight Crew Member" safety has now been shifted to a much lesser priority level, because of the insatiable greed of the current Corporate Leaderships running the airlines, which has automatically lead to more and more corruption, thereby more and more criminal behavior within the Aviation Industry, there is a more serious and alarming present danger facing the flying public as well as the Commercial Airline Flight Crew Members, regarding all of our "safety". To safeguard their all consuming monetary greed, or power, or both, these EXTREMELY powerful, "above the law" mentality Corporate as well as high Government official entities, such as American Airlines and the FAA for example, have developed an impenetrable liaison with one another, allowing the path for complete and mutual corroboration for the sole purpose of maintaining the "safety" of their very prosperous livelihoods, as well as that "ultimate" power they posses at whatever cost; consequently catapulting the once elite and completely

SAFE and airworthy Commercial Airline companies, as well as the entire Aviation Industry, into the currently depraved, perverted, defiled, morally decayed, debased and extremely deteriorated, and most importantly of all, "UNSAFE" condition we have all unfortunately come to know all too well! If we are ever to be able to once again know with certainty that when we take to the skies on Commercial Airline aircrafts, everything is being done that can be done to ensure our safety at ALL times, then it is IMPERATIVE, that together, YOU and US, have to immediately take on the most difficult challenge of all time challenges and begin the journey of the much needed reparation process, a "cleaning house" so to speak, in order for necessary CHANGE to happen that will permit us to restore the Commercial Airline companies as well as the entire Aviation Industry back to its original form of operation, before all of its criminal corruption began, which was that of a SAFE, DEPENDABLE, and incredibly EXCITING manner of transportation which the flying public and Commercial Airline Crew Members could indisputably depend on! Together, we must all STAND UP and SPEAK UP loudly in protest against the desecration of that very sanctity. We need to stop these people from hiding behind their many scapegoats such as High Fuel Prices, Competitive Ticket Pricing, Labor Costs, and the biggest and most shameful cop out of all time, September 11th 2001, and call them on misuse and mismanagement of company money. It's not like they didn't know all of this was eventually coming and they did NOTHING to prepare our airline companies for the challenges they knew we would sooner rather than later, be one day facing. They have been much too busy with their continuous glutinous obsession with their bonus money and they dropped the ball on everything else! To put this all in a nutshell perspective, they've been yacht and mansion shopping for years at the expense of all of us, meanwhile, the rest of us are dealing with cutbacks here, cutbacks there and cutbacks everywhere. Now they are taking it a step further and completely disregarding our SAFETY with cutbacks there too! If that is just too unbelievable for some of you to fathom, all you have to do is bring back the horrors of Septembers 11th, 2001 to your memory, which was a completely avoidable and unforgivably overlooked tragedy, that I will forever hold the leadership of the two airlines involved; American Airlines and United Airline's partially responsible for, because of their total lack of interest in spending the necessary money in order to train their Flight Crews properly, as well as give us the information we desperately needed and should have years ago already. AlQueda wasn't born on that day, and no one is going to convince me that American Airlines or United Airlines, and all the other airlines for that matter, didn't know about them or Bin Laden's threats regarding bombing the World Trade Towers in New York City. We should have been better prepared. If you find that you're still not completely convinced that these people who are in charge of running the airline companies are very "bad" and "unconscionable" people behaving "criminally", then take a real good look at how deteriorated our airline companies' have become. We are all just one very short step away from the catastrophic disaster of all catastrophic disasters, so ask yourselves this question; "Do I really want to find myself on a Commercial Airline jet, flying at 39,000 feet, when the light bulb finally goes on in my head, and I realize that not STANDING up with the Flight Crews and Labor employees in PROTEST for the blatant disregard these Corporate Leaders and High Government Officials have shown for my SAFETY, is about to cost not only my life, but the lives of my loved ones who unfortunately happen to be traveling with me"? Everything that you have seen on the news lately regarding the grounding of hundreds of aircrafts due to their poor maintenance, electrical wiring issues or cracks through the aircrafts fuselages, not to mention that little FYI, that American Airlines has the second oldest fleet in the United States of America, second to Northwest Orient, should show you without a doubt, that when these big airline company execs think about their constant cutbacks, your safety and mine doesn't factor into their decisions, otherwise the situation with those grounded aircrafts having maintenance issues, would have never happened. During those couple of weeks that we were dealing with all those aircraft groundings, I watched many of you being interviewed by the news media and I have to say, I was really amazed and shocked at how many of you had missed the severity of the situation, and didn't even bring up the fact that had the FAA inspectors not grounded those American Airlines planes, your flight might have taken off on one of the DC 9 (Super 80) who had loose electrical wiring problems. That is what all of you should have not only been complaining about, but you should have been SCREAMING at the top of your lungs about, letting all these airline company leaders know that your SAFETY cannot and will not be compromised! That should have been what every single one of you out there, should have found deplorable! Ask Arpey if he would have put his family on one of those compromised aircrafts. Trust me, even though he would lie through his teeth and say he would, the answer would be an unequivocal NO, yet he finds nothing wrong with transporting you and your family as well as mine on them, I know because that is the reason I am currently not flying, remember? I refused three trips in a period of 2 years because of SAFETY compromised aircrafts/flights. If I am a flight attendant and I won't go, what does that tell you? So many of you were stuck at airports waiting for straight shooting answers from the airline spokespeople about the absurdity of so many flight cancellations, and they did their usual song and dance routines for you instead the way they always do, because telling you the real truth would just make them all look like the dumb asses that some of them are. Many of you were extremely angry, and as far as I am concerned, you had every right to be, because your time is just as important to you as theirs is to them. Although I don't really know why they think their time is so important because from what I know as an employee and what I saw on t v, all they seem to be good at is creating passengers chaos! Anyway, the two main complaints that I heard from many of you out there were about the inconvenience of your delayed or cancelled flights, as well as the "oh well, that's too bad" attitude that you were receiving from some of the employees you spoke with. First of all, let me start by saying that I completely agree with your anger and frustrations with both of those issues you had to deal with. As a passenger, hell, as a non reving flight attendant traveling on my days off with my family, I would have been just as upset as many of you. Here's the difference with your anger as opposed to mine though, and this is the part I really need you to understand. Yes, the inconvenience of a cancelled or delayed flight is a nightmare, although many times there are legitimate reasons for them and they happen, that's just the nature of the beast, but the magnitude of the flight delays and cancellations you experience during those FAA groundings were not only completely inexcusable, they were also criminal because of the reasons for the groundings. Yes, the "I don't really give a rats ass" employee attitude towards you is uncalled for and just rude, and all I can say about that without sounding like an American Airlines corporate spokesperson with a bunch of lame excuses (I'd rather be dead), is that if you stop and think about it for a minute or two, perhaps those couple of employees who spoke to you in that cavalier manner had reached their maximum capacity for diplomatically handling one more excessively rude and belligerent passenger, and unfortunately by the time it was your turn to speak your mind about the distressing situation, he/she had already been showered with all of those colorful words many of you sometimes share with us, for the 50th time, and that's just in the last three nightmarish hours since he/she had reported for work, therefore, he/she shuts it down! Please don't think that I am in any way saying to you that shutting down and treating your situations with indifference is okay, because it is not. But unfortunately, it is what many of us do after a while, when we get one passenger after another screaming obscenities at us, as if it were us who caused your situation, and although we all wear the American Airlines uniform because we work for them, we don't own the company therefore have no say whatsoever when corporate employees make decisions that are irresponsible and affect all of us adversely, such as the negligent one American Airlines Corporate management made when they decided to check and defer the DC9 electrical maintenance. Not providing our passengers with SAFE airworthy aircrafts that the FAA has to then ground for inspections, causing massive delays and hundreds of cancellations for our passengers is absolutely not okay. But those complaints that I just mentioned, which were the only ones I heard all of you mention, are pale in comparison to the compromised equipment they were willing to have all of you board and take to the skies. I for one don't think that getting anywhere on time or without delay is worth risking your life for, and from what I heard from many of you on the television, is that you missed the whole point of why those hundreds of aircrafts were being grounded! It is an Industry known fact that because most of these huge powerful airline companies corporate leaders, have an FAA/Airline Company liaison with a few upper FAA management supervisors, who "strongly" instruct the inspectors they send out to inspect the maintenance of these airline companies aircrafts for safety violations, to conveniently not see things that are mechanically not kosher with the aircrafts when inspecting the planes, and clear them to fly. Now, try and tell me how that is not CRIMINAL behavior by the very people we depend on to police our skies as well as our Commercial Airline companies! If God forbid, one of those mechanically compromised aircrafts that the FAA inspector let slide by, unfortunately crashed and burned along with the hundreds of unsuspecting passengers that are on board, because of a malfunction caused by that very same "known" mechanical issue that was discovered while the aircraft was still on the ground and should have been repaired there, or taken out of service, would that not constitute holding the people responsible for the accident and the deaths of all those passengers, and charging them with MURDER? Let me use another example that is exactly in point. With all the information and all of the statistics we are all constantly bombarded with today, about the consequences that can come from drinking alcohol, getting drunk and then "knowingly" getting behind the wheel of your car and driving, thereby killing someone, we all know that there will still be those irresponsible idiots out there who "knowingly" drink and then drive, right? Well, when that drunk driver "knowingly" gets behind the wheel of his car, very aware of the information and statistics that are out there, but ignorantly and arrogantly thinks that the tragedy of killing another person while driving drunk happens to other people and not him, and then all of a sudden, someone is in fact dead because of his negligent attitude and behavior, shouldn't he be held accountable for that life or lives he took and be charged with MURDER? What I need to know that all of you out there understand is that there is only one difference between a drunk driver killing one or two people, and American Airlines Corporate managers or any other Commercial Airline Corporate managers killing hundreds of people, and that is the amount of people killed. Anyway you look at either situation, when people die at the hands of others who put them in a compromised situation that they "knew" could possibly have that kind of devastating outcome, should they not then be held accountable for their deplorable actions? Up until now, these airline company leaders have been very lucky that nothing catastrophic has happened from their negligence, but what are the rest of us going to do about the way they seem to be running many things they shouldn't be, on LUCK? What is it going to take for all of you to get as upset as I am about the constant disregard they show us for our very SAFETY? Is it going to take another September 11th? I pray to God, you're answer is NO! American Airlines management personnel is great at making a tremendous mess with things, and then putting us on the front lines to take all he heat for their stupidity! I am trying to fight for all of us so that things start to change, but a few of us can't do it by ourselves, WE need YOU, and YOU need US! The "corporate bullshit" conversations, led by our very own CEO, Mr. Arpey, held in their board room meetings sound something like this: "Hey guys guess what? You are all aware of how our airline, which is equipped with the second oldest aircraft fleet flying in the skies today, is in dire need of newer aircraft replacements, right? Well, to date, not a single one of those tough old birds have fallen out of the sky yet, right? Well, in lieu of that, what do you guys say, we hold off on replacing them until that happens, and we throw this and last year's extra profit that the company yielded, into our "bonuses bucket", alongside the remaining 2001 Government bail out money we still have in there, that we got from the September 11th tragedy from our buddies, and write ourselves some nice big checks? Everybody in favor of that say YAY! When it should have sounded like this: "Hey guys, guess what? You are all aware of how our airline, which is equipped with the second oldest aircraft fleet flying in the skies today, is in dire need of newer aircraft replacements, right? Well, before something catastrophic happens to one of our flights, that ends up unnecessarily taking the lives of hundreds of our innocent loyal passengers, as well as many of our "beloved" Crew Members (okay!

over reaching a bit), what do you guys say, we find that September 11th, 2001 Government bail out money that was given to us by our "keeping the skies airworthy police" (okay! over reaching again), that we seemed to have misplaced somewhere, and put that money, together with this year and last year's extra profits which the company yielded, and that, along with the billions of dollars in Labor concession money that our Labor employees have been giving us for quite a few years now, should be more than sufficient enough money to take care of all of our current financial woes, and start the process of the purchasing new and better fuel efficient aircrafts to begin replacing our current ones, instead of paying ourselves such "bloated undeserved bonuses", and while we're at it, let's get working on developing a program for our Flight Operation's Crewmembers, especially the flight attendants, who are the "front lines of passenger defense", instructing them more thoroughly on the current type of "suicidal bombing" hijacking as well as teaching them plausible self defense maneuvers, as opposed to the "take me to Cuba" beware of Stockholm syndrome hijacking, which is fast becoming "obsolete" and somewhat of an "ineffective" training, that they are still unbelievably receiving in their yearly emergency training as of late, which is of no real use against the terrorist type hijacking that exists today, to ensure that there is absolutely no room for any more needless HIGH FATALITY accidents involving American Airline's, in the foreseeable future, such as the horrifying, and completely unavoidable one that we're partly responsible for that occurred on September 11th, 2001! All in favor say, YAY! Okay, so, I know that's not the real world out there, and that that entire skit you just read, from beginning to end is only Alicia's current "pipe dream", but my God, I have to warn you, that it better start becoming Alicia's, as well as everybody else out there's "reality" if we intend on continuing to use commercial air travel as our number one form of transportation from one state or country to another, because the ramifications we will face if it doesn't, will be of the deadliest kind! Those entities who are currently in charge of the Commercial Airline companies, as well as the entire Aviation Industry, have been accorded with such immense power, and have been given an unlimited amount of trust from all of us, to represent us as and make the big decisions that affect not only our very livelihoods, but our very lives, and all you have seen fit to do for that great honor you've been given, is use it to your own capricious advantage, making yourselves wealthy at the tremendous cost, of not only all the rest of us, but our beloved airline company, American Airlines, as well! Much shame and dishonor shall walk the path alongside you for the rest of your lives, regardless of whether you understand that now, or sometime in your future! Hey, Corporate management at American Airlines, listen up! I don't know if you realize it or not, but right now there is a war going on between the US and Iraq which will probably cause fuel prices to soon take another huge flying leap, which will quickly become a scenario much worse than the one we are currently finding ourselves facing at the moment, so don't you think that maybe NOW would be an excellent time, for you to really start thinking about planning for that fuel price increase that's undoubtedly headed our way, and start "Hedging", like Southwest and JetBlue did years ago, to guarantee ourselves at least a "locked fuel price" of $4 to $5 dollars a gallon, as opposed to waiting a couple more years from now (like you unfortunately did before), where it will then probably be at $10 to $11 or even maybe $12 dollars a gallon, or is the "real" reason that you haven't "Hedged" our company yet, is because in order to do that, the amount of money, for whatever amount of years we would be "hedging" at the "locked in" price, has to be paid in full up front, and American Airline's ready cash flow, has been too financially sucked dry, from all of your corporate frivolous and wasteful spending, thereby making the company too financially strapped to allow us to participate in that incredibly smart and money saving strategy! How very, very sad for the rest of us, Mr. Arpey, who unfortunately will not be in the financially elite position that you and your friends are presently in, which is that of walking away from American Airlines, with the billions and billions of dollars you all have taken from this company, before annihilating it completely! My dear passengers and fellow employees, that is exactly what our corporate leadership has been doing for what has been quite some time now, with the unwitting aid, as well as blessing no less, from all of the rest of us, and our "do nothing", "non protesting", "non challenging", "non confrontational", "co dependency", "denial mindset" and last but certainly not least, the "endless excuses". I cannot begin to count the amount of times when I have heard my co workers, who I have first hand knowledge that they are most of the time, completely worldly and highly intelligent people, "whine" to me the most ridiculous verbiage, such as "it's not just our company that's suffering, Alicia", it's everybody, or "Alicia, it's the same way in every corporation out there", or "Alicia, we are never going to be able to change things back to how they once were", or "It's just the way things are Alicia, get use to it", or my favorite one of all time, which I actually heard come straight out of my ex APFA UNION President, Tommie Hutto-Blake's mouth during a brief telephone conversation we shared, and that one was: "Alicia, as long as the Republicans are in office, that's just how it is"! What? What was that? I mean, I am a registered Democrat (barely), not a Republican (definitely), so I sort of got the jest of what she was trying to say, which was basically that Democrats = Poor and almost non existent Middle Class, and Republicans = Dumb Ass United States President, Oil, an the Filthy Rich, and the Pretentious Wannabe Rich! I think that most of America not only gets that correlation, but we are actually living it! But Dear God in Heaven, how and when did the

Republicans become a scapegoat, and the mother lode excuse of excuses, for flight attendants not STANDING united and strong, while at the same time, demanding from our corporate leaders to cease and desist from their greed and corruption, as we remain completely focused instead, on making positive change happen, that can help us to start getting out from under this deplorable working environment we have been allowing ourselves to fester in for years now. I hate to burst your bubble Tommie, but as much as I would love to, we can't blame our airline's current financially pathetic woes on the Republican Party! You may have, maybe, the tiniest amount of validity possible for a point, as far as the fact that many of the corporate individuals at American Airlines, that are currently running this "dog and pony show" and are trying to pass that off to our passengers as a legitimate and respectable airline company, unsuccessfully I might add, I would venture to say are Republicans, but other than that, really, what's your point? The incredibly sad as well as embarrassing bottom line here is, WE, the American Airlines Labor employees, as well as all other non UNION employees, except for Corporate and even most of the "lower food chain management employees", have ALLOWED American Airline's Corporate people to slowly and methodically take everything many of us have worked incredibly hard for and for many years, by simply looking the other way, doing absolutely nothing, and hoping in vain, that somehow it will either all work itself out in time, or at least not completely blow up and dissipate before reaching that "Golden Age of Retirement! That, my fellow flight attendants, is the absolute TRUTH and whether you like it or not, doesn't really matter or change the very fact that we are our own worst enemies. Up until now, we, the flight attendants and all other American Airline's non Corporate employees, have been part of the "problem", and now we need to quickly become part of the "solution", and when I say quickly, that's exactly what I mean, because we are going to most certainly run out of time here pretty soon, in regards to being able to come up with a plausible plan that could help us save our company, American Airlines, from being taken under, by the current infestation of barracudas that are running it! The devastating affects that their malignant actions have caused through the years, have finally reached us all, employees and passengers alike, and there's nowhere to run and hide anymore. If you happen to be one of the already retired flight attendants, who considers yourself lucky, and quite truly believe yourself to be safe from the repercussions that would surely come, from our company's corporate leaders completely bankrupting American Airlines, or better yet, annihilating it to the point where it ends up being forced to take the oblivious extinction route, which is much the same route that Eastern Airlines, as well as many of the others have already been forced to take, you are living under much misguided misconception, and my suggestion to all of you is that you seriously might want to chew on this for a few minutes: If American Airlines is obliterated from existence, then there is no more American Airlines, right? So if there is no more American Airlines, then naturally, there is no more American Airlines retirement money to be allotted, for all of you already retired American Airline's flight attendants every month, that are currently feeling so "lucky!" In case many of you have forgotten, let me just give you a quick reminder; that is EXACTLY what happened to the already retired Eastern Airline's flight attendants, who were anything but "lucky" or "safe", when their greed ridden and power hungry company CEO, Lorenzo and his corporate buddies, forced the once elite and thriving airline company, which at one time was the largest and primary passenger Commercial Airline serving the entire Northwestern and Southwestern parts of the United States, into bankruptcy in 1990, and then complete and irrevocable liquidation by 1991! Way to go, Mr. Lorenzo "Corporate" genius sir! The logic I am applying here is really quite simple if you stop to think about it. Certain causes such as this one, have certain inevitable results, and simple logic, which is itself the science of pure reasoning conforming to rationality, causes you, the already retired American Airline's flight attendant, to become irrational when you truly convince yourself that because you are in the retirement phase of your flight attendant profession, that no matter what happens to American Airlines, your retirement pension and benefits are thereby secure. I am sorry to be the one to have to break this to you, but you are not in much better shape than the rest of us out here, still working towards that retirement, you are presently, and quite possible temporarily enjoying, and no matter how you want to paint your situation, that is a FACT! The huge problem with this "corporate" way of running the Commercial Airlines is that the very people placed in charge of these companies, are no longer about the incredible Aviation Industry that the more senior of us once knew , or these days, about the indisputable necessity for SAFETY that cannot be allowed to be compromised for any reason, but rather, these current corporate leaders serve allegiance to one, and only one industry, and that is the self serving industry of financially lining their own pockets. Their message to the rest of us through their disrespectful conduct and blatant disregard reads loud and clear: "It's all for one and one for ME!" As someone who has been in this magnificent industry for 32 years now, it breaks my heart to see such defamation and utter lack of respect being shown to these once regal airline companies, such as Eastern Airlines, Inc. I suppose I am saddened so because I can imagine the incredibly hard work, sacrifice, pride, perseverance and most important of all, the love of aviation it must have taken for those early pioneers who founded these airlines, and I have always been and will forever be, grateful to these amazing individuals, who through their diligence, made it possible for the little, unimportant people like myself, to be able to not only be part of their ingénues and masterfully created Industry, but they have given every single one of us, the gift of having the ability to be able to do today (with amazing ease and regularity, I might add), what was considered a ridiculous impossibility way back when, and that is the ability to travel by air, in a machine apparatus, consisting of basically metal nuts and bolts, formed in the shape of a graceful giant bird, with the ability to get me to any destination around the world in record times. I know I have simplified its description immensely, but my point is that to this very day, for me, it remains an awesome phenomenon to be sure! Eastern Airlines, Inc. company pioneers were a huge part of facilitating that very gift we all enjoy today. It was founded in 1928 by Harold Frederick Pitcairn, and was originally known as Pitcairn Aviation, Inc. It was sold a year later and became Eastern Air Transport, until March 29, 1938, when it was once again sold to Edward V. Rickenbacker and his associates for $3,500,000.00, which today, that monetary amount sounds like a ridiculous absurdity. Rickenbacker, who was a former WW1 Ace, and had been general manager of Eastern since 1935, became President of the company and incorporated it as an independent company under the name of Eastern Airlines, Inc. in 1938. He remained President of Eastern Airlines from 1938- 1959. The airline flourished over the years, until the mid 1980's (Lorenzo days of doom), when they began suffering financial reverses. Unfortunately, many other great airline companies have followed suit. The kind of planning ahead that the leadership at Southwest Airlines engaged in, was smart, responsible and savvy, in regards to "hedging", and will be what gets them through the tough times ahead that this industry is facing. Unfortunately for all of us who are employed by American Airlines, our present corporate leadership is not thinking with that pioneer type of mindset, and what American keeps demonstrating to us over and over again is that they don't really give a rat's ass about us, or this company or anything else except money that they can extract from the company and its employees and that's obvious, because if they wanted our company to stay operating successfully, our airline company would not be finding itself in the severely deteriorated condition it is currently in, and we would be in a much stronger position than the one we are finding ourselves in today. My dear Passengers, please allow me to explain in more detail for you, the tremendous difference in the outcome of whether an airline company chooses to "hedge" or "not hedge". Jet fuel represents a critical expense category for any airline that is responsible for and carries at least 80% of its own fuel costs, and the airline companies that fall into that category are: Airtran Holdings, American West, "American", ATA, Continental, Delta, Frontier, Jet Blue, Midwest Air, Northwest, "Southwest", United and US Airways. During periods of rising oil prices, airlines can derive tangible benefits from hedging fuel costs, but despite these benefits, there are a number of domestic airline companies that do not follow the examples of the other airline companies that have incorporated hedging into their balance sheets, and American Airlines is one of those! Fuel is probably one of the biggest expenses for commercial airline companies. In studies that were conducted in 2003, fuel costs represented an average of over 16% of the total operating expenses, and although these "non hedging" airlines attempted to offset fuel costs by increasing fares as well as surcharges by $5-$10 dollars in 2004, due to the fact that they were experiencing a 25.9% compound annual increase in jet fuel costs, while at the same time the average airline pricing decreased by 0.1%, which is measured by revenue per available seat mile, these attempts at that very strategy have continuously failed because the "hedging" competitors have not needed to respond with similar increases in order to remain competitive with the "non hedgers", and besides that fact, those futile increase attempts have not been sufficient enough to make any real difference in offsetting any significant increase in fuel costs anyway. In addition to the very obvious importance of any airline company being able to control their operating expenses, especially the fuel costs, studies done on measurable fuel "hedging" have demonstrated that that very process inevitably increases the airline companies' value up to but not limited to an estimated 12-16%. While there are several factors that influence the measurable value, as of December 2003, the value of the airline companies, as measured by the companies' price to revenue ratio, have a positive correlation that is coefficient with the airline companies' level of fuel "hedging". The tremendous impact of rising fuel costs on the profitability of "hedged" and "non hedged" airline companies is very apparent in the year 2004. By not "hedging", airlines like American Airlines, are taking the serious risk of rising commodity prices into the company. Zea reports that "airline executives often comment on how "hedging" is not a core-competency, and that as long as competitors are not "hedged", it will be a level playing field", they go on to further state that "unfortunately, when fuel prices rise dramatically, airline companies, such as American Airlines, will not be able to pass all of the costs on their customers". Well, thank God for that because that would be YOU, who our current corporate circus clown management people would try to pass all the costs to; our passengers! The corporate leadership at Southwest Airlines apparently does not have the same insatiable greed as that of the corporate leadership of American Airlines, which American seems to so proudly and demonstratively tout around (corporate exec bonuses). Southwest's CEO Jim Parker reported that Southwest's profit of $26 million in the first quarter of 2004 would have been instead a loss of $8million, had they not been "hedged" against rising fuel costs. Imagine that! They used the simple theory of PLANNING AHEAD, and because of that clever move by them, the high fuel prices that are currently ravaging our Aviation Industry including my company, are not devastating their company in the manner which it is adding to the devastation of ours (most of our devastation comes from your corporate salaries and bonuses paid over a span of 32 years and counting)! Thanks so much for watching out for the rest of us employees, on your lower Labor food chain, Mr. look at me, I'm so arrogant, I made it on the cover of CEO of the Year Magazine! Southwest Airlines and JetBlue are the Aviation Industry current leaders when it comes to jet fuel "hedging". They are "hedged" today, as they were in 2003, with at that time, 82% and 40% of their expected 2004 fuel consumption "hedged" as of December 2003. From 2001 – 2003, Southwest Airlines reduced its annual fuel expense by $171 million dollars, $45 million dollars and $80 million dollars, respectively, through its fuel "hedging" operations. That's not "Chump Change" Mr. Arpey, sir, and besides that, it doesn't look to me like Southwest Airlines, CEO, Mr. Parker felt the need to take that substantial amount of "hedging" savings and line his and his buddies pockets with it, instead of putting it back into the company. Apparently for some people, such as Mr. Parker, their moral ethics dictate to them that putting the money back into the company to ensure its success as well as the continued livelihood of its "lower food chain" Labor employees, is undoubtedly the right thing to do! To be perfectly honest with you, Mr. Arpey sir, you and your friends could learn more than a few things from Mr. Parker and his friends, on how to run a Commercial Airline in the Aviation Industry, and actually succeed at it! That almost sounds like another book title for me! Anyway, other than that ridiculous show of negligence on the part of Southwest Airlines a few months back, when their aircrafts were grounded by the FAA after inspectors found that the hairline cracks that had been discovered on the fuselage of a couple of their aircrafts a year earlier, had not been repaired as promised, and they knowingly continued to fly those aircrafts in that compromised manner for a year, Southwest Airlines is faring more than fairly well, I'd say, during these current difficult times! I will even venture to say that the most difficult situation Southwest Airlines has been recently faced with, is probably having to swallow that completely avoidable, self inflicted negligent call they made, which forced them to have to fork up a $40 million dollar FAA fine that they were slapped with, which is a   substantial amount of money, that I am sure they are thinking now, could have been remained in the company and better used. Call me silly, but I think that if everyone who owned their own business, whatever type of business that might be, chose to run and operate it in the same way the corporate management idiots at American Airline's have run our airline company over the past few years, their companies would end up exactly at the same place ours seems to be heading, and that is straight into the ground like a DART! (No pun intended). Who hired these bafoons anyway, I know it wasn't me! Unlike the completely mistaken perception that many of you out there who are presently reading this book may have concluded about me, and that includes my fellow flight attendants at American Airlines as well as all of our other Labor employees, I am not responsible for the financial problems we are experiencing lately. Those are completely Corporate inflicted, and contrary to popular belief, I am not trying to add to the current woes that American Airlines is currently facing, trying to bankrupt them or any such thing. Trust me, I do not posses that kind of power, nor do I ever want to. I am also not making you privy to the information in this book, for the sole purpose of being vindictive towards American Airlines Corporate management employees and CEO, Mr. Gerald Arpey, because of the appalling and horrendous behavior they have chosen to utilize and then shower me with, for what has been probably the last four to five years of my flying career, of which the last two have been the absolute worst! American Airlines is the company I have worked for in excess of 32 years, and is one I have given my allegiance to and have worked hard and given much of my life to, in order to secure its prosperity as well its success. My loyalty to American Airlines remains as strong today, as it did when I started back in 1976, but make no mistake that for me, the company known as American Airlines consists of Flight Attendants, Pilots, Mechanics, Cabin Service, Ground Personnel, Reservation and Gate Agents, Crew Schedule and Crew Tracking, and the people who work all of those departments within American Airlines. They are the "only" people I consider my piers. Sadly, the despicable treatment from American Airlines Corporate management and its "lower food chain management", that I have been on the receiving end of, is being shown and expressed to me for the simple reason that, it has not been convenient for them to have me, and other flight attendants like me, staying the course of doing the job I was hired to do in May of 1976, which is primarily that of keeping YOU, my passengers, SAFE, to the utmost of my ability, along with my fellow Crewmembers as well as myself. That has been my career's lifelong pledge, not only to me but to my fellow Crew Members as well as to all of you. That pledge which was heightened to an even higher level, if that's possible, after the needless tragedy that occurred on September 11th, 2001, the unspeakable day that took the lives of my beloved Flight Attendant and Cockpit Crew families, who I respectfully vowed never to forget, will remain strong and clear for the duration of my flying career. The souls of those crewmembers and passengers forever lost to us on that day, are what reach out to the very core of my heart, and give me the daily strength and the courage that I need, to be able to battle against the "Mighty American Airlines Corporate Machine", and others like it, in order to make sure without any questionable or reasonable doubt, that I did everything within my power, so that another unnecessary catastrophic tragedy such as September 11th never, ever happens again! That, dear passengers, is the most important description, of all the other many descriptions, that come attached to the profession of the commercial airline flight attendant. In closing, I can only say to all of you that even though flight attendants might give off the impression to many of you at times that we don't really care about you, or that we don't need you, nothing could be further from the truth! You bring us tremendous joy, more times than not, and no matter how much some of you piss us off, with your sometimes incredible arrogance and rudeness, every single one of us knows that deep down inside all of our hearts, if ever any one of us should find ourselves together with you at 39,000 feet, having to protect you, or your Mom and Dad, or Husband, or Wife, or Children, or Grandparents, or Best Friends or just anybody you loved from harm, believe me when I tell you that every single flight attendant I have ever had the privilege of working with, would fight like hell for all of you, even if meant protecting you with our very lives to accomplish that! I know that very fact to be true as well as I know my own name! If you find yourself doubting what I just said, I ask you to pay real close attention to the next few paragraphs you are about to read, and really digest them before you go on reading any further, because they will completely prove my case in point! The Webster's Dictionary defines a "hero" as a person of exceptional quality who wins admiration by noble deeds, especially deeds of "courage". When I read that definition, the person who immediately comes to mind, is American Airlines Flight Attendant Madeline "Amy" Sweeney. She epitomizes that very description. She stood by her passengers, protecting them to the best of her ability, until her final breath. She selflessly thought about all of them, and made them priority when she made the incredibly courage's call to American Airlines Flight Service at Boston's Logan Airport, giving them detailed descriptions of the terrorist, including the seat assignments they occupied, how many were on board, what kind of weapons they had, and most importantly, how many of her passengers and her Crew Member family they killed, as well as the details of the horrific manner the terrorist to accomplish those murders in. She remained amazingly calm and focused the entire time, while giving her report. She knew that the information she was relaying would be vital for the authorities in order for them to get a better handle on what type of hijacking they were dealing with, subsequently allowing them to take the proper and necessary actions to that would provide the flying public protection from further harm, and she accomplished exactly that! Within minutes, they knew Mohammed Atta, and the other terrorists that were traveling with him, belonged to a Muslim extremist group who called themselves, AlQueda, and were recruited and led by Bin Laden. Because of the bravery shown by Amy, numerous hijackings of aircrafts that were planned to be used as missiles of mass destruction that same morning, by being flown into other landmark buildings, including the White House, were foiled by Amy. The information that was received from her caused the FAA to shut down the flight system in the entire United States and ground all take offs and immediately land all aircrafts in flight and then ground those as well! Talk about a "hero!" She was beautiful, only 35 years old, had a Mom and Dad, siblings, family and a husband she loved with all of her heart. She was the loving mom of two beautiful little children that she worshipped and adored more than life itself. Yet in spite of all of those wonderful people in her life who loved her, as much as she loved them, she gave up what would be the last opportunity to spend the last moments of her life, talking to them, and instead made the decision to fight for her passengers and protect them from harm as best as she could, from where she unfortunately found herself at that point, all the while knowing that she was risking her own throat being slit, should she be seen by any of the terrorist, making that incredibly selfless phone call to American Airlines, as she kept fighting to keep you safe! Perhaps Amy's ultimate sacrifice is what will finally convince all of you of what your commercial airline flight attendants are truly made of, and why we are on board those aircrafts with you. Flight attendants are not your enemy. We are and always will be your last line of defense up there. Although September 11th 2001, has become a distant horror to many of you, who are seldom reminded about the tragic events on that day except maybe for a little while when you have to travel by air, for all commercial airlines flight attendants and cockpit crew members, it is now, and forever will be, a tragedy we all live with daily, which stays front and center for all of us. Most people cannot even begin to comprehend the incredible horror suffered by all of the people who lost their lives on September 11th, 2001. The Flight Crews and passengers aboard both American Airline's Flight 11, and United Airlines Flight 77, who by no choice of their own, came together on that fateful morning, to share one single commonage; that of total despair; they were the lucky ones, if that is even a possibility, because the impact alone, from both United Airline's 757 and American Airline's 767 aircrafts slamming into the World Trade Towers, killed all of them instantly. It was the horrifying manner in which all the others who perished, that was so tragic. From all of those people having to make a decision that would be inconceivable to the rest of us, which was that of staying in room burning up alive, from the aftermath of the raging inferno left by the aircrafts that crashed into the Towers, or jumping out of the windows from the 80th floor and plummeting to their deaths. Many were buried alive for hours, hoping against hope that someone would find them in time, and rescue them, and of course no one did.   I want you to try to put yourself on that 767 on the morning of September 11th. Close your eyes for just a moment (after you finish reading the next few paragraphs), and try to imagine that it is you yourself, who is getting ready to go on a trip that you have been planning for months. You're taking the entire family, your wife and two kids, to California, to see your parents whom you miss terribly and haven't been able to see for a couple of years now, because you live on completely opposite coasts which makes it a little difficult for you to just drop in for dinner, and besides that, work just hasn't afforded you the time off you've needed to be able to do that until now. Today is that magical day you have all been waiting for; September 11th, 2001. Your alarm goes off at 5 a.m. and everybody gets up, showered, and dressed. You made sure to have everyone pack the night before, so you throw your four suitcases in the trunk of your car, you make your final checks making sure the house is all locked up, pile everybody into the car and you're off! You're headed for the airport to catch your flight to California, and are looking so forward to spending some quality time with your wife and your kids, who can barely be contained at this point, from the excitement of knowing they will soon be reunited again with their adoring grandparents, who spoil them rotten, and who will no doubt be at the airport in Los Angeles, anxiously awaiting your arrival. You've had four seats reserved for weeks now, on American Airlines Flight 11 with non stop service to Los Angeles International Airport from Boston's Logan Airport. You finally arrive at the airport, park your car, check your bags at curbside check in, proceed to gate through security, where you receive your boarding passes, and you board your flight. You are sitting in 21A and your wife in 21B. Your kids are directly behind you in 22A and 22B, perfect! Everybody settles in, as the flight attendants are doing their walk thrus in their respective cabins, making sure all carry on luggage is stowed completely underneath the seats, closing the last few overhead bins that are still open, and making sure that everyone has their seatbelt on. You are instructed over the aircraft's PA system to "please direct your attention to the television screen monitors in the forward part of each cabin, where you will watch a brief instruction film, concerning the safety features of your Boeing 767 aircraft, your attention, please". When the short film is over, you observe the flight attendants walking through the aircraft's cabins, making one last check for passenger safety compliance, and you finally hear the words coming from the cockpit over the PA system saying: "flight attendants prepare for departure. Finally, you think to yourself, and your flight takes off to the skies. The take off was smooth. You look out the window of that Boeing 767, and see the most incredibly crystal clear blue sky as far as the eye can see, complementing the magnificent colors that the Fall Season has brought to that beautiful city's skyline, and it all takes your breath away. You give a quick over the shoulder glance to check on your kids, and see that they have already tuned in their Nintendo Gameboys, and tuned out everything else. They make you smile. You face forward once again, to talk to your wife, and quickly realize that your wife is fast asleep, and you start getting ready to do the very same exact thing, as you feel the aircraft still climbing to what will eventually be its cruising altitude for the flight. Just as you shut your eyes, you hear this loud, blood curdling screaming coming from the front of the aircraft, and extremely alarming loud commotion as well! Your body bolts straight up in your seat, just in time to look over at your wife, who is clearly frightened, because the look of horror on your wife's face is giving it all away, and all of a sudden you feel a chill run down your spine, and a tremendous sense of desperation starts to take over you, and there doesn't seem to be any way for you to control it. In the next instant you see all the first class and business class passengers as well as a couple of the flight attendants hysterically running back towards the coach cabin, and your mind now begins the incredibly difficult process, of breaking down for you, what you are actually now seeing as well as experiencing; a hijacking! Your mind uncontrollably races as you begin receiving information from the dialog of those passengers that were seated in first class and business class, who saw first hand what had transpired in those cabins. At first, you can only make out bits and pieces of what is being relayed, because everyone is talking at the same time and some are screeching over the ones talking. Their body movements seem exaggerated and excessively excitable, and you somehow end up in the middle of that massive hysteria. The first thing that you are able to decipher from what you are hearing is that two first class flight attendants while preparing to begin their in flight service were stabbed to death. Perhaps the terrorist needed the cockpit keys to secure entry into the cockpit, in order to take over the aircraft, or maybe it was just because they might have been in the direct path of Mohammed Atta and the cockpit door. He was the only terrorist on Flight 11, who knew how to fly the aircraft, and FYI; Atta was the terrorist you heard about AFTER the tragedy of September 11th, that was reported as having mentioned to his flight instructor in that Florida flight school, where he took flying lessons, that "he didn't need to know how to land a plane, only fly it". Remember that? Hello! Red Flags Anyone? Anyway, a First Class passengers unknowingly seated directly in front of one of the hijackers was also stabbed, when he perhaps made an attempt to stop the two hijackers, believed to be Wail al Shehri and Waleed al Shehri, who were the ones in the First Class galley, stabbing the first class flight attendants. As you stand there and listen to the hysterical voices of all these passengers, you turn to see that your wife and kids are now hysterical as well, and this incredible sense of helplessness and doom, begins to take over your complete existence. Suddenly, this thick cloud of burning smoke the terrorist released into the air, now starts making its way back to the

Coach Cabin from the First and Business Class Cabins, and your eyes and throat feel as if they were on fire, and you find yourself hardly able to breathe. Then, as if to solidify the fact that you are all indeed caught in a hellish nightmare, you hear a voice speaking over the 767's PA system to you in English, but with a strong Middle Eastern accent, and all of you know, at that precise moment that your Captain and First Officer have had their throats slit as well, and that the terrorists are now in control of your aircraft! He tells you over the PA system that all of you will not be harmed if you do exactly as instructed by the terrorist accomplices that are now in your Coach Cabin as well, finally informing all of you to sit down and be quiet and still! Everyone finds a seat and does exactly as told, hoping against hope, that what they are telling you is true, and that if you cooperate with them, they will not harm you. You sit back in your seating area, and huddle together embracing your hysterical and convulsing wife and kids, as you make an impotent attempt at whispering to them how it will all be over soon, and that everything is going to be okay after they get wherever they are going, and release all of you. Of course, the rest of us know all too well the way that whole story ended, don't we? The terrorist on that hijacked 767 aircraft had specific reasons for killing people in that animalistic manner. They wanted their heinous crimes to bring shock and sheer horror to the psyche of the remaining passengers, ultimately traumatizing and then paralyzing them into a completely submissive state. They knew that by killing a few individuals by slitting their throats in front of the other passengers would be so surreal and horrifyingly gruesome, that it would cause the enormous fear in the remaining passengers, thereby leaving them terrified for their own lives, causing them to become submissive and unobtrusive. That is the mindset they wanted to maintain the remaining passengers in, in order to be able to stay in complete control of the aircraft so that they could accomplish the atrocity they had been planning for many years! For me, every flight attendant on board that aircraft is what I now use as the definition of what a "hero" is, but one flight attendant stands apart from the rest because she possessed a courage unequal to any other I have ever seen, and from what I have read about the incredible strength she displayed that day, she went way beyond the definition of a "hero". Ms. Madeline "Amy" Sweeney is the very reason I was able to state to all of you earlier, that when it comes to protecting our passengers from harm, we will do it with our very lives if we have to. It is because of the selfless courage shown by Amy on that day, that hundreds and thousands of other passengers did not have to lose their lives as well. When you are on board our aircrafts, we look at most of you as our guests/friends who are visiting us for five hours, or whatever the duration of the flight may be. I think that is why we feel so responsible for all of you, because that is how we feel for those hours we are all together in flight, So now, after writing this chapter for you I hope that perhaps you will come to understand us a lot better, and realize that we are not the enemy, and have never been such, much to the contrary of what certain airline individuals have worked very hard for many years to convince you of, and that has been that we are, we need you as much as you need us. It has been a love/hate relationship I have shared with all of you for so many years, much the same kind as I have with my Mom and Dad, that I personally, have felt blessed to have experienced, and wouldn't trade for anything in this world. Considering the fact that I started interacting with so many of you when I was someone's granddaughter, I am today, someone's grandmother, so you see, you have been my teachers, and many of you have even been my mentors as well, during my very young years as an American Airlines flight attendant, and I have continuously learned so very much about life from all of you, throughout the many years of my career, and for that very gift alone, I now say thank you to all of you, and please know that I will forever be grateful to you all. It is my sincerest hope that when the inevitable time comes, and it will, when the American Airlines flight attendants have to STAND and FIGHT for not only the restitution of our profession, that we so dearly love, but also for our company, and all that is rightfully belonging to us, that I, along with the rest of my comrades, will look over our shoulders to not only find that all of you are STANDING behind us, but that you are FIGHTING with us as well. If and when that day should come, what a tremendous honor that will be! In complete solidarity, I bid you all farewell and

God's Speed!

American Airlines Flight Attendant,

Alicia Lutz Rolow

CHAPTER 19

AIRPORT SECURITY
OR
AIRPORT ABSURDITY?

Flying on a Commercial Airline today is about as much fun as going to your dentist and having a root canal procedure done without being provided the comfort of the standard Novocain injection that you always get to numb the pain that the procedure causes. That is the sad but true analogy of what the immense tragedy that September 11, 2001 has left in place for us, regarding our current Commercial Airline experience. It is really quite tragic when you stop and think about what an exciting adventure it use to be in the post 9/11 days. The excitement always started with the trip to the airport. Once we arrived there and went through security, which was a relatively painless experience back then, and got checked in at our departure gate, our excitement escalated as we anticipated boarding our getaway flight. Until that time came, we found immense enjoyment in the simple act of just relaxing, which was a luxury that was seldom afforded to us except maybe once or twice a year when we went on vacation. So we took full advantage of it, and sat back and people watched until we heard our flight number being called out and the passenger boarding process began, loading all of us into the aircraft that would be taking us away on that flight heading straight for the Cayman Islands or Tahiti or some other exotic place on the planet, where the survival drink was a Pina Colada, and our tanning booth consisted of a strip of private beach accessible ten steps outside the front door of our hotel accommodations. Today, the Commercial Airline traveling experience has been turned into a "stressed to the max" nightmare from beginning to end, that we make ourselves "endure" only when it is absolutely necessary. Besides the fact that the Commercial Airline companies themselves have been allowed to become deteriorated and have also been completely ravaged by the present Corporate greed that has been put into place to oversee and manage them, all prior amenities which were once provided on our flights and included in the price of our ticket, have presently either disappeared altogether, or we now have to pay an extra monetary charge in flight for those very same amenities. The airport security as well as the airport security screening the Government Homeland Security Agency, TSA (Transportation Safety/Security Administration) has in place today is nothing more than a ridiculous façade, intended to keep the flying public thinking that their safety is secure and cannot be penetrated. It is a deliberately false impression designed to create the illusion that the procedures that are presently in place for passenger screening are done with great care and attention being paid to detail. The more the hoopla, the safer the passengers think they are! The bottom line here is that they want to ensure that the flying public keeps flying, and if passengers feel like their safety is being constantly protected, they will fly! The reality of the present airport security system that the TSA has in place today though is one that actually leaves you with less "security" and more "absurdity"! If you are having your doubts about that, consider the last airport security screening you experienced. If you recall, there was constant chaos surrounding the passenger screening area, and that coupled with the nonstop yelling back and forth going on among the TSA Agents and the continuous loud beeping/buzzer sound in the background from the screening machines, manifests and maintains a complete state of confusion which we are now forced to have to suffer patiently through it. As if that alone wasn't bad enough, the "Gestapo" like treatment provided for us while we are going through the screening process from those TSA Agents, has us having to muster up all the self control we possibly can in order to keep our mouths shut from any protesting we might otherwise do, regarding the sheer stupidity of much of their process, in order to refrain from spewing out well deserved four letter words in the direct path of the TSA employees, whose arrogance and power tripping along with their stupidity, is just more than any intelligent person should have to bear! Don't get me wrong here. I am very much in support of having an airport passenger screening system in place that "truly" keeps our airports safe from terrorists, or just crazy, unbalanced, and dangerous people who want to bring harm to the flying public for whatever reasons they might have. I think most Americans as well as the rest of the flying public agree with that wholeheartedly. That isn't the problem. The problem is that what is currently being passed off as and referred to as airport security passenger screening by the TSA Government Agency, is nothing more than a Broadway Play Production, choreographed by an idiot, and performed by a bunch of dumb asses (not all of them), who are running the show, and unfortunately for the rest of us, the only way to get through that Barnum and Bailey Circus Act, which other than the complete TSA smokescreen it offers us in place of "real" safety, is nothing more than a tremendous passenger inconvenience, as well as annoyance. Nevertheless, it is a process we must all methodically undergo in a controlled and orderly fashion, in order that we may be allowed to proceed to our respective departure gates. So we dutifully stand in long lines filled with passengers that are already upset from the cavalier and rude attitude that they received from the unhappy, company abused, overworked and underpaid counter agents, at their "favorite airline's" ticket counter. When it's finally our turn to be screened by the TSA Agents, we place our carry on luggage on the x-ray screening conveyer belt and watch our suitcase conveying itself out of our sight momentarily, while at the same time we busy ourselves in what has now all of a sudden become a "rushed" pace as compared to the slow, snail like sluggish pace which we were previously moving in while we were standing in line; we hurriedly and nervously empty all our pockets from any items we may have had in them, into a plastic type container, along with any jewelry, metal hair ornaments of any kind, belts, jackets, purses, wallets and of course our shoes that we took off our feet. We do a final quick check for anything else on our bodies that might have any amount of metal on it, even if it's the slightest amount because we know how much longer this process will take should we cause the screening arch we walk through to go off, and it's getting close to our flight's boarding time, so we sure don't want to add any more stress to this already quite stressful enough experience by missing our flight altogether. So we place that container filled with our personal artifacts on the same conveyer belt we sent our suitcase off in. We proceed to walk through that screening arch that detects any kind of metal on our actual bodies, and we are amazed and shocked at the loud and disturbing buzzer/beeping sound that we hear go off as we walk through. So we gape around looking dumbfounded, to try to see where it's coming from because we can't possibly even begin to imagine that the sound we hear going off, is coming from the screening arch we just walked through, because at this point, we have taken off everything we could possibly take off, and if one more article of clothing had to be removed, we would surely be confused for either a performing male stripper, or a cathouse pole sliding lap dance girl, depending on if you were male or female! We do however quickly realize in horror, I might add, that it is in fact us who set off the menacing sounds catching everyone's attention, and the next thing we know, this big burley mean looking woman in a TSA uniform raises her baton looking stick at us, and points it in the direction that she wants us to walk over to, as she starts mumbling some kind of orders at us, which were extremely difficult to understand since her two front teeth were missing which caused her speech to come out sounding a lot like Donald Duck, and regrettably, we can't understand what she is saying to us because seriously, who out there has ever once been able to understand what Donald Duck is saying! So, not meaning to offend anyone and answer the TSA agent improperly, we make the serious mistake of asking her to kindly repeat herself, (next time we'll just pretend we comprehended), which when she did, not only did we not understand what she was saying any better than the first time she said it, but we made her really angry and now we found ourselves being backed up against the wall, hands up in the air over our heads, with our legs spread apart wide, and we were stripped searched and felt up, and the last thing we remember, was watching that big burley TSA woman coming towards us while donning on some rubber gloves telling us to bend over before we passed out, and that's just what was done to the Flight Crew! I can only imagine the horrors endured by the ordinary passenger. Heaven help you! All kidding aside though, Americans have been led down a very misguided road by the very people that are in charge of keeping us safe. The TSA is nothing more than another layer of bureaucracy in the vast land of the political arena that has been afforded much to much power, and they have little to none accountability. They are a Government Agency that thrives out of a culture comprised of fear, with constant "showy" displays of vigilance that they would have us believe are procedures that they are following, in order to keep us safe. They want us to see them as the final word in safety when it comes to keeping our airports as well as our Commercial Airlines secure, when in actuality, the whole spectacle just public relations band aid, which wastes much of the flying public's valuable time, by having them stand in ridiculously long lines that accumulate in length from the TSA agents "over focusing" on all the wrong things as well as all the wrong people, and that would constitute everyone, because they look and treat everyone as a potential security threat, and that is just wrong on so many levels! That mindset remains the same with these TSA Agents regardless of whether the passenger being screened happens to be a child//infant, as well as employees, as well as old people in or out of wheelchairs, and the most ridiculous of all, a uniformed Flight Crewmember carrying proper FAA as well as airline identification, who is not even a passenger at all! Call me silly, but in case the TSA agents and TSA department heads haven't noticed, the Flight Crewmembers are the very people that fly and work the aircraft the rest of the flying public will be traveling on. If a Commercial Airline Pilot or flight attendant wanted to hijack one of their own company's airplanes, and fly it into a building somewhere, I really don't think that the ridiculous screening of Flight Crewmembers by the TSA Agents will much matter because we have complete access to the very thing you're "over focusing" on us about, and that would be the aircraft itself! Whenever any TSA agent is "over focusing" on one of the Flight Crewmembers, and we question them about the absurdity regarding the way in which we are being screened and why they feel the need to dishevel everything we have so neatly packed in our suitcase for our "work flight", and then confiscate from us, certain items that we have with us that we need for our layovers, such as the plastic silverware we use to eat our morning cereal with while in our hotel room, their typical response they always seem to come up with, is that they have to make sure that we (Flight Crew) don't have anything in our possession that we can use to take control of the aircraft! I hate to burst the bubble of those TSA Agents, but I' am not aware to this day of a "spork" ever being used as the hijacking weapon of choice, and I do not foresee it becoming one in the near future! Can any TSA Agent please explain to me how even having to verbalize that very idiocracy, which by the way makes all of you seem as if your intelligence is severely challenged, isn't embarrassing enough to make you take it up with your superiors? Consider the very important fact that taking control of our aircraft is exactly what we are going to do as soon as we get on it! The Captain and First Officer will make their way into the cockpit where they will commandeer it to wherever our airline company has scheduled us to fly, and the flight attendants will take control of the rest of the aircraft as well as the passengers that are coming with us because that happens to be our jobs and what we get paid for, so what in God's name is your POINT! That is exactly the reason why the system completely falters, and is thereby "flawed" and not "secure"! Having a savvy intelligent running "airport security" screening system at all airports is a MUST! I don't think anyone out here is disputing that very fact. But that's not what we have! The "airport absurdity" which is what we do have, along with all the many other un pleasantries presently facing the flying public regarding the use of Commercial Airline companies, as a form of transportation, is fast becoming a deterrent for many people who just don't want to have to deal with any of it! The TSA passenger screenings at the airports today that dares to call itself "airport security" is more of a senseless, benign, illogical, and ineffective attempt at keeping us in a secure state! The only thing that's accomplished from all that stressful airport hoopla created by the TSA employees is that it makes passengers become irritated with all the nonsense, and anxious about the possibility of missing their flights due to the vital time wasted in those ridiculously long slow lines. The absurd "power tripping" demonstrated by the TSA agents only serves to anger and frustrate the flying public who are intelligent enough to know that the "over focusing" screening that is being done which is that of randomly selecting for example, an 89 year old women or man who need walking canes to get around, or a slow moving 8 months pregnant mom traveling with a her 1 year old toddler, is completely futile and unproductive, and the biggest absurdity of all absurdities, which is when the TSA agents find it necessary to hold up the security screening lines because of "over focusing" on Flight Crewmembers that will ultimately be in "control" of the flights, instead of "focusing" on the things they noticed that give them legitimate reasonable and probable cause for "over focusing", which there are plenty of red flags out there to watch out for! Doesn't that pretty much some up the Homeland Security TSA (Transportation Safety/Security Administration) stupidity and arrogance of it all? I'd sure say so, and being employed as an American Airlines flight attendant, working on the inside of the Aviation Industry and looking out for the last 32 years of my career, has not only given me the insight necessary for assessing potential security threats of all kinds, but it has given me the experience as well, to deal with them properly and without all the TSA hoopla! The other huge and ridiculous suggestions made to us as flight attendants by these Federal Aviation Administrations, is that of not profiling passengers in any way, which when you think about the absurdity in that statement, you can't help but wonder what kind idiots are running not only this Aviation Industry, but the entire country as well! That is completely absurd advice and believe me, it is not advice that any of us follow. It's real easy for these Homeland Security Government Agency officials, who are so hell bent on being "politically correct" when making these stupid policies for us, expecting us to adhere to them, as they sit in their safe little cubicles and tell us not to passenger profile. If more passenger profiling had been used on September 11th, 2001, all those people who died on that day would today be walking among us, and that folks, is a FACT! If Atta had been profiled when checking in for the flight he hijacked, they would have been looking for all the red flags he had out there, such as one way ticket, no checked baggage and Middle Eastern ethnicity, HELLO!!! There is absolutely nothing wrong with passenger profiling when it comes to the security of the flying public while using Commercial Air transportation. Nothing! This might be a good time to have it reiterated for many of you out there who after reading that are saying to yourselves that " profiling is an outrage", that the last time this country of ours experienced a massive attack on its people, the despots involved in that heinous attack were not blonde and blue eyed, nor were they 5 years old, nor were they 89 walking with a cane nor confined to a wheelchair, nor were they Commercial Airline Crewmembers! The ethnicity of the animals that strap on home made apparatuses with explosives attached to them, to make themselves into human time bombs for the specific purpose of MURDERING as many people, as they possibly can, whom they consider to be INFADELS when they blow themselves up, are of Middle Eastern Ethnicity and no other! That is a FACT! It's not a racist comment; it's not a hatred comment; it's not even an "un" politically correct comment! It is a PROFILED FACT! It doesn't matter whether we like it or not. It is exactly what it is, an indisputably well known PROFILED FACT! If there is a passenger who is of Middle Eastern ethnicity and is traveling on a Commercial Airline company such as American Airlines let's say, and let's even take it a step further and say that I am one of the flight attendant working the flight and am in fact working the business class cabin, which is the very cabin that passenger has been given a seat assignment in, as long as he/she shows no signs of nervous or strange and threatening behavior, he/she will receive the exact same treatment from me, as well as from all the other flight attendants working on that flight that I am displaying for all of my other non Muslim passengers, because that is in fact what he/she is up to that point, another one of my passengers. But do not make the mistake of thinking that he/she is not being continuously observed more closely than my "non" Middle Eastern ethnicity passengers, while he/she is on that aircraft from boarding to gate arrival. If he/she is a perfectly innocent law abiding person without any murderous intentions, the fact that we are observing them more closely should be of absolutely no consequence to them, and they should not be threatened by it either, but instead they should be able to completely understand the reasons why the flight attendants pay a little closer attention to their movement around the aircraft and such. That is our job! We are there to protect the flying public when they are on board our aircrafts. This is the present vigilant condition that the Aviation Industry, as well as the entire United States of America for that matter, was left in, from the gruesome and tragic events that transpired on September 11th 2001, which has forever changed us, whether we want to admit that FACT or not! I personally was born in New York City and had a parent who immigrated to this country from Cuba in 1959. Most of us can certainly recall when there was a time not so long ago when people who were of Cuban ethnicity were hijacking the planes belonging to American Airline carriers while they were flying over American air space, and after taking control of the airplane, would demand from the Cockpit Crews of those hijacked airplanes to fly them back to Cuba, and the Cockpit Crew had no choice but to satisfy their demand in order to keep their flight attendants and passengers on board safe! The big difference in the Cuban hijacking as opposed to a radical Muslim extremist hijacking, is that when the Pilot landed the plane in Cuba, the Cuban hijacker got off the plane without further incident, and the passengers as well as the Flight Crew turned around and flew back into American air space, unlike the Muslim extremist, who has a much more demonic plan for everybody on that airplane, including his own self sacrificing! Any way you look at it, both hijackings are of a terrorist nature, and even though I was born in this country and I am an American Citizen by birth right, my ethnicity on my Mother's side is Cuban, and as such, during the times when the Cubans were doing the hijackings in this country, I did expect when traveling on a Commercial Airline, to be observed more closely than the rest of the passengers by the flight attendants, and because I was a passenger of Cuban ethnicity who was law abiding and never had thoughts of ever hijacking an American Airline carrier and taking it to Cuba, it was not insulting nor was it threatening for me to be profiled and more closely observed. It is a "necessary" tool Flight Crews cannot work without in the Aviation Industry's Commercial Airlines, and anyone who thinks it wrong to profile, has evidently NEVER experienced the horror of being on a hijacked aircraft! All I can leave you with in this chapter is the knowledge of what is needed from the standpoint of the very people who are "truly" working very hard everyday to try to make it as SAFE as it can possibly be, for the flying public to travel, and there are many entities, to be sure, but that of the Homeland Security TSA, that in its orderly chaos leaves you with more rules of "absurdity" as opposed to "security", all I can say is that although it must remain in place such as it is for the moment, because many of its procedures are in fact being performed in an effective enough manner, and that does add to our safety when we choose to use Commercial Air transportation, but most of their current procedures do need to be readdressed in order that the airport passenger screening may become less of the chaotic confusion and drama that it presently insists on being today, and more of an informed and "truly safe" detecting procedure that runs more timely and efficiently and that ultimately provides less stress and aggravation for the traveling public. Regardless of if and when that should ever happen, the fact that the American Airlines flight attendants have got to stand united and strong during these increasingly difficult times, is not an option, it is our history and it is at stake, and our time is NOW! Flight attendants, it's time for us to STAND!

CHAPTER 20

U.S. COMMERCIAL AIRLINES AIRCRAFT MAINTENANCE "OUTSOURCING" ARE YOU KIDDING ME?

Since I have been off on leave from my flying profession *(not by choice)*, I have found through my researching for this book, that there is so much disturbing information out there that is documented, concerning the *Aviation Industry's commercial airline companies' corporate executive negligence* and total *disregard for passenger and flight crewmember "safety".* I strongly feel that the flying public has every right know and be made aware of any and all information that pertains to their safety when they are traveling on commercial airline transportation, and I am sure that there are plenty of people out there who *"conveniently" disagree with me wholeheartedly!* I also suppose that if anyone would have tried to tell me 32 years ago when I started flying for the once very elite commercial airline company known as *American Airlines,* that the deteriorated condition in which the *Aviation Industry's commercial airline companies* including mine have fallen victim to today would one day become a sad reality, I would have dismissed that person's statement as utterly ridiculous, and I would have thought him/her to be the biggest

IDIOT living on the planet! That thought process was not anything that was even remotely *fathomable* on any level back then. Those of us that have had the great fortune of working in this industry for as long as I have or longer were able to experience it when it was at the peak of its magnificence and glamour. *This was an industry that most people only dreamed of being a part of. We are the very people who today, are finding it extremely difficult to helplessly watch as it is catapulted towards inevitable destruction. Our hearts are broken. My heart is broken.* The reputations of the majority of major commercial airline companies *American Airlines* included, have become *defiled and desecrated* from the injurious aftermath that has materialized, after having been placed in the hands of corrupt corporate company employees, who although hired in *"good faith"* for their *"supposed" leadership abilities and managing skills* to oversee these airline companies and all pertaining to them in ways that would assure the companies' on going success; instead found endless amounts of avenues that allowed for complete deflection from these companies' original courses, to the deficient course that is in place now, which is that of the *sedulous kind, providing only self interest, self indulgence, self importance, self gratification, and self devotion for all company corporate executives, starting at the top with the CEO's.* This was the course that the leadership of *American Airlines* as well as many others elected to follow in the early *1970's* and they have remained on that course through the years, which is what has now begun the destructive domino affect we are all seeing and unfortunately experiencing as well, every time we use commercial airline travel as our form of transportation. The misuse and mismanagement of company funds and passenger revenue has become very apparent at *American Airlines* by just simply observing the deteriorated condition the airline company finds itself in today. *The passenger "customer service", which was once at the top of its game, has now been slashed with cut backs, after cut backs, leaving our passengers with nothing even remotely resembling what it once was; why is that Mr. Arpey? Hundreds of American Airlines employees have been laid off in recent months because of claims from our corporate execs that the company can no longer afford to pay those employees salaries anymore; why is that Mr. Arpey? American Airlines currently has an aircraft fleet that is older than my Great Grandmother, which desperately needs replacing or at the very least, a complete overhaul; why is that Mr. Arpey? You and your friends are "out of control" Mr. Arpey!* Just when I think I have heard the last of the most irresponsible or the most despicable behavior *AA's corporate management* can think of to engage in *"poof"* just like that, something else magically appears and proves me wrong! If I could only list one *"true"* thing that I could say about the people in charge of overseeing *American Airlines,* it would have to be that *they can never be believed or trusted about ANYTHING!* Not by the labor employees or passengers anyway. Our safety is overlooked on a daily basis and if any of you passengers and crewmembers out there can possibly still doubt that, let me just give you a few facts about just how *"deep"* the greedy pockets of the commercial airline companies' corporate execs' at *American Airlines* are. Since the late *90's and early 2000's,* the commercial airlines' corporate executives have been putting the lives on the line, of not only the flying public but the flight crewmembers who work for them as well, by *"outsourcing" the maintenance of our commercial airline aircrafts to "third world countries". The reason for this dangerous outsourcing that almost every U.S. carrier, including American Airlines participate in (American claims only 20% non-critical maintenance "outsourcing" but who really knows because they LIE so much), is for what else the bottom line dollar, but then isn't that what everything is about for them even if it is at the cost of our safety?* Besides putting the entire flying public and crewmembers in harms way, the money they save by *outsourcing* the maintenance of our aircrafts out to people who they can get away with paying less than the *"minimum wage"* to, regardless of whether or not these people know what they are doing, as opposed to the *"living wage"* they have to pay our *U. S. mechanics,* who are qualified and have the necessary required training as well as the certifications to back their knowledge and their work, is just more money added to the already growing pile of money that these corporate execs claim they have saved their airline companies'. Well, evidently that money that they have *"supposedly"* saved has not made its way back into the airline companies to be used for their continued upkeep as well as success, because if it had, these airline companies' *safety records* would be faring a lot better these days. So, because I work for *American Airlines,* naturally the question I have is directed to our very own *CEO, Mr. Gerald Arpey and his corporate management execs* who are overseeing my airline, and that question is; *"where the hell is all of this extra money that you are "supposedly" saving us by outsourcing 20% of our aircraft maintenance?"* Could it be that it somehow found its way to your executive's **pockets perhaps?** *Sara Kehaulani Goo,* a staff writer for the *Washington Post,* wrote an article on *Sunday, August 21, 2005* entitled *Airlines Outsource Upkeep.* In this article she states that *"Outsourcing of maintenance tasks has surged in recent years, raising concerns about the experience and the background of workers performing the upkeep on the nation's aircrafts. Fifty-three percent of all major maintenance on U.S. airlines is done by contractors rather than airline employees, an increase from forty- seven percent in 2003 according to the Transportation Department's inspector general. In 1990, only a third of the carrier's maintenance went outside the company."* *The people who have been given the vitally* *important jobs of maintaining the U. S. aircrafts that transports all of us from one place to another at 39,000 feet every day, live in such places as El Salvador, Mexico, the Philippines and of course my favorite place, China, the very place responsible for giving the global consumers lead laced toys for our children, tainted toothpaste for our teeth, and deadly pet food for our dogs and cats; oh and let's not forget those counterfeit drugs we are all enjoying, especially on the streets!* This information was obtained from an article written in *Business Week Dated July20, 2007 entitled "Danger In The Repair Shop"* which states that *FAA inspectors warn about the risks of outsourcing maintenance.* It's bad enough that the corporate executives of almost every U.S. major corporation are *"outsourcing"* their businesses/employment to people in these *third world countries*, and laying off their U.S. workers, but now, *the commercial airline corporate execs are joining the "outsourcing" club, and are contracting out the vitally important maintenance of the airplanes that you and I are flying on every day!* Why has the *FAA* allowed these airline companies to even start this aircraft maintenance *"outsourcing"* in the first place? Aren't they the ones who are suppose to oversee these corporate greed hogs and keep them in line in order that the American flying public and the commercial airline companies flight crew members safety is *NEVER* compromised? I am not trying to be high drama here or make too much ado about this, but come on! It gets worse, read on! According to a *2005* report in the *Wall Street Journal,* "*JetBlue, Southwest, America West, Northwest, and United* are among the carriers who *"outsource"* major maintenance of their aircrafts to contractors in other countries. *As *Jet Blue's* new *A320 Airbus* fleet ages, aircrafts are sent to a repair hub in *El Salvador;* *America West* also sends its jets to **El Salvador;** *Southwest* has always outsourced its major maintenance; * *Northwest* sends its wide body jets to **Singapore and Hong Kong;** *US Airways outsourced **2000** mechanics jobs and gave pay cuts to the remaining mechanics. *United Airlines* use outside contractors for the heavy maintenance of their aircrafts". **Keep reading!** The fact is that these people in these "*third world*" countries are absolutely **NOT** qualified to do that job, nor do they have the proper schooling or necessary amount of training required to do these aircraft maintenance jobs competently and as in thorough a manner in which our mechanics do in the United States. This situation is a very serious one and has high potential for immense catastrophic consequences which will no doubt fall on the flying public and flight crewmembers. **WE** are the ones who will ultimately be affected by the consequences of this dangerous aircraft "*outsourcing*". The blatant cavalier attitude that these corporate execs have regarding the compromising of passenger and flight crewmember safety, as well as the attitude of their high official buddies at the **FAA** who are looking the other way and are allowing this abhorrent situation to go on, is not just shameful, it is down right unacceptable! Are you kidding me? The **Wall Street Journal** article continued to state that "*Mechanics in these countries who are working for outsourcers on our aircraft maintenance don't have to have certification that proves complete competence and compliance with all FAA mandates regarding knowledge of commercial airline aircraft maintenance the way that our U.S. mechanics do! They are "unqualified", "untrained" and "unskilled" workers who are contracted to do the work for a third of the money, and they don't need to meet any FAA mandates or be licensed either, because as long as their "supervisor has all of those qualifications, that is all that is required in these "third world" countries' chop shops"!* That's all the reassurance any one of us should need, right? **WRONG!** Believe it or not, this is exactly how they are trying to justify this incredibly dangerous game of **Russian roulette** that they are playing with our very lives! I did not just make all that up! These are documented **FACTS!** All you have to do is ask any one of those **overpaid corporate execs or their FAA supervisor friends.** Every single one of them will not only defend their position on the issue, but they will go as far as telling you about how safe it is too, because after all, **if it wasn't safe, wouldn't there be more airplanes falling out of the skies?** Well, from the looks of the way things are going these days with regards to the **Aviation Industry**, that scenario is not too very far away at this point and if all of you airline corporate execs and your FAA sleepover buddies don't mind, I personally prefer not to take a chance on that happening! In the same **Business Week article dated July 30, 2007 entitled "Danger In The Repair Shop",** **FAA inspectors warn "there's plenty to worry about in Taiwan, and they have been deeply troubled by what they have observed at the Chiang Kai-shek International Airport where Boeing is currently modifying four 747's into extra large cargo freighters. In recent Congressional testimony, FAA inspectors** reported finding **"unsecured bins that are used for the disposal of discarded B747 parts, as well as other old parts that come off the airplanes, such as aluminum panels and generators which could end up finding their way back on commercial airplanes."** The aircraft maintenance work area of the repair shop, which is a unit of the Taipei based U.S. Evergreen Group, a transportation conglomerate, is supposedly mandated to be sealed off, and the old aircraft parts that have been removed are suppose to be destroyed.** But the inspectors are worried that scavengers are stealing the parts and then reselling them into the black market as counterfeit aircraft parts.** The FAA inspectors estimate that 520,000 counterfeit parts make their way back into commercial airline aircrafts each year! Boeing Company officials LIED and denied the statements made by the FAA inspectors, stating *that their company followed FAA regulations and that the parts in question have been destroyed. The senior Evergreen Group executive also LIED and agreed that the work that was done at their repair shop complied with FAA guidelines and that the parts were disposed of properly. Shortly after telling those blatant LIES, Boeing officials "conceded" that FAA inspectors' reports were indeed accurate, and even admitted that two years prior, parts that had been stolen from various 747 jets and were not identified, destroyed or disposed of properly. The FAA disagrees strongly with the Unions, regarding foreign maintenance facilities posing a safety risk for the flying public.* Imagine that, big surprise there! *James J. Ballough who is the FAA director for Flight Standards Service says: "the agency visits each foreign repair station annually" and coming from his own mouth he further states: "I am confident that we get a TRUE picture of the compliance posture of those repair stations; we have a great safety record."* Are you kidding me? Do you really think Mr. FAA director, sir, that checking on these 'third world" countries' aircraft maintenance repair shops once a year is going to get you a legitimate TRUE picture of what's really going on over there? With all due respect sir, if you're that STUPID, you need to apply for a job where your blatant incompetence doesn't have the responsibility of the public's safety and mine, the way your current one does! All of you *FAA "big shots"* keep falling back on constantly citing the impressive safety record of the commercial airline carriers in the United States. How long can you *idiots* keep running with that one before the horrendous corruption that you are very much a part of in the aviation industry, allows for the certain catastrophic commercial airline accidents that are undeniably heading our way, if someone doesn't do something to stop all of you and the current **"greed obsessed"** ridden manner in which you are all running these companies, and Lord knows that you are

359

getting plenty of help from your *FAA buddies* in high places that from the looks of things, are apparently sleeping with you, it's just a matter of time before disaster hits our skies! Instead of the **FAA** doing their real job, which is suppose to be that of *"overseeing"* these major airline companies and keeping them safe, they are *"overlooking"* many of these major airline companies' *FAA non compliances* instead! As far as I am concerned, every single one of you are completely ignoring the safety of the flying public as well as the safety of every flight crewmember that works for these commercial airlines and I don't care how much cheaper it is to *"outsource"* our U.S. commercial airline aircraft maintenance to unqualified people, you sir, *Mr. FAA director*, and all your airline buddies are all guilty of putting hundreds and thousands of people's lives in harms way every single day, including mine, every time we board one of your cheaper *"third world"* country maintained airplanes, and that sir, is noting less than **CRIMINAL!** Besides all of you being **CRIMINALS,** you are all **LIARS** as well! Some FAA inspectors (*not to be confused with FAA directors*), dispute your whole bullshit theory on the bogus statement you made about the FAA inspectors going to these countries once a year to check these stations for FAA compliance, as if once a year was an adequate enough inspection timeline that needed to be commended, even if it were true, which it's not, because you know damn well *Mr. Ballough* that the reality of it is, you can't get to all of these *"third world"* countries in a year. FAA inspectors say that the biggest problem your agency faces is getting the funds and the clearance to travel to those overseas sites. One inspector based in the Midwest said that he was documented and credited with your agency as having inspected dozens of facilities in *Asia and Europe*, but the reality of it is that he would only be able to visit one or at the most two such facilities a year, and then only briefly and certainly not thoroughly. He went on to say that once there, the inspectors were not able to oversee the work so as to ensure it was being done properly, and that the proper tools were being used, or whether they even in fact have trained technicians in these countries that are qualified and FAA certified to be able to properly work on these U. S. Commercial Airline aircrafts; Really? I wonder why? Could it be perhaps that those FAA inspectors, once down there, are **DENIED** access to those foreign mechanic chop shops because the people working down there do not want the inspectors to get a first hand look at the incompetence and negligence that is going on in those so called maintenance shops, and have the inspectors document the information and bring that information back with them when they return to the United States maybe? No foul play going on there! This particular FAA inspector also mentioned that when these facilities were located in the United States, FAA inspectors would visit those repair shops every day or at the very least, on a regular basis, and that allowed them the opportunity of continuously checking to make sure that the airline companies' mechanics and maintenance employees were always *FAA compliant*. After he finished testifying in front of the *Congressional Hearing Board*, he had to insist on anonymity for giving this information because he feared retribution and the loss of his job *(I'm feeling your pain buddy!)* These 3,000 FAA inspectors can see exactly what I and many others can also see coming, and that is the horrendous and needless commercial airline catastrophes that are already heading our way! *(Read up on Qantas Airlines August 2008)* The FAA inspectors that are currently speaking out against the current manner in which business is being conducted between commercial airline execs and top FAA supervisor officials, and are trying to warn us of what is to come from foreign maintenance shops, which receive *grossly inadequate oversight* and have become a risk for *shoddy work and counterfeit parts*, should be commended for their bravery and should be fiercely protected, from the harassment and intimidation tactics that these corporate execs and FAA supervisors/directors will no doubt try to inflict on them for doing the honorable thing, and STANDING for what is right for all of us, trying to keep us safe! FAA inspectors and Union representatives both say that of the 698 overseas maintenance contractors licensed by the FAA, they are only able to thoroughly scrutinize the work of only a handful. They have found that these facilities sometimes hire *"unskilled"* and *"untrained"* employees, and the FAA inspectors don't have the ability to oversee an unknown number of obscure maintenance repair shops that they know lack FAA certification altogether, and in these chop shops, no one seems to bring up the fact too often, that the *"unskilled", "untrained" and "unlicensed"* people working on our U. S. commercial jets, are also *NOT* required to meet stringent *"criminal" background checks,* or *pass random drug testing* the way the mechanics and maintenances people working directly for the airlines in the United States do! How scary is that? That is just INSANE! The *Aircraft Mechanics Fraternal Association at Northwest* ponder whether the safety and the security of our aircrafts in this country are being compromised by *"outsourcing"* the extremely important and precise task of major aircraft repairs and maintenance, to these countries that are not easily accessible to FAA inspectors, for assessing compliance with FAA mandates. *Northwest Airlines* has cut back its mechanics and maintenance workers from *10,000 in 2001,* to what they currently have today which is *4,400* through constant layoffs and maintenance *"outsourcing".* Are those numbers frightening enough for you? *Kenneth J. Hylander,* who is the *VP for Northwest's safety and engineering* said, quote: *"other airlines and aircraft operators are using the full range of competent maintenance opportunities available to efficiently maintain and safely fly their aircrafts. This is the world we find ourselves in and in which we must compete".* End of quote. Well excuse me *Mr. Hylander*, sir, but what the hell does **"competent maintenance opportunities"** mean exactly? Are you referring to the *"unskilled", "untrained," and "un-certified"* employees in these *"third world"* countries that our FAA inspectors can't even get to, in order to assess the work's quality as well as conduct FAA compliance checks on them? And exactly what is it that you mean when you say *"this is the world we find ourselves in and in which we must compete?"* Isn't this what you're really saying; *"this is the unconscionable and self serving world we have had a big part in creating and therefore, whoever is the most clever at being the most corrupt and looking the most sincere and legitimate wins, even if it is at the cost of our SAFETY!"* No *Mr. Hylander*, you don't have to compete with unsafe practices, you choose to compete with unsafe practices! If you were anything *forthright and honorable*, which you obviously are not, instead of *"competing"*, as you put it, you could instead *"protest"* this kind of deplorable situation that is running ramped and out of control for the sole purpose of the insatiable *"greed"* you are all obsessed with, and the unscrupulous determination every one of you possess for keeping your own pockets fully lined. You could choose to STAND apart from these other corrupt individuals who are putting personal greed over human life, and in so doing, force the others to have to stop these kinds of dangerous and criminal business practices, but you just join in instead don't you! Please sir, don't confuse the words *"compete"* with *"greed ridden"* because they have two completely different meanings! The information the FAA Inspectors gave at the *Congressional Hearing* also gave accounts of the myriad of problems they found the few times they were able to observe these repair shops, such as faulty engine installations and improperly documented parts, which is a red flag for counterfeiting. Another common violation the inspectors found was the critical rotating parts not being cleaned before they are inspected and checked for possible cracking, and they said that such cracks, if undetected, could cause the components to fail, and could thereby easily lead to an air disaster. *NICE!* This *"outsourcing"* trend poses much threat to the security and safety of the flying public as well as the flight crewmembers. *On January 31, 2000 Alaska Airlines Flight 261, a McDonnell Douglas MD-83 (Super 80) was in flight from Puerto Vallarta, Mexico to San Francisco. While cruising at 31,000 feet off the California coast, the aircraft suddenly became uncontrollable by the Crew, and the aircraft dropped to 24,300 feet. The pilots radioed in that they were having problems with the "stabilizer trim". They then were able to once again get control of the aircraft and descend it to 18,000 feet, at which time they asked for clearance to divert and attempt an emergency landing at Los Angeles International Airport. The request was granted to them, but sadly they would not make that emergency landing, because 11 minutes after they called in the problem, the jetliner plummeted in an uncontrollable dive and plunged nose first and "inverted" into the Pacific Ocean, killing 83 passengers and 5 flight crewmembers!* This information comes straight to us from the *American Red Cross – In The News by Cynthia Long, Managing Editor, Disaster Relief. org*. Well, when the **National Transportation Safety Board** (NTSB) investigated the crash, *they found a faulty/un lubricated jackscrew assembly , and the failure of the assembly's acme nut threads which controls movement of the horizontal stabilizer mounted atop of the MD-83 (Super 80) vertical fin, along with the excessive wear resulting from Alaska Airlines' insufficient lubrication of the jackscrew assembly from the improper maintenance, and the constant flying it back and forth, the airplane lost its pitch control, and those passengers and flight crewmembers never had a chance* *because they were left with an airplane they could NOT control! Also contributing to that fatal crash was an "extension" on the lubrication interval given to Alaska Airline's CEO John Kelly, from his FAA buddies, which allowed the excessive wear of the acme nut threads to progress to the point of failure without prior detection. The importance of the maintenance of the horizontal stabilizer of any aircraft, as well as the lubrication of the "jack screw" and the assembly is crucial. The horizontal stabilizer is a wing like structure that is located at the tail of the aircraft, and it is what controls the aircraft's pitch, pointing the nose of the aircraft up or down, and the gimbal nut moves up and down the jack screw to change the stabilizer's position. Both the jackscrew and gimbal nut when recovered from the wreckage of Flight 261, were both damaged. The NTSB performed a very stringent maintenance check at the Alaska Airline's maintenance facility in Oakland, California in September 29, 1997, and it was back then they found the gimbal nut to be worn to the maximum acceptable limits, on the very plane that would fly as Flight 261 on January 31, 2000.* That was a two year and four months window of opportunity for Alaska Airline's CEO John Kelly, and corporate management, to do the right thing and make sure that proper maintenance was done on that aircraft before it went up again. Had they been forthright and held our SAFETY as top priority, instead of the bottom line dollar as priority, the passengers and flight crewmembers of Flight 261 on January 31, 2000, would be walking among us today! Not only was that overdue maintenance issue not taken care of immediately, the way it should have been, but guess what? After that heavy aircraft maintenance check that the *NTSB agents performed on that airplane, where the problem with the gimbal nut and jackscrew had been discovered, according to Alaska Airline's maintenance records, the aircraft was supposedly inspected five times on the very next day, which was September 30, 1997, and it was repeatedly found all five times to be well within limits for continued use!* Just like magic! No foul play there! During that last major inspection of the horizontal stabilizer on that plane, the gimbal nut was not replaced! Imagine that! Apparently it must have completely slipped their greed obsessed minds that it is vital to the **SAFETY** of the flying public and flight crewmembers that these aircraft parts be properly maintained because of the significant fact that they are what provides the Captain flying the aircraft, the ability to control and maneuver it! Call me silly, but it doesn't take brain surgery to figure that one out! As far as I'm concerned, the accountability for the lives of all those who died needlessly in that crash belongs completely to *Alaska Airline's CEO John Kelly, and his corporate execs and the FAA higher ups* that allowed this criminal activity to go on in the first place. That Oakland facility had been the subject of many federal investigations over allegations that some maintenance records had been falsified. A federal grand jury had been investigating complaints of **"maintenance irregularities"** at the maintenance shop, prodded by a quitam *(whistleblower)* lead mechanic by the name of *John Liorine*, who said that in *October of 1998, Alaska Airlines* managers had signed off on maintenance work that was *never performed*, and on *March 15, 2000,* Sixty four mechanics at the *Alaska Airline's Seattle* maintenance base sent a letter to *CEO John Kelly*, telling him that they had been pressured, threatened and intimidated into cutting corners on **SAFETY!** Now, let me explain something to all of you. The reason I know for a FACT that those *Alaska Airline's mechanics* were telling the *TRUTH*, when they wrote that letter to *Alaska's CEO, Mr. John Kelly*, is because the *EXACT SAME* thing has happened to me with my company's *CEO, Mr. Gerald Arpey at American Airlines!* Exactly, I tell you; and I can bet you, knowing that I would win the bet, that it is with high probability that in the response letter that those sixty four *Alaska Airline's mechanics* received from their *CEO, Mr. John Kelly,* he stated to them that quote: *"those are some very serious accusations you make about our Oakland maintenance facility managers"!* Right guys, did I get that right on the money? Did he also mention that he checked things out at the facility, and everything is running as it should be? Did he also tell you guys that you were the one's that had some serious *"INSUBORDINATION"* issues and that you had better correct them, or you would be placed on *"Carrier Decision Day" Status?* Well, you know what guys, I completely, wholeheartedly believe every accusation you have made regarding your then *CEO, Mr. John Kelly,* and his corporate entourage and FAA buddies' blatant disregard for the *SAFETY* of the flying public and flight crewmembers. Do you know why? Because I am presently dealing with the very same *LIVING HELL,* provided for me by my company's *CEO, Mr. Gerald Arpey* and his *American Airline's corporate clowns and FAA buddies!* I am very proud of all of you who *SPEAK UP* as well as *STAND* for all of us out here on a limb. It takes guts to put everything you have on the line for making sure that people do not die needlessly for the **GREED** of others. I have said it before, and I'll say it again. The *"corporate mindset"* does not belong in the aviation industry's commercial airline companies! If it is allowed to continue to oversee our airlines, we are definitely heading for a situation which will surely provide for many more hundreds, perhaps thousands (*such as in September 11ᵗʰ*), of lives lost in needless mid air catastrophes, because corporate is all about the *"the balance sheets"* and commercial aviation transportation is about *"the human element"*, it is really that simple! The question I have for everybody is: why have these people involved in the cause of these fatal pane crashes, not been charged with *manslaughter?* Their complete indifference to the passenger and crewmember safety is completely demonstrated, and very clearly I might add, by their decision to not take the proper steps to ensure that aircraft's horizontal stabilizer's proper and timely maintenance. *Alaska Airline's* corporate insatiable greed is what led to that needless and horrifying passenger and flight crewmember experience, which ultimately left those people with inescapable death. That is my opinion, and it is also my strong opinion that their behavior was completely reprehensible and they should be held responsible to answer for all of those lives lost and families that were so sadly affected! So where are they now, and why have they not been brought up on charges? Are these *corporate execs* and *FAA big shots* exempt from the laws that everyone else has to answer to? You bet they are! They are powerful people with powerful friends in powerful places, don't kid yourselves! According to staff writer for the Washington Post: *On January 2003, a US Airway Express flight operated by Air Midwest crashed shortly after take-off from Charlotte, North Carolina, killing all 21 passengers and crewmembers that were on board, and it is believed to have happened because of an "inexperienced" mechanic at an "outsourced" maintenance contractor chop shop, who performed improper work on the aircraft. Did someone hold those execs and FAA supervisors accountable? In 1999, ValuJet Flight 592 crashed into the Florida Everglades after taking off from Miami International Airport. The crash was attributed to oxygen canisters that were improperly stowed in the aircraft's hold, by maintenance employees working for an "outsourced" chop shop contractor. All 110 people on board that flight were killed!* How about that airline's corporate people and their FAA buddies, are they in jail today? I don't think so! Let me update you on *Qantas Airlines*, and the problems they have had so far in *just 2008!* Keep in mind that *Qantas* at one time had a very impressive safety record before they began heavily *"outsourcing"* their aircraft maintenance to save money and in this year alone, they have not only managed to shatter that safety record with one mid air emergency after another due to aircraft malfunctions, but have prompted *Boeing* to put all airlines flying its planes on notice, as well as an all out international investigation that will most likely indefinitely ground all *747s* thereby affecting thousands of aircrafts around the world. The bottom line here seems to always remain the same. The flying public as well as the flight crewmembers are the ones who are paying the tremendous price for this *"money saving"* aircraft maintenance *"outsourcing"*, and we're paying that price with either our *SAFETY* which is constantly being disregarded and placed in harms way, or our *LIVES,* the way the people on all those *"outsourced"* aircraft maintenance flights paid with theirs, and absolutely no one is going to jail for it! Oh no. They all walk away form these devastated airline companies with their *golden parachutes* containing millions of dollars, for killing hundreds, NO thousands of people. As in the case of *September 11th, 2001*, I hold *United and American Airlines corporate management and our government* responsible for the atrocity. Should they had shown the very much deserved *RESPECT* and *CONSIDERATION* to those flight crewmembers who died on those fatal flights, by providing them with a *"heads up"* warning, as well as the much needed training that they lacked regarding this type of hijacking, it would have given them a much better chance of survival had they known ahead of time exactly what they were dealing with. Given the proper information might have allowed them the ability to combat that horrific situation in flight, and perhaps the ending of that tragic day would not have had to end so tragically! Yet no one protests against this irresponsible corporate leadership displayed by these commercial airlines execs and government agents, or holds any of them accountable for what happened on that day! That is what is unbelievable to me! Ironically enough, **Qantas engineers** had argued and warned that the cost cutting and moving of these aircraft's maintenance could put safety at risk! Well, what the hell would they know about the maintenance of the aircrafts, right? Wrong! They are the **"trained"**, **"skilled' and FAA "certified" mechanics** of this airline are you kidding me! Let's check to see if indeed those **Qantas mechanics** not only knew what they were talking about, then tried to warn their corporate execs about as well, just in case any of you out there could still possibly doubt that they do. For those of you who might choose to continue to buy into the blatant **LIES** and excuses that these airline companies' **CEO's and FAA** higher ups always seem to come up with, every time they have these mid air aircraft emergency situations arise that they conveniently try to deflect the attention from, because they know damn well that the emergency situations are occurring from the improper maintenance work done on these aircrafts, by the unskilled people working on them, in their *"outsourced "* chop shops: *January 7: Flight QF 2* with 344 passengers on board was about 15 minutes from Bangkok on the way from London to Sydney when the 747 lost main electrical power and landed on battery back up (outsourced maintenance). *January 13: Flight QF 93* carrying more than 200 passengers on a Boeing 747 from Melbourne to Los Angeles, made an emergency landing in Hawaii after an oxygen leak (outsourced maintenance). *February 19: A Qantas Dash-8* had the nose wheel malfunction during a flight from Gladstone to Rockhampton and passengers were ordered to get into the crash position for landing (outsourced maintenance). *March 2: QF 925* from Cairns begins leaking oil during its descent (outsource maintenance). *March 25: QF 12* from Los Angeles to Sydney carrying 217 passengers blows three tires and has to be stopped mid take off (outsourced maintenance). *March 29: QF 580* Boeing 747 carrying 420 passengers made an emergency landing when an external window in Business class "popped" (outsourced maintenance). **May 13: QF 805 Boeing 737-800** carrying 92 passengers from Sydney Airport to Canberra had two tires explode on take off, and passengers had to be evacuated (outsourced maintenance). **June 20: A Qantas Link Dash-8** operating as *QF2495* from Horn Island to Cairns was diverted to Weipa for an emergency landing after the flight crew shut down an engine due to a cockpit warning (outsourced maintenance). *July 25: QF 30* from Hong Kong to Melbourne was forced to make an emergency landing after an explosion blasted a hole in the fuselage of the aircraft (outsourced maintenance). *July 27: QF 548* from Sydney to Brisbane carrying 155 passengers was towed from the take off runway, after hydraulics failure (outsourced maintenance). *July 28:* A Qantas plane that was Melbourne bound had to return to Adelaide because the doors covering the nose- wheel bay did not close properly after take off (outsourced maintenance). Okay, here's the new story about the stabilizer. Today, *August 14, 2008: QF 31* from Sydney to London thru Singapore was delayed this afternoon by six hours, after it was discovered that the Boeing 747-400's horizontal stabilizer jack screw needed *"urgent" maintenance.* The jack screw is that very important component I mentioned earlier, that will seize up if it is not regularly checked and lubricated and it's proper maintenance is vital because corrosion poses a real risk and must be eliminated to prevent this key component from seizing up which will cause a catastrophic crash, such as the one on that *Alaska Airlines in 2000.* The passengers as well as the flight crewmembers who were on *Qantas Fight QF 31 on August 14, 2008* can thank their lucky stars that the mechanical problem on their aircraft was caught on the ground instead of mid air or they too would have faced the exact horrific fate that those poor passengers and flight crewmembers traveling on the *Alaska Airlines flight that crashed in*

2000 did. Sadly they were not as fortunate! Once your aircraft stabilizer is gone, guess what? So are you! The grave consequences arising from the commercial airline's irresponsible *"third world"* outsourcing is starting to finally rear its ugly head and it is definitely begun taking its toll on the flying public in this country. To make you, the flying public, as well as every commercial airline flight attendant out there understand the severity and ramifications involved in this atrocious and current on going situation that the FAA as well as other Aviation Industry Government protection agencies in this country should have stopped a long time ago, I have decided to count all the **Qantas passenger and crewmember** lives for you, regardless of whether or not the occurrences ended up being fatal because of the very fact that **ALL** of these mid air emergency incidents could have ended up in that very manner, *FATAL!* Maybe if we see the numbers, it will bring all of us exactly where it is that we all need to be; *UNITED in PROTEST!* Without counting four of the flights because I did not have exact passenger and flight crewmember count, there were, are you ready for this; *ONE THOUSAND, SEVEN HUNDRED AND SEVENTY FOUR (1,774)* passengers and flight crewmembers that could all be *DEAD* today. That's more than half of the people who died on *September 11th 2001!* What is even more alarming is that most of those lives that were placed in such needless peril were from just *ONE* commercial airline, and that's *Qantas!* This information has to shock the most hard core flyer out there, which I would consider myself to be, since I am a commercial airline flight attendant after all, who spends roughly *eighty percent of my life at 39,000 feet*, and I can honestly tell you that I am horrified! All I can think of after researching and reading all this information is how *LUCKY* I have been the last few years of my career that I have been flying, because *American Airlines Flight Service* management at *LAX (Los Angeles International*

Airport) has been behaving quite badly, and I am no stranger to the harassment and intimidation tactics they use in order to get their flight attendants to fly safety compromised aircrafts/flights full of unsuspecting passengers. I unfortunately have been dealing with the repercussions that come from not engaging in such ***criminal activities*** since roughly **2003,** but it doesn't matter what they choose to inflict on me because I will ***NEVER*** allow myself to take an aircraft up or work a flight that I do not feel is ***safe!*** Besides the fact that I feel I'm too cute and too young to die, I've just never had the desire to find my self up at **39,000 feet** asking myself; *"what the hell were you smoking?"* I suppose my question to all of you out there who use commercial airline companies as your long distance form of travel is, are you willing to take a chance with yours or your loved one's lives? On ***August 14, 2008***, a second ***Qantas Airlines*** mid air emergency occurred where a **747** engine switched to idle as it was on approach to **Auckland Airport**! *QF 25 from Sydney to Los Angeles thru Auckland* had begun its descent when its engine just rolled itself into the idle mode. The cockpit crew however, was able to restore the aircraft's power quickly, and the **747** landed safely. Let's address the huge ***SAFETY*** issue that this current outsourcing situation is providing us, the flying public and flight crewmembers with shall we? According to the ***Washington Post***, in March, the ***Immigration and Customs Enforcement Agency*** made 27 illegal immigrant arrests at one of this country's largest *"third party"* contract aircraft maintenance facilities located in ***Greensboro, North Carolina.*** The illegal immigrants came from **Central and South America, Sudan and the Philippines**, and although none of these people had terrorist ties, what do we do? Do we wait for the next illegal immigrant *"round up"* comes around to find out if the next group will have terrorist ties? Maybe the next roundup will turn up some of ***Atta's (9/11 flight 11 hijacker)*** family members, or maybe some of ***Bin***

Laden's merry men that have been employed by these outsourced maintenance facilities, and have been working diligently on the very aircrafts that the people of the **United States of America** will be flying on! What the Hell is wrong with this entire picture! Why is it that the American people have become so complacent, that we completely roll over and allow these **morons** who really don't care if any of us live or die, as long as they are getting the numbers they want to see on their damn balance sheets, so they can continue living their *"privileged"* and self indulged lives in the Cayman Islands, to get away with their bloody criminal behavior? What is wrong with us? We are all *"sitting ducks"* waiting to be turned into **Duck Le'Orange**, and I don't even like duck! Why does it take tragedies' like **September 11th** to happen, before we start paying serious attention to the injustices that we clearly see, and put up with, such as the inexcusable, self indulging behavior of all of these IDIOTS that for some reason seem to be calling all the shots that affect the rest of us in our daily lives. For instance, take the not only embarrassing but stupid and dangerous *idiot of idiots* that we have allowed to run our country into the ground, and not for just one term. That would have been bad enough, but for two! How in the name of all that is sacred, did we ever let that one happen? We have become a society of *"self entitled"*, *"non accountable"* and *"complacent"* people, and by the way, hold off from blowing up those balloons and throwing yourself a party over the fact that we are all bearing a strong resemblance to those descriptions, because they are not attributes by any means. We are giving ultimate power to individuals who are using a **Me, Myself and I approach** to every thing they do, and every decision that they make which ultimately affect all of **US**! They are literally playing a chess game with our very lives! I know we're better than that, aren't we? Does anyone out there besides me, remember watching one of **Bin Laden's** videos on television where he is ranting on and on about *"death to all infidels" (in case any of you have forgotten, he's referring to all of us)*, and how **September 11th** was going to look like a picnic in comparison to what he and his merry men had planned for us "down the road"? What? Did you think he was just kidding with all of us and he really didn't mean it? I'd venture to say that *"down the road"*, is actually right around the corner. It's coming up on seven years this **September 11th**, and what have we done to make ourselves any safer than we were on that God forsaken day! Not a thing, that's what! Our airport security is a joke. Our borders are still wide open, and illegal aliens are coming in by the droves. We are faced with moral and ethical corruption at every turn, including much of our government entities, and now we can add commercial airline companies *"outsourcing"* the extremely important job of maintaining our aircrafts that are flying throughout the **United States of America** and abroad, to *"third world"* chop shops that have people working on them, who are no where near qualified in any capacity, to do that job and who don't even have to answer to the **FAA** the way to which our guys here at home do. What a perfect opportunity we are placing right in the hands of AlQueda, and all the many other different terrorists groups out there, that would like nothing more than to blow us all up to kingdom come. These U. S. commercial airline companies' are leaving the door **WIDE** open, for terrorist having complete access to our airplanes, with their aircraft maintenance **"outsourcing!"** But hey! As long as the TSA has grandma taking her shoes off at that airport security line and checking them for bombs, or they strip search that 8 months pregnant woman and her two year old toddler's diaper, in case she's stashed *"anthrax"* in it, we're bound to stay **SAFE** right? As ridiculous as that sounds, that's how ridiculous it has become. Have we not learned anything from our unnecessary losses and our tragedies? We keep falling back to that unrelenting state of denial that many of us live in and let rule our lives? Is that really where we are the most comfortable? Why do we insist on remaining ignorant of what is really happening all around us, or just burying our heads in the sand, thinking that if we don't see it, it will just go away. Well, it's not going to go away, unless we all **STAND** up and make it, and all of them go away! We continuously demonstrate to the rest of the world how out of touch so many of us really are. Has this just become our lazy way of life? Always waiting for somebody else to take care of things and fix our problems? We have to fight against the *"inside destruction"* that is currently happening to our country, by the greed of our very own people! I suppose what really chaps me the most, is the nonchalant statements that ***Mr. Peter Gibson from Australia's Civil Aviation Safety Authority*** made to the press about the passengers and flight crewmembers on that ***Alaska Airline's*** flight that had the smoke coming out of the back of the aircraft in mid air, and had to return to the airport for an emergency landing. He had the audacity to say: *"the passengers had not been in any danger"*, like we are all a bunch of dumb asses who are suppose to believe that eleven **Qantas** flight emergency situations, most of them occurring in mid air and in one year mind you, with three of those eleven in a period of **EIGHT DAYS**, is nothing to worry about. That's really easy for you to say, **Mr. Gibson**. You were not up there worrying about whether or not you were going to make it back down on solid ground and walk away from that airplane alive! I suppose exposing hundreds and thousands of passengers to extremely dangerous and life threatening situations, with a possible catastrophic disaster ending is just another day at the office for you, **Mr. Gibson!** Star light, star bright, I wish I may, I wish I might, have the wish I wish tonight; and you know what I would wish? That every time any one of you people opened your mouth to give your lame excuses and your *"cover ups"* downplaying explanations and **LIES** regarding your negligent and unconscionable behavior, that every single person watching you would be able to know you were all lying because your nose would start growing like Pinocchio's, and the more you talked, the more it would grow! God, wouldn't that be great! *Mr. Gibson*, sir, how easy it is for you to be on solid ground, running your ridiculous mouth with your incredulous statements to the press about how the passengers and flight crewmembers *"had not been in any danger"* when that **Qantas Boeing 767** had to return to *Sydney Airport* for an emergency landing. The visible smoke coming from the back of the aircraft on take off that the air traffic controllers noticed and reported to the Captain is alarming! The fact that it turned out to be hydraulic fluid spewing from a spoiler actuator near the wing is also alarming! How do you even verbalize all that *"never in danger"* nonsense with a straight face! Then you have the audacity to go on talking your stupidity as if you could be taken at face value about anything you were saying at this point, and you continued with quote: *"the 767 has three independent hydraulic systems on board, so if one springs a leak, there are two others to back it up, and the safety of the aircraft was not at risk"*. Are you kidding me! It doesn't matter whether that *767* has three hydraulic systems on board, or ten, because that leak alone was not the severity of the problem, and you know it! The problem was that the air traffic controllers could see **SMOKE!** The fact of the matter that you damn well know sir, is that in order for there to be visible smoke, which there was, any number of circumstances involving extreme heat or even fire were probably involved in some way that combined themselves with that hydraulic fluid leak thereby allowing cause for a possible aircraft fire, and as an American Airline flight attendant who has been around for 32 years, trained for these kinds of emergencies, we know that where there is smoke means there is probably fire, and fire is not anything you want to be dealing with on a *767* flying mid air, with 200 passengers on board. We know how quickly an airplane of any size can be consumed by fire within minutes. The sheer fact that the Captain circled the ocean dumping fuel before he brought that aircraft in for a landing, so as to not bring that aircraft down *"heavy"* with fuel says it all doesn't it, **Mr. Gibson**, sir. There's also two little facts that magnifies the absurdity of your *"passengers were never in any danger"* statement that, if you haven't noticed yet, I happen to resent tremendously, and those would be that one: when the air traffic controllers informed the Captain that they could see smoke coming out of the back of the airplane, the cause of that smoke or the exact location of where it was coming from had not been determined yet, and two: hydraulic fluid doesn't *"smoke"* without extreme heat being added to the mix, and if you should mix extreme heat with hydraulic fluid, you should be able to make yourself a perfect combustion cocktail that would probably engulf that *767* and everyone who happens to be on it, in a matter of minutes, if you were in the wrong place (*the middle of the ocean*) at the wrong time, don't you agree sir? So why in the hell would you make a public statement about how the passengers and flight crewmembers on that aircraft were never in danger? That is a blatant LIE and you know it. HOW DARE YOU! Then there is the brilliant leadership from **Qantas Airline's CEO and the CFO, Mr. Geoff Dixon and Mr. Peter Gregg**; the two corporate *"big shots"* that the employees, labor and otherwise, can thank for leading **Qantas Airlines** to where they find themselves today. I am sure they are all so grateful for that! Just months prior to the numerous mid air emergency abominations **Qantas** is currently dealing with now, I'm sure those two egotistical corporate heads couldn't get enough adoration and praise from their piers and were eating up all the compliments and indulging in the many *"pats on the back"* they were receiving from their shareholders and fellow corporate executives who revered them and referred to them as *"integral to the success of the company for the past eight years, serving their shareholders with distinction!"* as quoted in the **National Brisbane Times on August 3, 2008**. That's really what it's all about for you people isn't it? All you CEO's just love to hear other CEO's and execs spew about how you are greater than great and how you know how to make money for those shareholders! Well, my, my, my. All that glory and adoration has been coming your way non stop (**no pun intended**) for the last eight years hasn't it, and you have just been wallowing in all of it, haven't you? You made a big mistake though, when you decided that the money that you saved the company by paying an unqualified, unskilled and un certified laborer in a "third world country $8 dollars an hour, instead of paying a completely qualified and trained mechanic that has attended hours of classes in order to receive his/her FAA certification, would better serve all of you if it ended up in your own pockets instead of back into the company and it's employees. For as smart as you and your piers and shareholders think that you are, you turned out to be quite lacking in the intelligence department didn't you? Especially the part where you didn't figure out the fact that *"outsourcing"* the maintenance of your airplanes to "third world" countries and allowing people who didn't know what the hell they were doing, was bound to come back and bite you in the ass, and bite you it did! So what is not only protocol, but typical behavior for people like you to display when as some of us put it; **"the shit hits the fan?"** You run like the cowards that you are, and resign! Yeah; you jump right into those million dollar parachutes that are built in and guaranteed in your contracts back when you were signing up with the company as the new and brilliant CEO and CFO! How nice for you both, and I am sure what makes it even nicer for you is the fact that you get all those millions on your way out regardless of whether you run the company into the ground while you're there or not! Both of you literally resigned/retired within hours of the current *Qantas Airlines* debacle you helped create, leaving the mess behind for your labor and other employees to clean up. You know the ones who never made the exorbitant amount of money that the two of you have made. The same ones that need as well as depend on their jobs and salaries and benefits from the continued success of their airline company *Qantas*, so that they can meet their mortgage payments and pay their medical bills and send their children to college. Those hard working people who, unlike you two, really ARE what makes up *Qantas Airlines*! Remember them? I am going to ask both of you two questions, *Mr. Dixon and Mr. Gregg*, that I am hoping you could answer for me, because I have put this question to many of my own *American Airlines* scumbag corporate leaders and supervisors, and when I do, all they ever seem to do is just glare at me! Maybe you can answer for me exactly how it is that you can sleep at night knowing the horror that you inspire from the self serving decisions that you make daily, that detrimentally affect everyone around you, except your *"chosen few"* of course? What do you tell your kids when they want to know what you do for a living? Do you tell them that you are egotistical and self absorbed and consumed with such salacious greed, that you can't care about anything or anyone that doesn't monetarily satisfy you, and you mow down anything that gets in the way of your achieving that goal in order to get that greed pacified? If that's not how you are describing yourselves to your families, then they are not really getting the true picture of who you are and what you are capable of doing to others, because greed is most definitely who and what you people are all about, and you've proven that by demonstrating such little regard for the lives of the passengers you transport everyday, as well as your very own flight crewmembers that are on those very aircrafts that you gave the thumbs up for having their maintenance outsourced to *"third world"* chop shops! Well, as you are now seeing for yourselves, that corporate mentality that you both operate and work under may be great for the office, and in your big shot fancy board rooms where you make your decisions on whose throats you're going to slice up next, oh, I beg your pardon, that's what you people call mergers and acquisitions, right? Sorry! Anyway, this is what I consider to be your biggest problem when overseeing a passenger commercial airline company as opposed to a huge conglomeration type business that you people are usually overseeing, such as ***Enron***, for example. When you take your ***"corporate mindset"*** into Enron, for instance, the employees as well as anyone involved, except for you and your ***"chosen few"*** of course, end up being swindled from everything they've worked hard for and sacrificed all their lives for, and as bad as that can be, and I don't want to downplay or disrespect their horrific situation in any way, but they still get to walk away with their very LIVES and start over! On the other hand, when you bring your ***"corporate mindset"*** to a passenger commercial airline company, you end up literally ***"killing"*** people because the manner in which you conduct your corporate process of overseeing the company, usually entails that of applying cut backs after cut backs, until you reach the monetary amounts on your corporate balance sheets that are pleasing to you and your stockholders. Well, if you haven't figured it out by now, the ***"corporate mindset"*** which you possess and the ***"human element"***, which is what keeps all passenger commercial airline companies operating and running, are like ***"oil and water"***; they do not MIX! Corporate is about the numbers on the balance sheets at the end of the day, and how much is left for the ***CEO***, ***top corporate executives*** and the ***stockholders.*** Commercial airlines are about ***first and foremost*** having the safety in place for the passengers they transport and the flight crewmembers that work for them, and everything else having to come after that! Therefore, once again, in order to ensure the **SAFETY** of all passengers and flight crewmembers, the immense and critical danger that the *"corporate mindset"* poses for the a*viation industry* has to be removed so to accomplish that, the entire *corporate leadership* has to be removed and replaced with a system that assures not only the success of the commercial airline companies, but the entire *aviation industry* all together! All I can tell you is that if the proper authorities don't start getting a handle on this currently ongoing and incredibly dangerous and frightening *"third world"* commercial airline aircraft maintenance *"outsourcing"* that is based on complete corporate corruption and greed, it is only a matter of time before it will surely begin to take the lives of many of us, unfortunately in huge numbers at a time, when you think about how many people a *Boeing 747 or 767* can carry on board just one flight. We have to begin protesting this kind of *immoral and unethical* business practices and misconduct to the government departments that are suppose to protect us, until we are heard, starting with the *Homeland Security* and all of their aviation departments. They need to spend less time in their ridiculous *TSA airport drama productions* that we are being subjected to, which provide nothing more than a false sense of security, and spend more time truly overseeing these airline companies' execs and start putting a halt to their shady, and very avariciously inventive corporate business practices such as, but not limited to, ordering *company cut backs after cut backs*, as well as the *constant concessions demands* from their labor employees, because apparently they are so determined to walk away with *exorbitant amounts of money* to line their own pockets, that in their estimations, if achieving that very scenario for themselves means that a few of *US* go down with the ship, than so be it! Well, for all you *self serving, irresponsible, money grubbing CEO's* out there that are overseeing the aviation industry's commercial airlines with a *complete disregard for your* *passengers and flight crewmembers well being as well as safety,* I'll leave you with this; *If you people find that you do the despicable things that you do because you're all under the delusional impression that you are somehow special and therefore think that you are entitled above everyone else, so you live your lives as if you were going to exist forever, you might want to re-think that absurd philosophy of yours, because you're NOT!* In the meantime, while you're re-thinking, *I will hold no ill will towards any of you whatsoever; on the contrary. I will say a prayer for all of you tonight, and honestly, may God have mercy on all of your souls!* In any case, *American Airlines Flight Attendants,* and all other commercial airline flight attendants, including *Qantas* flight attendants, we have been left with no other recourse but to *do what we know is right*, and what is right is for all of us to take a united **STAND!**

CHAPTER 21

"IN CLOSING" FROM ONE AMERICAN AIRLINES FLIGHT ATTENDANT TO ANOTHER

What could I possibly have left to say to all of you that I haven't already said in the previous 20 chapters? If we want *American Airlines* to start making its way back out of the *abyss* it is presently being guided directly into by the *unconscionable* and *inordinately desirous* corporate executives and corporate employees that dare to call themselves our leadership, we are all going to have to stop groveling for the scraps they have the audacity to call our salaries and benefits that are thrown our way. *Every single one of us need to come together and focus on finding a new and different approach for "successfully" (key word there) demanding from these so called self appointed leaders, what is rightfully and respectfully ours on every level, not because we have entitlement issues, but because we have worked hard and earned it, and then take it back!* Then, we have to use all of the resources available to us, such as our *APFA labor attorneys, The President of the United States (not the current one), Congressmen, Senators, Lobbyists and every other body of legislation out there, along with all existing government regulators and lawmaking entities that are responsible for governing and policing our skies,* and begin a powerful movement to *rid* the aviation industry's commercial airline companies of all *corporate mindset executives, who place "above all" importance on revenue rather than on passenger and crewmember safety and lives.* Laws need to be passed that will protect the flying public as well as the flight crewmembers that work for these commercial airline companies' from the catastrophic harm that *can* and *will* most certainly come, from the *excessive desire for wealth* that is currently being used by the corporate executives and stockholders as their *example* and *inspiration* for overseeing the airline companies'. The aviation industry's commercial airline companies' simply cannot be allowed to continue conducting business with the flying public in the current manner in which they are. The devastation that has happened to this country's economy which was made possible by the abundance of *insatiable corporate greed* belonging to the many in *Wall Street*, who were left to wheel and deal on their own without any kind of oversight whatsoever, is the perfect example of why we can no longer afford to keep that very same *"corporate mentality"* in the aviation industry's commercial airlines. *Wall Street's horrendous negative impact on our country's economy, as bad as that most certainly is, pales in comparison to the horrendous negative impact there would be on the immeasurable loss of "human lives," should the current conditions remain in place as to the manner in which the aviation industry's corporate executives oversee this country's commercial airline companies.* Was the morning of *September 11th, 2001* not enough proof for all of us, of the horror and detriment that can come from the *corporate greed that presently has such a strong hold on our entire country?* The *unsafe* aircrafts *we "allow"* ourselves to be intimidated into flying, the all too short, non recovery layovers *we "allow" American's* execs to force us to have, the numerous hours that we work for **FREE** that **we "allow"** them to get away with not paying us, the **FAA mandated** flight attendant equipment that **we "allow"** them to force us to pay out of our own pockets, the list goes on and on and on, and you know what? **We are the ones that "allow" AA's** corporate management to get away with all of it, and that's not even inclusive of the literal abuse **we "allow"** them to bestow upon us on a daily basis! Let's go there, shall we? The harassment that our worthless supervisors show us on a daily basis **we "allow"**, the **"illegal"** and **"ridiculous"** company sick time and attendance policy harassment **we "allow"**, the flight attendant reprimanding for passenger misconduct **we "allow"**, the **disrespect** and complete **disregard** shown to us by **Flight Service** management employees **we "allow"**, the rude, embarrassing, demeaning, power tripping uncalled for behavior and treatment that many **American Airlines reservation/ gate agents shower us as well as our families with, every time we non rev, we "allow"**, or how about my favorite the **"don't speak up"** about any **unethical** or **criminal Corporate/Flight Service Management behavior** that endangers the lives of flight crewmembers and passengers alike or you will be labeled **"insubordinate"** and we will make your life miserable threats, **we "allow"**. Let's keep going because I am on a roll here! How about the embarrassingly dirty aircrafts we continuously take off and land with, **we "allow"**, or the filthy **un-sanitized** passenger blankets and pillows they have us offer to our passengers, flight after flight, after flight **we "allow"**, or the needlessly intense and harrowing boarding experience that the **"stressed out to the max"** gate agents provide for us, **we "allow"**. Have you had enough yet? I know I have, and in case you haven't noticed, that **whining gig** that we are constantly doing for each other about everything that is wrong with **AA's** current corporate management, well **IT'S NOT WORKING!** **Whining** to each other when we get on the airplanes, **about the horrific depletion** *of the high standards once belonging to not only our beloved profession but our beloved company as well, isn't going to get us anywhere except exactly where we are finding ourselves today. In dire straights!* We are hanging on to the minimums on every aspect of our jobs, and therefore we have exhausted all leeway for any more company *"bankrupting"* threats coming from *AA's* corporate management, mandating labor employee concessions, to make up the money that they have paid themselves in unearned *"bloated salaries"* and unearned *"bloated bonuses",* instead of putting it back into the company. The *morally* and *ethically* vacant **IDIOTS** that are running *American Airlines,* right into the ground I might add, are the ones who now need to make all necessary concessions to keep the airline afloat, until we can restore it to the prosperous airline it was before the corporate executives took it over. After all, when you stop and think about it, it is their *genius brainstorming* as well as the many *disastrous* and *financially unsound decisions* based on their absolute *"GREED"* that have adversely affected our company as well as all of its labor employees. It's not just *us* that they are hurting it's our *passengers* and our entire *aviation industry* as well! We can't just sit back and think that it's the job of the *APFA,* or that it is they who are responsible for getting the despicable people who are running our airline company ousted from the company, or at the very least, removed from their current managerial and decision making positions in order to begin the long process of getting this company turned around. We are the *APFA!* Did we all forget what the letters in *APFA* stand for? For those of you that can't remember let me refresh your memory. Those letters stand for; *Association of Professional Flight Attendants.* That's *US!* Remember? *You and Me!* We need to get off our ambivalent and complacent asses and start fighting and taking back what is ours. *Flight attendants, we are so busy running scared of losing our jobs that we* *haven't had time to notice that our jobs are being lost for us!* If the people who are presently in control of *American Airlines* are not held accountable for the detriment that they have caused this company and all who respect and work for her, we won't have to worry about our disappearing benefits, or our current measly *1989 retro* wages that we are currently working our asses off for every month, not to mention the retirement we earned and were promised for the many loyal and diligent hard working years of our lives that we dedicated to our company. At the rate that things are going, *American Airlines* will cease to exist in the not so distant future, and even if it did somehow manage to keep from going under all together, *if it is allowed to continue in its current infamous infrastructure, they will surely step up the lack of conscience and accountability for everything that they do, which is almost the very manner in which it is operating in today anyway!* What we need to asks ourselves is; how much worse can our aviation industry and our flight attendant profession deteriorate? It is a rhetorical question that I think most of us know the answer to. If for some reason what we do for a living and where we do it momentarily escapes any of us, let me quickly remind you once again that we are *American Airlines Flight Attendants whose profession is performed at roughly 39,000 feet above sea level for approximately 80% of our lives give or take a percentage or two. We work in a long but relatively confined space that is pressurized and always moving. Our profession requires and demands much from all of us in the way of any or all emergency situations we encounter in flight. We are responsible for saving hundreds of lives in a matter of minutes when commanding an aircraft evacuation in an emergency landing, and during a hijacking (and we all know those are no longer the "take me to Cuba" kind), we become the buffers between the passengers and the hijackers, as well as the cockpit crew and the hijackers.* Then there's the smaller, *less magnified* problems we encounter frequently and have to take care of, such as a *passenger having a heart attack* in flight, as his/her family look to us and depend on our skills to save their loved one's life, or the passenger who is crying hysterically because he/she is *petrified to fly.* So we take turns sitting next to them throughout the entire five hour flight, trying to reassure them that everything is going to be okay. Then there's the mother traveling with her infant who starts screaming *"my baby is choking"*, as the baby is turning blue! Or how about the *diabetic woman who doesn't take her medication* before the flight, and by the time we find out about it, she is *lying in the middle of the aisle* convulsing from the full blown insulin shock she is having. Let's not forget about that *"extra fun"* emergency situation of having a *FIRE* break out in the middle of a flight when you're up at *39,000 feet* that we are all so fond of! This particular emergency situation happened to me personally, a few years ago during the days when I worked the *Boeing 747.* My flight crew and I were returning home from a two day trip and were en route from *JFK to LAX on American Airlines Flight 1.* The flight was completely full, and there were fifteen crewmembers on board. Incidentally, it was one of the first flights that took off under new *Federal Aviation Laws* that were now in effect, where *smoking was now completely prohibited on any U. S. domestic commercial airline passenger flights.* Moments after we had completed the meal service and the in-flight movie was playing for our passengers, the *"All Call"* button on the *aircraft's PA/phone* system chimed at every flight attendant station. When each flight attendant picked up the call on her/his phone at his/her respective cabin area, what we heard on the other side of the line was the voice of one of the coach cabin flight attendant's who was in the very rear of the aircraft, *calmly* calling us back there, so that we could help assist her in an emergency that had transpired. There was a *fire* in one of the aft lavatories. It was started by one of our passengers who was a smoker, and had decided at that point in the flight that she could no longer keep herself from smoking a cigarette. She went into the aft lavatory to smoke her cigarette, and after she finished it, she then irresponsibly disposed of it in that lavatory's trash receptacle, where the embers from the cigarette that was still lit quickly attached themselves to the paper products that had also been disposed of in the same trash receptacle, ultimately igniting them. When I picked up the phone on the **ALL call** chime, I was working in the **upper level of the first class cabin** area at the time and after hearing the information, I immediately hung up the phone, headed for the curved stairway that would take me down to the **main level** of the aircraft, and **I distinctly remember how I literally jumped on the stairway railing and slid all the way down on my butt to the main floor, where I jumped off the railing, grabbed a fire extinguisher, and continued running to the back of the airplane!** I will **NEVER** in my lifetime forget the tremendous feeling of anxiety that came over me, and the intense manner in which my heart was pounding at that precise moment on that flight! To this day, I have never moved that quickly again. As the other flight attendants and I got closer to the affected area, the passengers who could clearly see what was happening were screaming **"there is a fire in the back!"** Smoke was already billowing out from the inside of the lavatory through the door frame, and the rear of the coach cabin began quickly filling up with smoke, already making it difficult to breathe! Just as I was getting back there along with four of the other flight attendants, all of us having our fire extinguishers in hand and ready, one of our male flight attendants opened the lavatory door after spraying the frame of the door first, then began spraying the source of the fire that was located in the trash receptacle, until it was finally extinguished. **When we finally discovered what had caused the fire and identified the passenger** *responsible for providing the adrenaline rush for the entire flight crew and the hundreds of passengers that were on the flight,* we informed the cockpit crew that all was well once again in the rear of the aircraft. The captain then informed us that he had radioed ahead for the authorities to meet the flight upon arrival at *LAX,* where they would be personally escorting off our *"nicotine addicted"* passenger, who nearly caused what no doubt would have been a fatal plane crash of enormous proportion, especially with an aircraft the size of that of our Boeing 747. What most passengers who travel on commercial airlines don't realize is that if there is a fire that breaks out on an aircraft in flight, and the working flight attendants don't get it together up there fast enough, and quickly locate the source of the fire and completely extinguish it before it escalates to a degree where it is no longer extinguishable, the chances of passenger and crewmember survival are nil to none! "There is a *table from a UK CAA report from 2002,* which supports the generally held view that, from the first indication that there is a fire on board an aircraft, the crew historically has approximately *seventeen minutes* to get the aircraft on the ground. A fire in the air is one of the most hazardous situations that a flight crew can be faced with. Without aggressive intervention by the flight crew, a fire on board an aircraft can lead to the catastrophic loss of that aircraft within a very short space of time. Once a fire has become established, it is unlikely that the crew will be able to extinguish it." *(http://www.skybrary.aero/index.php/In-Flight_Fire).* When it comes to *fires* in flight, *"time is of the essence"* is quite the understatement! I feel that all of us who were on that *Boeing 747* were very fortunate to have caught that fire in time. Many of us have been around long enough to remember the catastrophic *aft lavatory fire incident similar to ours,* that happened on a *McDonnell Douglas DC-9 (Super 80)* aircraft and caused an emergency landing on *June 2,*

391

1983. Air Canada's Flight 797, en route from **Dallas Fort Worth International to Toronto, Canada** had a fire on the aircraft in flight and ended up making an emergency landing. In an abstract synopsis taken from the *official report published by the National Transportation Safety Board* (**NTSB**), it was stated that "The flight left **Dallas, Texas, to Montreal, Quebec, Canada,** with an en route stop **at Toronto, Canada.** The flight had *five crewmembers and forty one passengers on board.* While en route at flight level *330 (33,000 feet),* the cabin crew discovered a fire in the aft lavatory. After contacting air traffic control *(ATC)* and declaring an emergency, the crew made an emergency descent and **ATC** vectored flight 797 to the **Greater Cincinnati International Airport.** As the pilot stopped the airplane, the airport fire department, which had been alerted by the tower of the fire on board the incoming plane, was in place and began firefighting operations. As soon as the airplane stopped, the flight attendants and passengers opened the left and right forward doors, the left over wing exit and the forward and aft right over wing exits. About *sixty to ninety seconds after the exits were opened a flash fire enveloped the airplane interior.* While **eighteen passengers and three flight attendants** exited through the forward doors, slides, and the three over wing exits to evacuate the airplane and the **captain and first officer** exited through their respective cockpit sliding windows, *twenty three passengers* however, were not able to get out of the plane and *died in the fire. The airplane was destroyed".* Even though the **FAA** claimed they could not pin point exactly where the fire had started, *(how convenient for Air Canada and the FAA),* it was believed to have been started from *a passenger smoking in one of the aft lavatories*, and although it doesn't seem like it, they were lucky, because only twenty three passengers were killed in that *"passenger cigarette smoking" incident* instead of everybody who was on board that aircraft. Luck, however, was unfortunately not on the side of the passengers who were traveling to Atlanta from Miami on *May 11, 1999,* when a *ValuJet* aircraft crashed due to a cabin fire that broke out in flight, killing *ALL* passengers and flight crewmembers that were on board. According to a report given by *Consumer Affairs on January 22, 2005* on *airlines outsourcing maintenance,* they reported that *"In 1999, ValuJet flight 592* crashed into the *Florida Everglades after taking off from Miami International Airport,* killing all one hundred ten on board. The crash was attributed to oxygen canisters improperly stowed in the aircraft's hold by maintenance employees working for an outside contractor."* Every single time commercial airline flight attendants take to the skies, we go up there *"knowing"* that anything could transpire at any time during the course of our flight that would require us to hopefully be able to *successfully* handle whatever that may be, and we go up there *"willingly",* because that is who we are, and this job is what we love to do! It is after all, what separates us from the rest and what we are most proud of. Call me crazy, but I for one believe that very fact alone deserves to be shown a little more respect than we give it; and if we don't respect ourselves for what we do, how or why would anyone else! *With everything that I know to be true about all of you; the good hearted and caring people that you are, the selfless, hard working, loyal and highly intelligent and world traveled qualities that you all possess,* it is really difficult for me to understand how some of you could come to the conclusion that allowing Flight Service management to put you into the despicable position of flying compromised aircraft/flights oversold with *unsuspecting passengers,* is justifiable in some way! *Our passengers deserve better than that. We deserve better than that!* What if your parents or your husband and kids were going to be traveling on that compromised aircraft/flight you were scheduled to fly? Would you risk your loved ones safety by taking that aircraft up to 39,000 feet, or would you rethink it, making the ONLY decision you know to be *right?* Your *FEAR* of company retribution is causing you to forget that *protecting our passengers, as well as ourselves and each other, is the most important description of our job! To keep our passengers, our fellow Crewmembers and ourselves SAFE is the very reason we are up there isn't it?* If that is not the reason, then *WHY* are we up there? These corporate despots that are running our airline want you to think that flight attendants like me, and there are others thank God, who speak out against their *immoral* and *unethical* business practices are the one's who will be responsible for the demise of our company. How convenient for them if you *"allow"* yourselves to believe that ridiculous *scapegoat that they will no doubt try to use!* What I, and others like me are trying to do, is head off at the pass the inevitable catharsis of terror and horror that is most certainly on its way, especially for the passengers and flight crewmembers who will unfortunately be finding themselves on those very compromised aircrafts/flights that will be affected! If *American Airlines* gets driven to extinction like so many other commercial airline companies have, it will not be because of me or others like me trying to desperately turn the tables around. If the corporate execs are allowed continue overseeing our airline in this present deplorable manner, it's just a matter of time before we end up needlessly losing hundreds of innocent lives, and it will be *American Airlines corporate leadership who will have to own the responsibility for driving our airline company into extinction with their corruption and greed. Let's not give them any assistance in accomplishing that by allowing it to happen through our blatant complacency and paralyzing* FEAR (*F=alse E=vidence A=ppearing R=eal!*) I don't want *American Airlines* to become just another commercial airline to join the rest of the many great commercial airlines that have been driven into extinction by *corporate greed!* Do any of you? *It deserves better than that. We deserve better than that! My beloved flight attendant family please, I really need all of you to listen to me.* I need you guys to think long and hard about the question that I am about to ask you, and before your are quick to answer it, *PLEASE* take a moment to digest it and reflect on it before you answer, then only answer it *"honestly"* or not at all! *If any of you could have seen September 11, 2001 coming at us ahead of time in the same exact way that many of us see our safety compromised aircrafts/flights causing possible future needless catastrophic loss of life, would you have done everything within your power to attempt to stop those tragic events from occurring; thereby saving the life of flight attendant Amy Sweeney and her entire 767 Crew and passengers on Flight 11, as well as all the other flight crewmembers and thousands of innocent people who died needlessly on that day from HELL?* If you answered with an *unequivocal YES*, which I know that all of you did, then tell me now, *how is it that today you are allowing yourselves to be harassed into flying aircrafts/flights that you know damn well at times, are not airworthy or safe and they could have possible devastating outcomes when they are taken up in that manner?* Why aren't you *STANDING* for your fellow crewmembers as well as for yourselves in the same way that I know you would have for Amy and the crews of flights 11 and 77 *on September 11th? What is the difference?* If we don't start making some serious demands from this company's leadership, and force them to provide us with working conditions and a working environment that is *SAFE* at all times, *what in God's name are you going to say to yourselves if in fact those catastrophic accidents should be allowed to happen, and you KNEW it was only a matter of time before they would, but you chose to do nothing to attempt to stop them from occurring! Our complacency is going to KILL us if we don't start making our way out of the "co- dependant" and "cowardly" mental state we are presently in and heaven help us if any of us should find ourselves in a similar situation as that of Amy Sweeney's and her fellow crewmember's on 9/11! If you think that any of those corporate suits at AA are going to give a DAMN about any of us; crewmembers and passengers alike, you better think again!* Those of you that could possibly be having difficulty believing that, examine closely the manner in which our very own *CEO, Mr. Gerald Arpey* blatantly demonstrated that very fact to us when neither he, nor any other representative from *American Airlines* corporate management, showed up for the *9/11 Aircrew Memorial Dedication Service* that was held on *July 4, 2008 in Dallas Fort Worth Texas*, honoring the 33 Fallen Crewmember Heroes, who were *murdered on September 11ᵗʰ 2001 in the line of duty. Seventeen of those Crewmembers were taken from our own American Airlines family*! If that isn't a slap in all of our faces, letting us all know they just don't give a rats about any of us, I don't know what it's going to take to *wake you guys up!* The manner in which *American Airlines* is being overseen has to **STOP!** What I and others like me are trying to do, is the complete opposite of what these corporate execs want you to think we are doing! *I am desperately out here on a limb, putting everything I have worked so hard for all these years on the line, fighting for all of us. I am fighting for the respect and restitution of not only our profession but for the respect and restitution of our airline company as well!* I want my granddaughter to know the incredible a*viation industry,* not in the way that it finds itself today, *ravished and deteriorated by corporate greed*, but in the way it was once, and not so long ago either, when it was *elite and astounding and enormous and SAFE!* I want her to feel as completely astonished and amazed as I was, and still am for that matter, at the sheer magnificence of watching *a Boeing 747 or a 767 taking off with* *the ease and the grace of a huge beautiful eagle taking flight.* I want her to think as highly of the flight attendant profession as I did once and still do, so that if she should one day choose to follow in her grandmother's footsteps years from now, she will have chosen an honorable profession; one of having caring and virtuous distinction. I want her to see and experience the vast world outside of her own that offers her all of the different types of people and their unique customs and wonderful traditions, in the same way that I was able to experience it. *I want the once brilliant profession of the commercial airline flight attendant to be that brilliant profession once again, for her. The teacher of the many life lessons that she will learn, from the many incredible and wonderful human beings from all over the world, who will cross her path through the years, and will broaden her perspectives and strengthen her tolerance for all people and things that are so different from her, in the same way that it has taught me.* We **CAN** get all of that back! I know that we can, we just have to start believing in the strength within ourselves, the strength in each other, and the strength of our passengers. If you don't think our passengers want to be as **SAFE** as we do think again! *It is our passengers, not this company's corporate execs, who will be up at 39,000 feet with us if, God forbid, we find ourselves experiencing any catastrophic horrors in flight! WE truly* are those passengers and each other's **LAST LINE OF DEFENSE!!** Every single one of us needs to completely ingest the awesomeness of that responsibility because it is huge, and those of us that cannot or will not take that responsibility on, **DO NOT** belong up there in the first place! Just as corporate has taken *American Airlines* from us and have turned it into the *nightmare* company that we all know today, we can take *American Airlines* back from them and restore it to the *respected and admired airline company we were all so very proud to be a part of once and work for.*

Let me leave all you with a famous quote that was sent to me by a dear and beloved fellow flight attendant friend of mine *Ms. Gloria Gail Newman.* The famous words came from the great writer, *Ralph Waldo Emerson* who once wrote: *"TO LEAVE THE WORLD A BIT BETTER, WHETHER BY A HEALTHY CHILD, A GARDEN PATCH, OR A REDEEMED SOCIAL CONDITON. TO KNOW THAT EVEN ONE LIFE HAS BREATHED EASIER BECAUSE YOU HAVE LIVED …. THIS IS TO HAVE SUCCEEDED!!!!* *American Airlines Flight Attendants*, in solidarity, I implore you, it's time to **STAND!**

Acknowledgements

In the last two years I have come to know and realize the strength that I possess within myself, when I am facing some of life's tough challenges and adversities. *Life has a way of teaching all of us what it is that we need to learn in our individual journeys, but it is the "people" who come into our lives during that journey, that allows us to develop and nurture that strength from within so that it can manifest itself in a way that makes it possible for us to call upon it when needed.* The special people that I want to give my most heartfelt thanks to for guiding and supporting me through the two most difficult years of my life are first and foremost *my loving husband/best friend Shanon Rolow* whose belief in me never once wavered in those two years, *my two sons Brandon and Isaiah and my "baby girl" Mckaylah Rae,* who somehow managed to survive my many moments of inconsolable weeping and desperation, *my first and hopefully last therapist, the great Dr. John W. Hayden,* who provided me with countless hours of untroubled and undisturbed peace by giving me the tools that I needed in order to be able to revert back to that exact state of mind whenever I find it necessary, thanks Doc. My thanks go out to *Doctor Paul Corona,* who kept my physical health in check during some very difficult and emotional times, *Doctor Thomas J. Meyer, my orthopedic surgeon, and his incredible medical office staff,* for making it possible for my husband to walk on both feet again after a horrible accident he incurred, incredibly enough, during this already very difficult time *(God never puts more on us that we can handle),* *to Doctor Richard Anderson, my chiropractor,* who worked endless hours on me, relieving debilitating back and neck pain caused by stress, *my sister Annette Garcia,* who provided *Chapter 16* for this book by allowing me to include the college essay paper that she wrote for her English class; *my sister Penny McKnight,* who stayed up on a couple of "all-nighters" and put her whole heart into helping me draw all the parts from this book and put it all together, in order to finally send it out for publication, *my little Cuban Mom,* for all her worrying, daily prayers, love and motherly encouragement I couldn't imagine doing without, *my good American Airlines flight attendant friends Gloria Gail Newman and Diane Olsen* for keeping me e-mailed on current events at Ame*rican* in my absence, *my close friends Marilyn Saenz,* whose beautiful photographs adorn the cover of my book and *Michael Lockett,* who seems to have the uncanny ability to somehow know just exactly when to send his hysterically funny cards that lift my spirits high, and to all of the many other people in my life who have encouraged and supported the writing of this book. *My biggest thanks I reserve for you, Madeline "Amy Sweeney". The ultimate gift that you have given me, which is that of your "life", has allowed me the capacity to find the courage and the tenacity to exert the forces within me that resists any fear from all retaliation and retribution which I have faced and may continue to face from this book. There are no adequate words to describe the "heroic" courage which you displayed on September 11, 2001, that helped save the lives of countless others who cannot even be measured by numbers. You are the example I try to follow daily, to help me try to "head off at the pass" the inevitable aviation catastrophes which are undoubtedly coming our way in the very near future and will claim countless more lives, should the current "greed" of the commercial airline* *companies' corporate leaders in the Aviation Industry be allowed to continue. On behalf of all American Airlines Flight Attendants including myself, we send you our thanks and our love. We will never forget.*

About the Author

Alicia Lutz Rolow was born in Manhattan, New York in 1954. She is the second daughter of a working class family. She has lived most of her adult life in Southern California, where she currently resides with her best friend/husband Shanon Rolow, her two sons Brandon, Isaiah, and her granddaughter McKaylah Rae. She is an avid runner and enjoys her family time with her boys and granddaughter. She has been a veteran American Airlines Flight Attendant for over 32 years. The deteriorating condition of the Commercial Airline Companies in the Aviation Industry has compelled her to share her story in order to prevent possible catastrophic disasters that could claim the lives of her passengers and her flight crew member family such as the one that occurred on September 11th. She writes this book in the hopes that it will empower her fellow flight attendants who may not be able to presently share their stories, to STAND in solidarity and FIGHT!